Oh, Give Me a Home

For Ellen —
with best wishes from
the Humanities Institute —
hope it has been fun ?!

Ann Ronald
July '07

LITERATURE OF THE AMERICAN WEST
William Kittredge, General Editor

Other Books by Ann Ronald

Zane Grey (Boise, 1975)

Functions of the Setting in the Novel (New York, 1980)

The New West of Edward Abbey (Albuquerque, 1982; Reno, 1988, 2000)

(ed.) *Words for the Wild* (San Francisco, 1987)

Earthtones: A Nevada Album (Reno, 1995)

GhostWest: Reflections Past and Present (Norman, 2002)

*Reader of the Purple Sage: Essays on Western Writers and
   Environmental Literature* (Reno, 2003)

Oh, Give Me a Home

WESTERN CONTEMPLATIONS

ANN RONALD

UNIVERSITY OF OKLAHOMA PRESS : NORMAN

Oh, Give Me a Home: Western Contemplations is Volume 16 in the
Literature of the American West series.

Library of Congress Cataloging-in-Publication Data

Ronald, Ann, 1939–
    Oh, give me a home : western contemplations / Ann Ronald.
        p.   cm. — (Literature of the American West ; v. 16)
    Includes bibliographical references.
    ISBN 0–8061–3799–1 (alk. paper)
        1. West (U.S.)—Civilization—21st century. 2. West (U.S.)—
    Description and travel. 3. Landscape—West (U.S.) I. Title.
    II. Series.

    F595.3.R66 2006
    978'.034—dc22

                                        2006040462

The paper in this book meets the guidelines for permanence and durability of the Committee on Production Guidelines for Book Longevity of
the Council on Library Resources, Inc.∞

1   2   3   4   5   6   7   8   9   10

To all my WLA friends and family of thirty-plus years
Thanks

Contents

Oh, Give Me a Home

A Home on the Range

Oh, give me a home where the buffalo roam,
Where the deer and the antelope play,
Where seldom is heard a discouraging word
And the skies are not cloudy all day.

> Home, home on the range,
> Where the deer and the antelope play;
> Where seldom is heard a discouraging word
> And the skies are not cloudy all day.

Where the air is so pure, the zephyrs so free,
The breezes so balmy and light,
That I would not exchange my home on the range
For all the cities so bright.

The red man was pressed from this part of the West,
He's likely no more to return
To the banks of Red River where seldom if ever
Their flickering campfires burn.

How often at night when the heavens are bright
With the light of the glittering stars,
Have I stood here amazed and asked as I gazed
If their glory exceeds that of ours.

Oh, I love these wild flowers in this dear land of ours;
The curlew I love to hear scream;
And I love the white rocks and the antelope flocks
That graze on the mountain-tops green.

Oh, give me a land where the bright diamond sand
Flows leisurely down the stream;
Where the graceful white swan goes gliding along
Like a maid in a heavenly dream.

Then I would not exchange my home on the range,
Where the deer and the antelope play;
Where seldom is heard a discouraging word
And the skies are not cloudy all day.

Home, home on the range,
Where the deer and the antelope play;
Where seldom is heard a discouraging word
And the skies are not cloudy all day.

Chorus

INTRODUCTION

Home, home on the range,
Where the deer and the antelope play;
Where seldom is heard a discouraging word
And the skies are not cloudy all day.

Seventy-five miles an hour, my pickup truck rides like a smooth-gaited steed. No traffic from either direction slows me down on this two-lane highway that sloughs south to Sheridan. I could have taken nearby Interstate 90, but the anonymity of a divided highway doesn't appeal to me. I picked Wyoming 343 instead. Humming "Oh, give me a home" as I push down on the accelerator, I stare out at squared alfalfa and timothy fields, at fat cows and calves enjoying late morning siestas, at an occasional faded ranch house hidden behind a row of lombardy poplars. Typical panoramic western cattle country, with occasional valley settlements and long-range vistas in every direction. The Bighorn Mountains, still tipped with snow, glisten in sunlight, though this hot July day will fester into thunderstorms by late afternoon. I sing aloud the line about "skies are not cloudy," and look in vain for tumbleweeds, for antelope, for deer.

Forty years ago, about a hundred miles from here, I drove squarely into the largest herd of antelope I've ever seen. Hundreds, maybe thousands, bounced ahead and beside my car, their white rumps flashing in the twilight. I had a turquoise Chevy convertible in those days, so the top was down and I could smell the feral air. I slowed to a crawl, barely moving, while I listened to the hoofs beating on pavement and sand. It was one of those "click" moments in the West—I even remember moonlight graying the sage—an instant when the scenery suddenly mirrors the imagination and when your mind photographs something you remember for the rest of your life. I can't recall how long the antelope played, or how many miles I traveled before they disappeared. A long time, though, and a long time ago; my memory exaggerates.

Up ahead, in real time on Wyoming 343, animals of a different sort appear. A herd of cattle blocks the road, ambling slowly along as if they had the right-of-way. Braking sharply, I once again slow my vehicle to a crawl, then stop when a pink-shirted cowgirl holds up her hand as if she were a flagger in a construction zone. Unlike the free-ranging antelope, these critters are under supervision. Other Levi-clad riders, with red and blue bandanas waving in the wind, scatter left and right. Watching them, I realize that many ride like newcomers to the game. They sit their horses awkwardly, some with stirrups too short, others with reins too tight. So this cattle drive must be a made-for-dudes, Billy Crystal kind of operation, where old cowhands ply their trade and try to keep the neophytes—who are spending substantial dollars to be jolted along in their saddles—out of trouble. One Stetson-hatted guy rides back and forth along the ditch, shouting directions, nudging cattle left and right, motioning my truck forward at a petty pace.

I roll down my window, wave and shout "hello." Inching along, I smell the aroma of barnyards and hear fresh cowpies sludge against my tires. The midsized calves are particularly recalcitrant, moving from side to side almost by whim and ignoring the riders' commands. When one matronly brown cow bellows her dismay, three more Hereford voices join the bawling chorus. Most of the dudes look sunburned, uncomfortable, probably saddle-sore, but they're "home on the range" after all and they're content. That they're riding on pavement, that their chuckwagon dinner will include foil-baked chicken, corn-on-the-cob, fresh watermelon, and cold beer, that their beds tonight will be softly indoors—all this is immaterial. What unfolds before their eyes and mine, after all, is the West that is, a twenty-first-century replica of the cowboy's idyllic song. I gun my truck through the last of the herd, and pick up the pace to Sheridan. "The West at its Best," a welcome sign announces.

A cowboy balladeer crooning "Oh, give me a home," probably was picturing a spacious stretch of uncut tall-grass prairie and a cloudless horizon free from smoggy particulates. He was voicing a nineteenth-century innocence about the prospects and potentials of the American West. In truth, the songwriter, Dr. Brewster M. Higley, was describing windswept Kansas, not Wyoming, and not really the West that I call home. Dan Kelley set Dr. Higley's words to music, and the first "public perfor-mance" of "Home on the Range" occurred at the home of Judge John Harlan in April 1873. "It was a hit from the start and it spread over the country as if magic," old-timers recalled. The song soon became a stan-dard, its origins obscured and its romantic vision of the Old West fixed in the American imagination. "Home on the Range" came to be synony-mous with a cowboy's cloudless sky and a settler's eternal optimism. The original verse, in fact, insists that "*never* is heard a discouraging word" (italics mine).

I don't believe anyone attending the Harlan dance that night in Kansas could have dreamed up the real landscape where I live today, with urban barrios and rural ranchettes, snowbirds and ski bums, Indian gaming and boutique wineries, endangered species and invasive weeds, water transfer schemes and open-pit heap leach mines, Fee-Demo parking lots and pay-per-view scenery. Even as we cling philosophically to the values of yesteryear, we westerners of today are letting progress run wilder than the wilderness.

In some key respects, however, the idyllic West and my own western terrain still echo one another. We love it here. We see the sweeping landscape as a projection of possibilities, its spaciousness a doppel-ganger of our own aspirations, its potentialities a mirror of our dreams. Our interactions with the land are simultaneously romantic and practical, concurrently emotional and extractive, always physical and psychological at the same time. The American West is changing, to be sure, but it still carries an aura that seems to differ significantly from the inherent spirits of other parts of the country.

Spatial geographer Yi-Fu Tuan distinguishes between space and place, calling the former the physical boundaries of a particular landscape and the latter everything created by ongoing cultural interaction. Space becomes place after a human presence defines it. But I think that his observations can easily be reversed. It seems to me that a landscape like the American West dictates the course of our cultural interaction with it. Not only does space become place but space engenders the nature of place as well. Just as a seafaring economy shaped a young New England consciousness and just as cotton did the same for the antebellum South, so the "wide open spaces" of the West advance a particular attitude, a distinct habit of mind that in turn promises a vision both optimistic and opportunistic. This jackpot mentality prevailed in the goldfields of Colorado and California, invited the ill and elderly to Arizona, fostered the growth of San Francisco and Seattle, created Silicon Valley and Aspen Mountain, and continues to characterize the ways we operate today. The West of the twenty-first century, no less than the West of the nineteenth, exudes an attitude that not only exaggerates the American Dream but also exacerbates its rough edges. Wallace Stegner called it "the geography of hope." I call this landscape the spirit of space, the spirit of the wide-open spaces, my own particular home where I ride on the range of my imagination.

My personal experiences define the scope of my range. I've always lived in cities, but enjoy most of my free time in the near and far corners of the rural West. City-bred but country bound at every opportunity, I'm typical of one subset of urban westerners today. While I love to read anywhere, I'd rather do so when sprawled alongside a desert seep beneath the shade of a cottonwood tree. While I seek out backpacking and hiking and camping opportunities, I cherish creature comforts, too. While I appreciate open spaces, I also respect the realities of economic necessity. While I earn my own living by teaching philosophical debates about the wilderness and civilization or nature versus culture, I secretly question the long-term relevance of such conversations when so many shades of gray enshroud every black or white intellectual posture. I love abstractions, but I prefer thinking about them in tangible terms. Tossing a pebble into an icy mountain tarn, I watch concentric circles ripple water into wishes into wisdom, then see the imagined patterns turn back into water again. While I watch I wonder—how might "a geography of hope" become a viable twenty-first-century home on the range?

Evans Creek edges into Reno's northwest quadrant. A half-desert, half-suburban kind of stream, with an erratic flow of water, an accompanying trail both dusty and muddy, and bird trills and highway cacophony alternating in the air. It's the sort of eclectic setting I like for a morning walk. A recent June stroll alongside the banks led me to a sleeping gopher snake, lethargic and fat from a morning meal. The snake's semi-coiled body, two or three feet long, blocked the path completely. After I talked loudly to it, and stomped my foot a couple of times, it finally lifted its head and slithered away. Such a natural occurrence, I thought, as I headed on down the trail. Then I imagined all the people who might find this encounter unusual or even disquieting. Most of us who played in the natural world when we were children have few such trepidations, but anyone raised in an entirely urban setting might be quite alarmed by the sudden appearance of a snake underfoot. "A whiplash / Unbraiding in the sun," mused Emily Dickinson, that leads to "a tighter breathing / And Zero at the bone." I admit I was momentarily startled, but as soon as I checked for rattles, and saw none, I was more interested in the snake's behavior than concerned about my own safety. "Was it perversity, that I longed to talk to him?" asked D. H. Lawrence of another ophidian encounter. "Was it humility, to feel so honored? / I felt so honored."

I suppose something morphs itself into our unconsciousness when we grow up closer to dirt than to cement. Is it true that, for the rest of our lives, we will always perceive the natural world in a more relaxed and immediate way? Among my urban friends, I see a direct correspondence between our youthful games, our adult affinities for the out-of-doors, and our senses of self in an uncitified environment. Whether we built tree houses in Douglas fir or hid in red rock niches, whether we caught spiders or scorpions, whether we swam in salt water or high mountain lakes—or lived in arid spots where water was a luxury—we interacted one-on-one with our environments. That close contact, I believe, has spilled over into our adult lives. Given a choice, most of my good friends would rather hike than hibernate, would choose a walk over a movie, would prefer snowshoeing or skiing over stasis.

We live and work in cities; we want our nature close at hand.

Our early intimacy with the natural world also dictates our conservationist leanings. Here I use the word "conservation" not as an overtly political gambit but in its most pristine sense—to conserve our natural surroundings in sustainable ways. Not to preserve the past, necessarily, but to respect the future. To want for our children sufficient opportunities to see certain landscapes uncluttered and undeveloped by human hands. To offer them wild places and open spaces, to show them distances and the potential for dreams. To retain—on the ground—the West of my imagination.

What do people actually mean when they speak of that American West? Early geographers defined this elusive space as the territory beyond the hundredth meridian. Others said it's the land beyond the Missouri River. Still others, whatever landscape west of either of those lines of demarcation that receives less than fifteen inches of rain each year. This, of course, leaves out my birthplace, the West Coast, which has always seemed western to me. So I can't quite accept the notion that the West includes only arid lands where irrigation is imperative. Nor can I agree that the West embraces only those lands where the rivers flow toward the Pacific Ocean. What about Texas? What about Nevada? Every geographical definition immediately raises a question in my mind. Physically, the American West is some place—every place—west of the Midwest. Intellectually and emotionally, it's something far more complicated.

Historians, I don't believe, have done much better with their definitions. They design the West even more abstractly than geographers, describing a frontier where men and women sought to push forward the boundaries of the new nation, to domesticate the apparently open spaces, and to utilize the available resources. Contemporary historians reject the conventional pattern of the frontier. Patricia Nelson Limerick argues, for example, that the West is "a place undergoing conquest and never fully escaping its consequences." She sees domestication and utilization in the negative shades of colonialism rather than as steps on a rainbow trail leading toward the desirable taming of a hostile land. Instead of praising the frontier spirit, she and her fellow new western historians reassess and reinterpret the frontier's unfortunate violence and debate its ongoing consequences. In some respects their conceptualizations suit me, but because of their professional focus on the past, historians' views seem narrowly defined. How might we talk about the West that we live in today, or the West that we predicate for tomorrow?

Literary critics originally applauded the route of conquest and conflict, too, calling *The Virginian* a model for subsequent westerns like *Shane*. I like those novels, but they always seem removed from me, as if they were located in a time and space far from my own. Recent serious western fiction openly questions or has completely outgrown the myths of masculinity, so contemporary scholars have turned their attention elsewhere. Now literary critics describe the West as a place of borderlands, of crossroads where differences intersect. Matters of gender, of ethnicity, of religious fervor, of value systems, of economics, of attitudes toward the land itself are important in western literature, and those matters help define the American West in imaginative yet truthful ways. I'm more comfortable in the literary West than in some of the other Wests, but the storied West of fables and fiction has its limitations, too.

It has always seemed to me that the real West is a habit of mind. I think of myself as a westerner, even though I grew up in an urban setting. I think of myself as a westerner, even though I've never saddled a horse or ridden the open range. I think of myself as a westerner, even though I currently live in a metropolitan area that is consuming open spaces with a voracious appetite. I think of myself as a westerner, even though its legendary violence has little to do with the ways in which I perceive the world. The legacy of conquest means nothing to me personally, yet I remain western to the core. Without hesitation, I think of myself as a westerner—not as a Washingtonian, where I was born; not as a Nevadan, where I have lived most of my adult life—but a westerner who embraces the unlimited vistas, the vast distances and dreams. We westerners see the world not through rose-colored glasses but through a prism of peaks and canyons and big sky that continuously promises freedom and optimism and infinite possibilities.

This is a true story. Until I was twenty-one, I had not seen any territory east of the Rocky Mountains. Eager to correct this parochial deficiency, I nailed down a summer job in New Hampshire. On my first full day in New England, while we were driving toward the White Mountains, a proud Bostonian pointed out a prominent peak. "Wow," exclaimed the other newcomer in the car, a young woman from Ohio. "I've never seen anything like that before."

"Where? What are you looking at?" I responded.

"Right there." The Bostonian jabbed her forefinger toward the window. "Dead ahead."

While the Ohioan continued voicing her enthusiasm, I was still trying to figure out what they were looking at. Even as I nodded agreeably, I thought to myself, "Looks like a foothill to me." I never did figure out why anyone could get excited about such a minimalist bump on the horizon.

Fast forward. Some years later I actually found myself living in the Midwest, in an Evanston, Illinois, studio apartment located at the busy intersection of Chicago Street and Dempster Avenue. Just three blocks away, Lake Michigan curled onto the shore—crashing waves there on windswept summer afternoons, creating icebound sculptures when winter's chill froze the water. I walked to the lake almost every day. Its expanse was the only open view within miles, and the scope drew me to the beach as surely as the library drew me to my graduate studies. I remember trying to get my midwestern friends to walk down to the little park where Dempster dead-ended at lakeside. No one ever would join me. "Why?" they would ask, "Whatever for?" "There's nothing to see." Years later, I recall my astonishment at their disinterest.

Another strong midwestern memory involves a trip to the zoo. I don't remember anything else about the day, but I recall standing for a long time before a caged bobcat that was pacing back and forth behind bars. Once, when backpacking in Washington's Cascade Mountains, I woke to find bobcat prints all around my head. So I've always thought of the species as free-roaming, curious as housecats, and liable to turn up almost anywhere in the woods. This captive bobcat would never leave its cage. Neither would I, until I graduated and could finally flee from the Midwest back to the solace of someplace on the far side of the Rockies. In fact, I never once applied for a teaching position that would force me to live east of the West.

My forays far from home always felt strange to me. Ever eager to return, I would bide my time until I could head for the mountains of Washington state or the sagebrush stretches of Nevada or almost anywhere among the red rocks of canyon country. Since the Seattle vacant lots where I played as a child haven't existed for half a century, and wall-to-wall houses have long since replaced the Douglas fir, I literally can't go home again. Nor can I describe my childhood scenes in terms of western settlement. There's nothing romantic about moving to a house on the edge of a city, then watching the city swallow every tree in sight. There's nothing romantic, either, about my heritage. My mother was born in Washington, lived on a farm for a few years, then moved to town. My father was the son of an illegal alien—I smile as I write those words—who caught a boat from Vancouver to Seattle one day, and stayed. Dad often told me about his first boyhood home, destroyed when the hillside was hosed hydraulically to level more space for downtown Seattle. My mother's stories were eerily parallel. One day she and I watched a mudslide on television, where a whole series of houses tumbled into one another like jackstraws. "That's where the farm was," she said laconically, "when I was little. No mudslides then, before they began clearing the hills."

No one in my family grew up anywhere that still exists exactly; perhaps that's "western," too. No one came from a home on the range, either. My father's Scottish ancestors were urbanites, born and bred in the dingy environs of Glasgow. Mother's grandparents were Iowa farmers, their fields of corn rigidly aligned. No one in my family would be at home in Dr. Higley's utopian Kansas setting. But we would be at home in the vistas described, and we would understand the verses' inherent longings. Metaphorically, if not literally, his simple rhymes do suggest some crucial characteristics of the American West, some significant criteria for explaining what it means to be a westerner today.

The stanzas also remind us of the sweep of history. Their bountiful innocence foreshadows the way westerners still tend to view the land. In this respect, "Home on the Range" opens up the future, as we muse on what we dreamed in the past and what we continue to dream today. Western-ness—a habit of mind, a habit of mine, that ranges over a very wide range indeed.

CHAPTER ONE

Oh, Give Me a Home

Slowly, with deep feeling
Oh, give me a home where the buffalo roam,
Where the deer and the antelope play,
Where seldom is heard a discouraging word
And the skies are not cloudy all day.

A slap of wind against the derelict side of a tin trailer. The honky-tonk howl of a midnight coyote. Then a second howl. And then a third. Another slap of wind. In from the east rides the 3 a.m. train, a little late, with a Doppler wheeze that rises and falls as the engines and cars churn toward the west. Another slap of wind. Another truncated chorus of howls. A rooster, mistaking the moon for a rising sun, crows once, twice, and then falls silent. Breaking that silence, a diesel drags itself along Main Street. No need to stop. No traffic signals bar the way in this rural community so far from city lights. Still, the truck coughs its way slowly along the three blocks that constitute the town, looking for cars that never appear, for people who have long since gone to bed. Population 354, and falling, day by day. Another slap of wind. Another howl. Then silence.

An hour or two later, the sharpness of dawn in the high desert. A dozen miles from town, or more, a clapboard house leans into the acrid morning breeze. Flanked by a beaten-down lean-to on one side, a broken corral on the other, the unpainted building mirrors its empty surroundings. Sagebrush, a cottonwood shattered by age, a windmill with spokes spinning idly in the air. A porch aslant, with steps akilter. Inside the house's vacant shell, a field mouse skitters across a faded ragtag rug. Above it, at eye level, a tattered curtain rustles in and out of a fractured window frame. The wind jostles the calico threads from side to side. Another slap of wind. And still more silence.

In the distance, the hum of highway trucks and cars. More eighteen-wheelers hustling from here to there, intent upon efficiency and speed and estimated times of arrival. The occasional Winnebago proceeds more slowly, more curiously perhaps, but without stopping until the landscape softens and the desert air warms at least to room temperature. SUVs, too, their racks stacked with bicycles, tents, and other toys, charge forth across the corrugated terrain, as do battered pickup trucks, their mud-flaps pasted white with alkali and dust. As each vehicle passes by, a burst of desert dirt joins forces with the rising wind, whirling the sand to blanket the arid land. Not dust devils, exactly, just dervishes and dreams out of control.

This is the West we dreamed of. This is the West of our stories.

My grandmother came west at the dawn of a new century. After her Iowa father remarried, there was no place for a twenty-something spinster daughter. When a passing entrepreneur caught her eye, she understood that he was a means of escape. A few months later, she rode a westbound train alone, joining a relative stranger in holy matrimony. If this all sounds familiar, it should. My mother, reading Wallace Stegner's *Angle of Repose* for the first time, remarked definitively, "This is the story of your grandparents. Even though your grandmother wasn't an artist and your grandfather wasn't anything so romantic as a mining engineer, it's the same story," she said. "A relatively well-educated woman (my grandmother had a nursing degree, three of her sisters graduated from college) marries a strike-it-rich young man, follows him West, and spends the rest of her life trying to domesticate both him and her surroundings. And fails," my mother added.

My grandparents settled, not in the unforgiving desert but in beneficent Washington state, where a mild climate and a phalanx of pioneering settlers paved the way to success. But for the young Kellers, the pattern of settlement, disruption, settlement, disruption held true. Shopkeepers one year, farmers another. Never quite broke, never quite fortunate either. As time passed, illness took over the texture of their lives, for my grandfather had been sorely damaged by a stint in the Spanish-American War. Malaria, synonymous with service in the Philippines those days, finally incapacitated him, until he no longer could work at all. Grandma, wholly responsible for the family finances, fell comfortably back into her Florence Nightingale guise. She toiled as a factory nurse for decades to follow, mending the sniffles and bruises and mangled extremities that inevitably accompanied production-line workers in an early twentieth-century cannery.

I never knew Grandma when she was young, if she ever was. I imagine I knew her best when she was about the age I am now. Sitting here at my computer, wearing Levis, a '49ers sweatshirt and Birken-stocks, I think about her starched blue housedresses, her sensible black-laced shoes, her stiff demeanor that bent only when her granddaughter came to visit. Even those visits were regimented, however, with fixed hours for breakfast, dinner, and supper; with scheduled pauses for favorite radio programs; with set days for marketing, laundry, and housecleaning; with bedtime rituals as unvarying as the rest of her rigid routines. Even so, I can recall aberrations. Much to my mother's horror, Grandma taught me how to shoot a gun. Tending her carefully cultivated backyard garden, she gave me a lasting taste for fresh fruits and vegetables. Strawberries juicy and often misshapen, fresh young beet greens boiled in vinegar, baby potatoes still redolent with a clinging smell of black earth, peas and beans that readily snapped open, peaches that oozed. Grandma even showed me how to bake an omelet soufflé, though I cannot imagine replicating the airy concoction that she so handily achieved every Sunday, on a wood-stove no less. If she couldn't domesticate her husband, who died from malaria complications long before I was born, she could train her grand-child in the higher arts.

I don't mean to equate my grandmother with tin trailers and lone-some train whistles, or with dilapidated farmhouses and itinerant Winne-bagos, but I do see a connection between lives imagined and lives endured or enjoyed. Like so many other young men and young women, Grandma came west to pursue her private version of the American Dream. I'll never know quite what she expected, but I suspect that the subsequent narrowness of her later years, the tense rigidity of her nights and days, the intensity of her preoccupation to control every facet of her surroundings, had little correlation with how she imagined her future as she rode that train from Iowa's fertile farmlands to Puget Sound's timber and salt water and drizzle. No young woman, aged twenty-something, ever pictures the transitory vagaries of the future, the tragic realities of illness and ill fortune, the impossible distance between her dreams and her day-to-day life.

Is such a distance necessarily western? Of course not, but the palpable detritus of dereliction and decay is characteristic of pioneer trails. When I first moved to Reno, I could still find discarded wagon wheels, fractured pieces of furniture and broken tools. Square nails, bent horseshoes, and bits of cloth. Pioneers crossing the Forty-Mile Desert from Lovelock to Carson City or tracking the Black Rock Desert to Double 0 Hot Springs dropped every expendable item, lightening their loads so weary oxen could keep moving westward until they reached the next available water. By the end of the twentieth century, such leavings have been picked clean by curiosity-seekers. Today, if I follow any dirt road that steers away from dilapidated desert towns like the one described in the first paragraph, I find modern disposable treasures instead. The rusted frame of a Model T, or a Studebaker, or a Chevy pickup truck, windows gone, doors pocked with gunshot holes, upholstery ripped by nesting rats and birds. An icebox or two, equally targeted by random shooters. A torn Frisbee, a shredded T-shirt, an empty six-pack, the odd shoe.

The Pacific Northwest doesn't preserve its remainders in quite the same way as the desert. Because of the dampness, things disintegrate faster. A shredded T-shirt, for example, would soon molder away. And because of the extraordinary building boom in and around Seattle, there are fewer and fewer odd-lot places where people can dump unwanted trash. Yet there's garbage of a different sort, at least in my opinion. Grandma's little frame house was leveled dozens of years ago, victim of urban expansion. Her garden turned into an IGA parking lot, striped asphalt replacing the neat rows of strawberries, peas, and beans. There's a kind of irony in exchanging one kind of food bank with another, but somehow I don't think my grandmother would be amused. Once she sold her property, she never went back; so she never saw the demolition. Before she died, however, at age eighty-eight, she talked often of her garden, of how much she missed the fresh fruits and vegetables, of how much she missed turning over the rich brown dirt with her spade. I never heard her mention good times with my grandfather, not once.

At the beginning of the twentieth century, a difficult economy led to widespread unemployment in the British Isles, hitting Scotland's workers especially hard. At the same time, Canadian booking agents, commissioned to recruit Scotsmen to the Saskatchewan and Manitoba prairies and to points farther west, were particularly active and successful in Glasgow and Aberdeen. In keeping with the times, many of my own Glaswegian relatives decided prosperity would be possible only if they immigrated to Canada. While most of the family went directly to Vancouver, my great-aunt Maggie, her husband John, and their five daughters sought their fortunes in a more rural landscape.

In 1905, Uncle John's brother, James Campbell Ritchie, gained title to 350 acres of fertile Indian land alongside Lake Okanagan in eastern British Columbia. Local historian Sherril Foster hints at unsavory circumstances, implying that Salish native Antoine Pierre was "bamboozled" and "coerced to accept in trade" 370 acres of "mostly inferior hillside." While the details of the transaction remain murky, I can be quite certain of one thing—none of us whose families have been long-time westerners can claim total innocence for ourselves or can point our fingers at the machinations of figures of history. If our families emigrated west, they probably were indigenously culpable in one way or another.

Anyway, James Ritchie proceeded to plat a township called "Summerland," and sold lots to all comers. Ever the wheeler-dealer, he also orchestrated the Kettle Valley Railway survey, guaranteeing Summerland and West Summerland's expanding fruit crops direct access to lucrative coastal and interior markets. His brother, no such entrepreneur, seems more typical of diligent Scots settlers in the early twentieth century. My great uncle John Stevenson Ritchie, a harness maker, came to Summerland in 1906. Like most new arrivals, the family immediately set up housekeeping in a tent. How I wish I had talked with Aunt Maggie about that first Canadian winter. The temperature must have been below freezing nearly every night, and the dilemma of mothering five girls under the age of ten *in a tent* must have been a nightmare. "Cold and Draughty," says a sign on a tent house replica standing inside the Summerland Municipal Museum. I look at the flimsy canvas, the tiny iron heating stove, the lack of privacy and space, and wonder how Aunt Maggie managed to make such a place a home.

Nonetheless, she succeeded. Aunt Maggie lived into her nineties, as did four of her five little girls. I've always been struck, though, by the fact that these women clung together as if the sudden climatic shift from wet and temperate Scotland to the distant dry climate of Lake Okanagan and that first tent-bound winter bonded them in some special way. Uncle John died in 1926. 'The girls,' as my parents called dad's cousins, lived on for decades. Two married, and moved only as far as next door, Eliza with her husband and two daughters on one side, Peggy with her husband and three sons across the back alley. Two of the remaining 'girls' worked for the municipality, while the third kept house and tended the aging Aunt Maggie. Homebound and home-content, the Ritchies rarely ventured very far.

A year after the Ritchies settled into the Okanagan Valley, Aunt Maggie's brother, Peter Ronald, headed from Glasgow to Vancouver. No scrabbling rural existence for this city-bred man. Pop Pop, as I called my grandfather, came to Canada without his wife and sons, intending to secure a job and decent lodgings before bringing his family across the ocean. By this time, however, economic hard times had reached western Canada, too. The family mythology goes like this. Walking along the Vancouver waterfront one rainy morning, still unemployed and wholeheartedly discouraged, Pop Pop spotted a sign that read "Boat Trip to Seattle, 25 cents." That's what he had in his pocket, 25 cents. By nightfall he found himself in Seattle. By the next afternoon, he had secured a job as a printer, his old familiar Glasgow trade. By evening he had settled into his newly adopted country.

In these days of passports and border patrols and intense security issues, Pop Pop's arrival on United States soil sounds unbelievably uncomplicated. Technically speaking, he was an illegal alien. Moving from Scotland to Canada required no particular papers at the time, so he had none. Paperless Pop Pop then could boat casually across the border, followed a year later by Granny and their two sons who immigrated legally to this country without any authority checking on their breadwinner's status. I don't understand the immigration policy that allowed this odd transaction, but for years Pop Pop was illegal while the rest of the family was not. He couldn't, in fact, visit his brother and sisters and his nephews and nieces in Canada, fearing that he might be prevented from returning home to Seattle. Finally, an amnesty window opened that allowed him to apply for citizenship. My mother tells me that the day my grandfather and my father joined a formal ceremony making them both naturalized United States citizens was perhaps Pop Pop's proudest moment.

So the flip of a coin, in effect, made me a citizen of one country rather than another, a United States westerner instead of a Canadian westerner. Is there a difference? Laurie Ricou thinks so. His recent book, *The Arbutus/Madrone Files*, examines the ways in which one country's corner touches the other, how affinities and separations interact. His title is a riff on the fact that Canadians in British Columbia and Washingtonians call a single plant by two different names. While I grew up referring to the tree that "keeps its leaves but is always losing its papery bark to reveal a burnished, well-oiled salmon-colored wood" madrone, my British Columbia relatives were calling it arbutus. Just so, Ricou extrapolates, do our regional languages differ. He goes on to compare literary patterns of rhetoric, diction, and theme; I compare my familial ones.

I think about language patterns, for example, and the fact that my Scottish ancestors had bleached-white Gaelic skin and spoke English, of a sort (my mother always said she could hardly understand my father's parents when she first met them, and I still recall the lilting brogue of everyone on that side of the family). The fact is that my family assimilated easily in this new world, whether into a Canadian landscape or a United States milieu. Skin color may have predicated success, while a common language surely contributed, too. And education was another crucial ingredient. Unlike many other ethnic groups, most Scots could read and write. Such universal literacy—higher even than in England—enabled them to find jobs more quickly, especially in the cities. Ferenc Morton Szasz, in a book titled *Scots in the North American West, 1790-1917*, cites other factors as well. "A sense of adventure, a self-confidence, a familiarity with harsh landscape, a work ethic, an individualism that combined nicely with group loyalties, and, often, a set of industrial or agricultural skills," talents "sorely in demand in nineteenth-century America." He might be describing Aunt Maggie and Uncle John in their tent, making a hospitable home in the aptly named town of Summerland. He might be characterizing Granny and Pop Pop, who welcomed more and more Scotsmen—Granny's widowed sister and her children moved in almost immediately—into an extended family that quickly outgrew available space but never outgrew available love. In this New World environment, the Ritchies and Ronalds possessed the skills, the fortitude, the loyalties that augured success.

A twisted old madrone tree grew in my parents' backyard. Its uneasy elegance, somewhat dwarfed by the two Douglas fir that towered beside it, characterized our backyard ambience. Mother didn't like it, I recall, because of that slippery bark which constantly marred the perfection of her rockery and flowers. Her annoyance, however, seems problematic. The sloughing imperfections made the tree beautiful, in a way, certainly a touchstone of my childhood but perhaps an emblem of all those doughty Scotsmen on their new world adventures as well. Like the Ritchies of Summerland, the Ronalds of Seattle never became rich and famous, at least not in the paparazzi sense. On the other hand, the entire family achieved a kind of personal fit, a new world suitability that reminds me of that tree.

Every New Year's Day, my grandparents' wedding anniversary, the generations from Canada and the United States came together to party and play. Amid interminable cups of tea, and quite probably a bit of sherry, Granny's clear soprano lifted above the tenors, singing Glaswegian songs of their Scottish homeland. I recall a curious juxtaposition of the Old World and the New, the brogues that thickened as the day progressed, the house on Dearborn Street so Americanized in spirit. If my grandparents' home, with its welcome mat always at the door and its tea kettle always on simmer, differed from the Summerland enclave, it wasn't a madrone/ arbutus kind of disjuncture. It was the unity of a single tree with strong, vigorous branches. Both enclaves of relatives embraced everyone enthusiastically. Every summer, for example, my parents and I vacationed on Lake Okanagan, where I'm sure I spent more nights with Aunt Maggie than I ever spent with Granny and Pop Pop. I never learned to like undercooked bacon; I never managed to say "aboot" instead of "about"; I never loaded our luggage into the car's bonnet instead of its trunk. But I definitely learned the meaning of home, the hearth blazing both physically and psychologically. Home on the range? Not precisely. But home in an American sense, in the spirit of immigrants then and now.

When we think of home today, we tend to think of private space, of enclosure, of shelter, of sanctuary, of a place where we can retreat from a larger impersonal world. Such a concept, however, is something quite modern. Arlen Mack has edited a collection of essays called *Home*, where various scholars muse about the origins of our denotations and connotations of home and about the current English and American meanings of the term. John Hollander, for example, traces the etymology of the word, and finds it uniquely Anglo-Saxon. Other languages use a single term more closely affiliated with hearth, thus blurring the distinction between house and home in ways that English speakers do not. For us, house implies the physical structure of a space, while home suggests the more domestic implications of that shelter. House means bricks and mortar; home means haven. House is external; home, internal. Hollander argues, in fact, that Robert Frost cemented our understanding of home with his poetic lines:

> Home is the place where, when you have to go there,
> They have to take you in.

For Frost, home is a particular domicile, an environment with familial overtones, an unquestioned sanctuary, the one place where the proverbial welcome mat—even if undeserved—is always out.

Social scientist Tamara K. Hareven explains that, in earlier times, an understanding of the meaning of home was much more communal than we think of it now. "Rather than catering strictly to the needs of the family, the household served the entire community, by taking in dependent members who were not related to the family and by helping maintain the social order." Before the days of automation, home was characterized more by sociability than privacy. Often, "public and private activities were inseparable." This notion explains why the Brewster verses struck such a responsive chord in the hearts of the Harlan listeners and in the imaginations of so many subsequent songsters. It also explains how the generic "Oh, Give Me a Home" can make even the wide-open spaces of the West into communal territory that will always welcome a cowboy "home." It further explains the social interactions along the river corridor where the Snake divides Idaho from Oregon, a neighborly place ironically called Hells Canyon.

Grace Jordan's memoir, *Home Below Hell's Canyon*, narrates one woman's triumphs and tribulations as she struggles to convert rural isolation into domestic space, to replace frequent discomfort with the solaces of home, to make a community for family and friends alike. At their sheep ranch in Idaho, Len and Grace Jordan provide a social center for many of the canyon dwellers and visitors—"going out of the canyon for frivolity was neither practicable nor in Jordan style. We preferred to get together with our neighbors." Like the Jordans, those 1930s neighbors had sought economic refuge in inhospitable surroundings.

The name "Hells Canyon" implies a fearsome place of black depths and immeasurable distances. Washington Irving, for example, catalogued the difficulties of traversing the Snake River's "rugged defile," with its "deep channel through rocky mountains," its "banks so high and precipitous," and its impenetrable terrain that reduced men "to the utmost extremity." Although the Shoshone people occupied the more accessible stretches of the canyon, few explorers approached the inner gorge and no one initially thought of making a home on the sides of its incredibly steep reaches. As the nineteenth century progressed, however, men hunting for gold began poking through the nearby mountains. Downstream from Hells Canyon, they found substantial amounts of copper, and they discovered that the land between the inner gorge and Lewiston, Idaho, had a modicum of ranching potential. Entrepreneurs, hoping to furnish supplies to miners and homesteaders alike, were eager to capitalize on the waterway. A steamer called *Norma* provided river transportation at the turn of the century, while sternwheelers *Imnaha* and *Mountain Gem* took her place a few years later. Somewhat regular mail delivery came to the ranches south of Lewiston, and settlers came and went. Raising cattle, and then sheep, less than five percent of those homesteaders were successful, while the remainder either defaulted or sold their land to larger livestock operators.

In short, Hells Canyon was living up to a name that slowly was making its way into the local vocabulary. First used in print in 1895, made popular by Oregon senator Richard Neuberger in the 1950s, the sobriquet now denotes the deepest gorge in North America. Arizona's Grand Canyon, by comparison, is only 5,500 feet from canyon floor to rim, whereas He Devil Mountain summits out at 7,900 feet above the Snake River in Hells Canyon. (Tim Palmer, in his meticulously researched *The Snake River: Window to the West*, argues that California's Kings Canyon is deeper still, but he's in the minority, and I think he's splitting hairs.) So it's not an exaggeration to call Hells Canyon "the deepest gorge in North America." By the time of the Great Depression, people were desperate enough to seek food and shelter almost anywhere. In the spring of 1933, the Len Jordan family moved just below "that deepest scar on North America's face, through which the river is not navigable and where even foot travel stops." For the rest of the decade, while the Jordans ran sheep and eked out a sufficient living, Grace busily worked to make her house a home.

Just getting there in the first place was a trial. A sixteen-hour boat trip from Lewiston took Grace, her father-in-law, and the Jordans' three small children to Kirkwood Bar, where her husband already was settling onto their new property. She arrived long after dark, able to see her new home only by moonlight, exhausted, "with three dollars to spare!" The next morning, however, her spirits soared when she looked out at "the dreaming light on field and river," and discovered "straggling lilacs" and "ancient apple trees." Although a green alfalfa field was the only "bit of ordered life against all the rock and crag" that she could see, and the shadow of Kirkwood Rock created "a shade so dense it seemed almost sinister," she happily began to explore and to set her new house in order.

Some readers relegate *Home Below Hell's Canyon* to the category of "children's book" or dismiss it as something "for young girls to read." The straightforward prose and the profusion of domestic detail do indeed simplify the complicated subtext that in fact epitomizes day-to-day household activities in the rural American West. But even decades after the so-called 1890 closing of the frontier, this particular woman's tasks are archetypal. Grace Jordan alone was responsible for feeding her family, for feeding any hands who happened to be at the homeplace, and for feeding anyone else who arrived at suppertime. And despite the distances and difficulties, a surprising number of people did arrive at Kirkwood Bar.

The task of homemaking was not particularly easy, especially with the nearest groceries downriver and distant. After one festive Thanksgiving, for example, Grace generalizes that her husband "hadn't the slightest conception of the planning and labor that had produced the wonderful dinner." Turkey, oysters, mince and pumpkin pies for adults and children, followed that evening by sandwiches, hot chocolate, and more pie. "Len's praise," says Grace, "was the final crown of my day." Along with her hostessing, she alone was responsible for childcare, for medical emergencies, for finances, for the thousand and one domestic decisions that informed every day in the canyon. "You'll have to do on twenty-five dollars a month," Len declares. Twenty-five dollars a month "for clothes, medicines, reading matter, insurance, vacations, and the children's school courses." Without complaint, she manages. Indeed, she fares so well that she even saves money. A used organ, which she buys for fifteen dollars, is one of her few extravagances. Comfortable with her role as wife and mother, confident in her contributions to familial prosperity, she communicates a strong sense of self-confidence and self-worth. As she remarks in one perceptive passage—"Women are a luxury; yet when they leave, so do profits." No luxury in fact, Grace Jordan alone was responsible for the details of domesticity. I surmise that she helped keep the profits up, too.

The only time she directly confronts her husband about the difficulties inherent in their lifestyle provides one of the most endearing vignettes in the book. Promising to spend time on their house, Len procrastinates and delays crucial domestic projects. Knowing that farm and camp work always rated "unlimited attention," Grace realizes "the house was due for little or none." Finally tiring of the situation, she threatens to pack up the children and move to town. Horrified, her husband sets to work that very afternoon. Immediately, a new addition and needed repairs take shape—the pouring of four-foot concrete walls and a new concrete floor for the kitchen, the construction of a sleeping porch, the moving of another wall, and, most important, the creation of a new bathtub and washbasin. Grace helps, too, mixing just the right combination of mazama ash, flour, and water to whitewash the dark kitchen walls.

The house still stands today, as does the precious addition. The washbasin, made of concrete hand-poured over a chopping bowl mold, is still usable. The bathtub, extending on two sides of a single wall because little excess space was available, looks as quaint as ever. Because Grace's homemade paint combination did the job better, and cheaper, than store-bought enamel, the original whitewashing still lightens the kitchen. The fruit cellar, sunk behind the kitchen wall, sits just as she describes, too, with an immovable boulder jutting in from the back. With *Home Below Hell's Canyon* as my guidebook, I could trace the provenance of almost everything added for Grace and the children's comfort, could see the detail work that made this house a home.

In fact, the place remains livable today. Home this past summer to Linda Mink, a Forest Service volunteer, the Jordan living quarters are little changed, although the out-of-doors environs appear professionally cultivated. While eating lunch in the house's shadow, I sat beside a carefully mowed and tended lawn. Further shaded by an orchard of cherry trees redolent with ripe June fruit, I enjoyed flowering orange daylilies and a symmetrically trimmed rosebush not yet in bloom. The domestic scenery seemed more in keeping with a resort than a homestead. Nearby, several dozen visitors sat at picnic tables, their lunches catered by concessionaires and their conversations like the murmurings of bees. The once-isolated Jordan home no longer seems so far from civilization.

Kirkwood Ranch is now a domestic centerpiece of the Hells Canyon National Recreation Area, a 652,488-acre preserve that was designated on December 31, 1975. The Forest Service invites the public to experience the ambience of the Jordans' home below Hells Canyon. Just as I am amused by the name "Hells Canyon," created more for publicity than for practical reasons and bureaucratically spelled without an apostrophe, as are all place names these days, I smile to myself about the designation of this sanctuary. The Kirkwood Ranch, so named because the Kirks initially homesteaded here, is preserved primarily because Grace Jordan—whose husband went on to become governor of Idaho—wrote about it. Popularity and politics, in this case, went hand in hand. Given shorter shrift is Dick Carter, who lived there and operated a whiskey still— "five-star double-rectified moonshine"—before the Jordans arrived. Or the Bud Wilsons, who bought Kirkwood Bar from the Jordans and actually resided there longer than anyone else, for more than thirty years. Or Dick and Bonnie Sterling, who ran the Wilson sheep camp and lived there for awhile, too. All these names are part of the Kirkwood history, but the Forest Service, like the rest of us, has selective retention.

Alongside the Kirk/Carter/Jordan/Wilson/Sterling home sits an old bunkhouse with a story all its own. Originally built in 1952 by Dick Sterling, constructed of 120 trees bucked into twenty-foot lengths that were handcrafted and "feathered" together, the building housed Bud Wilson's herders and crew. When the government took over the area, the structure was in jeopardy because it wasn't old enough to be considered "historic." After some debate, however, the Forest Service finally went against its own regulations and left the building standing. Although Structure No. 13-B "does not meet the 50-year-old criteria," the Sterling Cabin "is architecturally unique in design and detail" and thus "can be considered to have both local and regional historical significance," says the official decree.

Bonnie Sterling describes the actual construction in her book, *The Sterling Years*. Weighing only ninety-five pounds, she helped her husband buck the timber. Then "for many an hour I sat on logs with a draw knife taking the bark off." She notes, too, that she lent a hand with the building only "as soon as I finished my work each day." The import of her work, of course, was significant. During shearing season, for example, she "ended up with 27 men to cook for. It was a little crowded but we did fine," she reports. Her first night at Kirkwood Bar foretells the pattern of her days. "Instead of having three for supper, I had seven. Somehow I got through it and the next day everything was put in order. I had no leisure time to get used to my new home." Like Grace Jordan before her, Bonnie Sterling uses the word "home" almost immediately upon her arrival at Kirkwood Bar. Her intention, clearly, is to make this gathering place into a domestic sanctuary, a home.

Years later, the Forest Service has turned the Sterling Cabin, ultimately left intact, into an interpretive display of settlers' artifacts, cookware, tools, and Hells Canyon NRA T-shirts for sale. Yes, this deep and distant canyon is now moderately accessible to tourists. Overland, getting down to the Snake River is still a rather difficult proposition, though passable routes do exist. On the Idaho side, travelers can drive the old dirt road to Pittsburg Landing. Its corduroy surface, smoother now than it used to be, turns formidable when the weather acts up. Hikers might also drop down from the Seven Devils Wilderness, although this access involves several thousand feet in elevation loss and gain. I managed to hike about a mile and a half downriver from the dam on the Oregon side before running into impassable cliffs and impenetrable poison ivy. That little foray showed me how truly difficult it is to negotiate this terrain.

Farther downstream, however, the Oregon side is somewhat easier to manage on foot. One May, I hiked down Saddle Creek, along the Eagles Nest Trail, which literally was blasted out of the rocks and narrowly—too narrowly for my tastes—parallels the Snake River, then back up Temperance Creek. Llamas, carrying our gear, were much steadier afoot than I as we negotiated the precipitous trail. I mention this trip because of the weather. Almost ninety degrees the day we started from our cars, the temperature dipped well below freezing a week later. A blinding snowstorm battered humans and llamas alike as we hiked out over aptly named Freeze-Out Saddle. My llama, Billy, simply sat and refused to move over the crest. Curling his front legs under his chest, he sat Buddha-like, blinking his long brown lashes while the snow began to cover his face and back. I was not amused, although I now see the adventure as a paradigm of Hells Canyon extremes. Making a home amid such vagaries of hot and cold cannot have been an easy task.

If backpacking down from the rim is unappealing, tourists also can approach the inner gorge by water. The river below Hells Canyon Dam is called "wild," a designation posited by the Wild and Scenic Rivers Act. For 31.5 miles, foaming whitewater scours the rocks, and kayakers and rafters relish the rollicking excitement. Floating to Kirkwood Bar takes a couple of adventurous days on the water. Even beginners find the rapids somewhat manageable in the summertime, but a spring flood can pose almost impossible challenges. Not only do the rapids run swift and deep, but cascading tree trunks and roiling boulders make the route horrifyingly dangerous. Below Pittsburg Landing, the river is called "scenic." There, where the water is tamer and the landscape more accessible, the stark green-brown hills fold into themselves with remarkable beauty.

Upstream, the water drops twice as far in half the distance. On the wild section of the river, water craft reign supreme. One hot sultry afternoon, I watched river runners and their bright, high-tech toys line the narrow Snake River shore below Hells Canyon Dam. Ready to ship off downstream, they were making last-minute adjustments to colorful outfits and wildly misshapen loads. One man floated his kayak into the shallows, then flipped and re-flipped the narrow red craft, doing so with ease. A green kayak with a woman paddler joined him and, in unison, heads down, heads up, they repeated the routine. Beached nearby, a yellow pontoon boat shuddered under the weight of coolers and gear. A bearded man with a floppy straw hat shouted instructions, while younger concessionaires hauled waterproof bags of gear and food. Another float craft, bright purple, was quickly loaded, too. Then a bus pulled into the parking area, disgorging a dozen apparent neophytes. Their pale skin and wary looks contrasted with the studied nonchalance of the boatmen. Glancing at the river and then looking away, the newcomers lined up for lifejackets and donned them wordlessly. In their eyes, I suspect, the Snake River looks immensely powerful, but they refuse to flinch while they prepare for the adventure they hope will lie ahead. Like the *City Slickers* look-alikes on the Wyoming cattle drive, these particular young men and women spent good money to pay for their vacations.

Immediately downriver from the dam, the river spews quickly into a Z-shaped rapid that zips from the Idaho shore to the Oregon side and back again. That crest will be the first test for these voyageurs, the first chance to hold their breaths and try out their neophyte skills. Finished with their exercises, the two kayakers, red and green, spin away from shore, head straight for the whitewater, and easily negotiate the turns. In a matter of moments, they disappear around the bend. Half an hour later, a second set of kayakers launches from the river bank. These three, orange and blue and maroon, spin slightly out of control, so that a pontoon bowsman has to push the orange craft sideways, then turn it downstream again. I watch with interest, glad I'm not the one hung up in the rough water. For several hours the sideshow continues, with fresh faces and mountains of gear arriving, departing, arriving, departing. These eager and intrepid travelers are running a waterway that was essentially unnavigable until a collection of dams made the water more predictable and sophisticated equipment made the rapids more manageable. Now, for thirty miles below Hells Canyon Dam, the place is an adventure paradise, a spot where city folk can test themselves against the forces of "nature," a scenic "wilderness" where the river runs "wild and free." As I think all this, another pair of watercraft spins fluidly away, riding the Z at exactly the same spot as all the others, as if this were a well-rehearsed path. No different than hiking an overused mountain trail, I guess. This sweet-spot downstream through the gorge, like all the other rapids on the river, is accurately charted and almost routine to those who run the Snake with regularity.

Counting the kayaks and pontoon boats today, I find the nether world terminology hard to fathom. The sunlit river seems anything but hellish, and the carefree spirits of the river runners are almost paradoxical to the history of this place. Kayakers, rafters, the whole phalanx of floaters setting out from below the dam are joined by jet boats, noisy gas-guzzling affairs filled with mom and pop tourists, not a hair out of place. As a long-time environmentalist, I ought to say that I'm appalled by the notion of jet boats grinding up and down a wild and scenic waterway. As a paying passenger, I confound my purist attitude. A jet boat takes Class 4 rapids with ease, curls through the whitewater with hardly a bump, splashes along the shallows, and covers a remarkable distance in a single day. Where Grace Jordan took sixteen hours to travel approximately fifty miles by packet to Kirkwood Bar, I can zip from Hells Canyon Dam all the way down past Pittsburg Landing and back again, more than sixty miles, in less than seven hours.

Such speed enables me—and dozens of other tourists—to cover a lot of territory. Indeed, the river is almost crowded with forty-passenger jet boats, especially below Kirkwood, where tour-guide concierges from Lewiston conduct a lucrative business. Less traveled is the whitewater above Kirkwood, where Hells Canyon Adventures, Inc. runs only two or three jet boat trips per day. Those watercraft speed up and down the wild and scenic river as if there were no obstacles at all. Wild Sheep Rapids, with a seventeen-foot vertical drop in 150 feet, the longest deepest rapid in Hells Canyon; Granite Creek Rapids, a pour, with a fourteen foot drop in only 75 feet; Bernard Creek Rapids, a drop-off, seven feet straight down. All Class 4s, all negotiated with only a bit of a bounce. At Wild Sheep we watched a collection of rafts ricochet through the rocks, splashing pell mell from one whirling eddy to another. To show off the jet boat's contrasting prowess, Brian, our boatman, cut cookies, spinning us around and around in 360s, then stopping on the proverbial dime.

The fleet June boat ride also took us past more wildlife than I would normally see in a day or even a week of hiking. Two khaki-colored big-horn ewes, with a young lamb in tow, munched placidly in an abandoned Oregon alfalfa field. Like antelope, they showed off their "see and flee" technique—running a short distance, then pausing to look at the contraption in the water, racing a bit farther, stopping again to stare. After lunch we saw more bighorn, a herd of perhaps a dozen males edging up a steep slope on the Idaho side, a typical bachelor conclave during the spring birthing season. Just north of the rams' precarious positions, Suicide Point gleamed in multiple colors of brown and orange, gold and tan. I was reminded of Grace Jordan's fear of that three-hundred-foot drop-off—"a virtual stairway, one rock step above another, each one sloping out, with a flimsy coping of small stones to mark the edge." Away from the trail, where the wall falls even more sharply, the bighorn showed no such trepidation.

Sheep I expected to see, but not two moose wading placidly in the shallows. Although moose frequently are sighted along the Salmon River, which runs into the Snake a little farther downstream, their appearance in Hells Canyon itself is quite unusual. Even our boatmen, who traverse the river every day, thought that finding two young cows was a rare treat.

Late afternoon brought another photo opportunity—a pair of yearling black bear feasting on fish just paw-caught along the shore. One was so busy eating it barely noticed the jet boat eddying nearby; the other seemed less sanguine, although it too remained visible in the bushes as it peered out at the ogling tourists. "Who's in the zoo?" we said, gawking and laughing. "Who's in the cage and who's free to leave?" My fellow passengers, including five white-haired sisters from Malad City, Idaho, a party of gay men from southern California, and three generations of camouflage-clad males from some unknown rural spot, were all having a wonderful time. One of the sisters spotted a rattlesnake, the kind of creature most feared by Grace Jordan, who cautioned her children over and over again. I think I saw an eagle high overhead, though the sun was in my eyes and I couldn't be sure. All together, the Hells Canyon zoo was most satisfactory.

We rubbernecked at man-made objects, too, like a set of amber pictographs, painted onto the rocks with a cinnabar mixture. The dating was unclear, but the combination of bars and shields attests to an aboriginal presence in the canyon many centuries ago. Home, for them, was a modest cave to provide shelter from the elements. More than two hundred Hells Canyon rock art sites, similar to this one and dating from just 200 to more than 7,100 years old, have been placed on the National Register of Historic Places. These sites, however, are in some danger of being eaten away by corrosive lichen. Fed by nitrogen pollution along the riverbed, "greenish *Xanthoparmelia* [seems to be] spreading over the canyon's rocks and petroglyphs." Scientists can prove that ammonia from upstream fertilizers and feedlots is causing the rock art to pit and fade, but so far no measures have been taken to prevent the damage and the ultimate dissolution of the artifacts. Future visitors may eventually find no trace at all of aboriginal Hells Canyon residents.

Nearby, the McGaffee Cabin remains a different sort of musty sign of pioneering fortitude. Built in 1905 by Frank Hiltsley, a blacksmith, the well-preserved structure is also on the National Register of Historic Places, although it nearly met its fate during a 1986 wildfire that swept down from above. The roof of the root cellar burned off, but firefighters saved the cabin itself. Grapevines now grow where the blacksmith shop once stood, apricot and locust trees surround the requisite old alfalfa field—where the rattler was avoided by our group and where edible "Chinese lanterns" edge the well-worn paths. Inside the cabin, we could see where Mrs. McGaffee, in an effort to add warmth and, perhaps, to make the place more homey, had papered the burlap-covered walls with pages from magazines and newspapers.

Lenora Barton and her son, Ace, lived here at the same time Grace and Len Jordan were settling in downstream. Their contemporaries used to smile and say that the farther up the canyon a person lived, the tougher a body had to be. Kirkwood Bar was the line of demarcation. Sociable folk made their homes below Hells Canyon; the more reclusive sorts sought shelter deeper in the gorge, so they said. Yet when the Bartons lived there, "the house had a washing machine, a phonograph to play classical music, and a library, which included the complete works of Dickens, shelved in the front room." Thus does her son recall his youth, in *Snake River of Hells Canyon*. He uses the word "house," but I believe "home" would be a more accurate appellation. In the modern sense of the word, Lenora Barton created a domestic sanctuary with as many amenities as she could gather. A half-century later, though, souvenir hunters have stripped much of her décor. The rest of the cabin—two rooms plus a loft—remains intact, except for the original porch that was used by boaters for firewood many years ago. But the niceties have vanished. Sometimes so-called preservation leads to unwanted consequences.

As a matter of fact, governmental action has dictated much of the recent history of Hells Canyon, with a variety of outcomes. Until the 1950s, the river ran relatively wild and free, although dams around Boise already must have been affecting its flow. Robert G. Bailey speculated in 1942 that perhaps "two score people living today . . . have been through this great chasm which is absolutely inaccessible except by boat." Now, perhaps ten or twenty times that many see the inner canyon every summer day. Between Bailey's heyday and mine, however, other interests sought to lay claim to the canyon. Engineers, eager to tame the wilderness and ready to claim the potential hydroelectric power, began making plans. Some thought a ten-million-dollar road through the canyon would be a fine idea. One such highway, in fact, was planned, but the unexpected costs of World War II made the project prohibitively expensive. Next, developers realized that a series of dams could control the Snake River all the way from eastern Idaho to its confluence with the Columbia. Agricultural interests, especially enthusiastic about making the interior Pacific Northwest accessible to shipping, lobbied hard in Washington, D.C.

After much argument and much debate, authorization was approved for three dams to be constructed immediately upstream from Hells Canyon—Brownlee, Oxbow, and Hells Canyon Dam itself. As one local colorfully said, "On August 4, 1955, the FPC issued a construction license for all three and within weeks company equipment was raising more hell along the river than a turtle when the tank goes dry." A decade later, engineers had effectively blocked three thousand stream miles and replaced 1,421 acres of riparian habitat with 18,450 acres of flatwater. Hells Canyon Dam, farthest downstream of the three new structures, sits right where the deep gorge begins, and effectively controls the flow of water through the canyon. Consequently, today's "wild and scenic river" designation is a bit specious. Not only are jet boats allowed, but the whitewater actually flows through rocks ringed with minerals. Just like a reservoir, Hells Canyon's wild and scenic shores are marked all the way downstream by an indelible white bathtub ring. The sportsmen may dream that they are floating free, but the reality is less exotic.

Meanwhile, the few settlers who lived in and just below Hells Canyon were fighting furiously to prevent the flooding that would ensue if further dams had been built as planned. Their voices essentially went unheard, until outsiders joined the conversation. Authorization had already been obtained for a fourth dam, and serious surveying had taken place. The exploratory markings, in fact, are still visible on the amber cliffs not far below Pittsburg Landing. If the 670-foot High Mountain Sheep Dam had been constructed, at a projected cost of $667 million, the entire canyon would now be under water. Ironically, a lawsuit by power companies left out of the consortium that would have benefited most from the additional dam actually stopped the construction. The Department of the Interior, a number of Oregon and Idaho politicians, and some well-known personalities like Arthur Godfrey brought pressure to bear, too. Within a decade, plans to build High Mountain Sheep Dam had been abandoned and efforts to somehow preserve the entire area were underway. In 1975 the House and Senate finally agreed, and the Hells Canyon National Recreation Area became a reality.

As a city-dweller who finds pleasure in the pathless woods, as someone who believes firmly in the preservation of scenic places like this one, I am grateful for the visionary decision. However, as someone perusing the words of the settlers who actually lived through the times, I realize that the NRA designation was not necessarily good for everyone. Greatly relieved that their homeplaces would not be inundated with water, the landowners almost immediately were confronted by a different sort of takings. The federal government appropriated four million dollars to buy them out, to empty the canyon of its permanent residents, to set the land aside for strictly recreational purposes. Doris Wilson, author of *Life in Hells Canyon*, offers "a private view" of the government's actions. Most particularly, the Wilsons took issue with the appraisal process. "We were not 'willing' sellers in any sense of the word," she declares.

First of all, governmental condemnation in the guise of "Eminent Domain" seemed to the Wilsons a step backward in time. As Doris explains, "Many hardships were withstood by our attempt to 'settle the wild west.'" Taking back the land not only didn't seem fair, it seemed downright anti-thetical to the pioneering spirit of her forefathers. Second, she considered the money offered in payment quite insufficient. She complains that the men of the Forest Service pinched pennies, trying to get the land for as little as possible. The *Idaho Statesman* quotes the family spokeswoman's forthright opinion. "We believe the Forest Service officials are using the ranchers to set a precedent of acquiring farm ground for recreation, then they could move in and take over anywhere and wherever they see fit." She added, "This is about as personal as they will be allowed to get with me. When anyone threatens to take possession of my home, that is taken very personally."

There's that word "home" again. This time its intensely personal connotations conflict directly with the philosophy of preservation that came into political favor in the late twentieth century. As environmentalists saw fewer and fewer tracts of undeveloped land, they argued persuasively that the remaining "wilderness" must be saved. What they ignored, in the eyes of the Wilsons and according to a sheaf of angry newspaper articles, was the fact that real flesh-and-blood people actually called this ostensible wilderness "home." At issue, too, was the question of subdividing. Since the surrounding terrain was officially off-limits to any activity other than recreation, ranchers like the Wilsons and the Carters were no longer allowed to graze their sheep on the public lands. In effect, this policy put them out of the ranching business. Subdividing their own property—which had become attractive to potential vacationers—became the only viable way for these landholders to recoup their investments. "We don't have any choice now," insisted Mrs. Wilson. "We have sold our sheep so now we are going to develop the land ourself for lots and dude ranches."

But subdivision was anathema to the concept of a National Recreation Area, which did not include riverside resorts and vacation homes in its blueprint for recreational lands. Large-scale NRA dreamers, envisioning "undeveloped" lands open to all the public, were adamantly opposed to the practice of subdividing. The government, in bureaucratic lingo, was willing to "accommodate the needs of the occupants insofar as possible," but selling lands piecemeal was never an option. Nor was large-scale grazing, even though the government was prepared to allow a certain amount of grazing under special-time permits. The Jordans, for example, ran 3,000 sheep on 17,000 acres of range; Bud Wilson ran 4,800. By the 1970s, however, this kind of ranching had become financially marginal. Perhaps the government thought it was doing the in-holders a favor, but families like the Wilsons didn't see it that way. One day Lem Wilson arrived at their Pittsburg house, located ten miles downstream from Kirkland Bar, only to find it filled with Forest Service personnel. "This was still our home, and all our household furnishings were still in place," reported the irate Mrs. Wilson. The men left, but the psychological damage had been done.

The Wilsons sued. Two years later, the case came to trial. Both sides paraded expert witnesses into the courtroom, attempting to prove the validity of their claims. Lem Wilson actually tried to settle out of court, but at that point the government refused to negotiate. The tables were turned, however, when the chief evaluator for the Forest Service admitted that "he really was not familiar with the Hells Canyon Gorge, that he didn't even know the names of the rivers and creeks flowing into the Snake River, had not even been on the various homesteads, but had just made an appraisal more or less as the Forest Service had dictated. He had tried to 'knock down' the value in order to get the land at a reduced price!" The jury deliberated only two hours before finding for the Wilsons. Although the family still had to vacate their property, they received suitable monetary compensation. Even so, they weren't happy about their eviction. Doris Wilson concludes her version of the government's betrayal with a vignette that summarizes the whole process. "As I cleaned up the house and made ready to depart, I discovered that there was a skunk family living in the wood pile." What had been a home becomes a "house," and, more telling, a refuge for the wildlife that had always made this place a home. "After giving some thought about how to get them out of there, I realized that it was no longer my duty, and just left them there!" The skunks, in her opinion, now owned the place.

Only one small Snake River getaway evaded the government's dicta. Kirby Creek Lodge sits on one-fourth acre of personally owned property on the Idaho side. Chinese placer miners originally took possession of the spot in the late 1870s and early 1880s, but their operation soon went defunct. Jack Kurby tented on the bar for awhile, leaving only his misspelled name behind. Then several generations of the Reid family made their homes there, only to sell out to the Jordans during the Depression. It's ironic that a spot never particularly profitable has lived on to become the only privately held riverfront property in the entire National Recreation Area. Some say the lot was missed by the surveyors, but local gossip suggests the outfitter-owner was a close friend at the time of the Idaho governor. Whatever story is true, the popular place is certainly profitable today. When we motored by in our jet boat, half a dozen watercraft were tied up at the dock.

Just as the economics of the past differ from the economics of the present, so the old tales of Hells Canyon settlers differ from the stories told by today's visitors. My carefree day on the jet boat, replete with wild animals safely on shore, bears little resemblance to the financial hardships and ongoing struggles experienced by families like the Jordans, the Sterlings, and the Wilsons. My trek with the llamas soon ended anticlimactically, in the bar of the Imnaha Hotel, where a warm fire blazed on the hearth and draft beer made the storm nothing more than an adventure to recount. For my pleasure, and for the pleasure of thousands like me, the National Recreation Area offers a respite from everyday life. For those who earned their living in Hells Canyon, for those who made the canyon "home," the governmental decree and its subsequent takings signify something quite different. My metaphoric home in the wilderness of the West still exists; their literal home has disappeared as surely as if the waters of High Mountain Sheep Dam had inundated the Snake River shores.

Life in Hells Canyon ends with a winsome verse. Although the logic gives way to the rhyme scheme, Doris Wilson's thoughts are unmistakably straightforward. Home, as hearth and haven, meant a great deal to these latter-day settlers along the Snake River.

> So ended an era never to be repeated.
> Still we didn't go home just to be seated.

Indeed, the Doris Wilsons of the West equated home with a busy, energetic, and hospitable daily life. No matter what obstacles might get in the way, they were willing to work hard and their optimism prevailed. Dozens of other Idaho poets express the same sentiments. One such anonymous effort marks the frontispiece of Robert G. Bailey's *Hell's Canyon: Seeing Idaho through a Scrap Book.*

> Bright star, lighting the place to go,
> To find the sweet peace and happiness sent,
> My home in the west we call Idaho.

Rose McFadden Shinnick, in the same privately published book, pleads "Oh, take me home to Idaho, I'm lonesome for the very air, / Of the place where I was born." Home, for these rural poets, was a domestic haven in time and space. Even though times may have been tough, personal memories of "sweet peace and happiness" prevailed. Home always connoted shelter, safety, and sanctuary.

To finish my personal Hells Canyon exploration and to conclude my own sense of what home means and meant to all these old-timers, I drove to the town of Asotin. Far below the downstream opening of the canyon walls, Asotin was once the take-off point for the paddle-wheel steamer that brought supplies and mail upriver to the early settlers. It's the downstream antithesis to the float trip put-in at the Hells Canyon Visitors Center some sixty miles away. The town began to dwindle when the mail boat stopped its service and the lucrative tourist jet boat trade moved totally to Lewiston. At the City Park, where I paused briefly to consult my map, the Flatt Family Reunion was in full swing. Twenty-eight vehicles in the parking lot, five guitars and a fiddler, cowboy hats and baseball caps, and too many people to count. Were they all from around here? Did they all make Asotin their home? I spoke to the patriarch and his wife, a couple in their eighties. "Too many of the youngsters have moved away," they said, nodding in unison. In a single sentence, they spoke the words so true of so much of the interior West today, where rural economics have stymied "home"-making as the Jordans and the Wilsons and the Flatts might designate the term.

Leaving the picnic grounds, I then drove upriver as far as I could, along a narrow winding road that accesses riverfront homes outside the National Recreation Area. I stopped for awhile at Buffalo Eddy, where the ancestors of the Nez Perce, the Nimiipuu, lived from 4,500 to 300 years ago. There I saw another panel of pictographs somewhat like the smaller drawings upstream near the McGaffee/Barton cabin. (Writing that line, I recognize my instinctive reliance on the pioneers for points of reference. Their historical impact, I'm afraid, remains the touchstone for the older human and geographical scope of the canyon.) Beyond the figured bighorn sheep and the more geometric designs, the grand sweep of the Snake River opened long views in either direction. Too long, perhaps. This part of the waterway is widened by downstream's Lower Granite Dam, and resembles a constricted narrow lake more than a river. Even the kayakers and rafters take out miles before getting to Asotin. Not enough action; not nearly enough.

Jet boats still ply their trade, however. *Rapid Runner* and *Gusto del Rio*, snub-nosed and splashing, sped past, pausing only for a moment at Buffalo Eddy and a tour guide's spiel. Even on-shore, I could hear the quick, slapdash allusions to prehistoric times. Back toward town, I drove past dozens of well-kept ranchettes—a twenty-first-century version of home—lining the river banks. Occasionally, I saw a double-wide or a prefab building, but most of the houses were built of stained logs with vast expanses of glass. Retirement dwellings or second-home vacation getaways, the permanent edifices looked larger than I might have expected to find hundreds of miles from the nearest metropolis. Asotin itself boasts some homes from a profitable past, neatly painted Victorians with large well-kept lawns, but it also has its share of seedier places, rough shacks in need of repair and look-alike houses mirroring each other. None of the places inside the little community is as spacious as those recently built outside of town.

Near the Asotin city limits, though, I saw the true harbinger of home for future generations in the West. "Riverpointe . . . where the river flows free." Riverpointe is a planned community where the "river," puddled backwards from the downstream dam, may be visible but looks more like a lake. Riverpointe, where optimism runs freer than the river itself. "Asotin's finest properties for custom built homes," the sign proclaimed, and "every lot is a view lot." That view, a backwash river; each lot, an unbuilt dream. The sign shuddered in the afternoon breeze, while dust from the square-cut construction sites blew fiercely across the Snake's undulant waves. Riverpointe certainly did not look like a place where I would choose to spend my golden years.

I suppose I could call this another sort of "takings," where newcomers are building look-alike "custom" dwellings on the periphery of what once was a close-knit western community and where open space is giving way to streets and sidewalks. Complete with its faux elegant appellation, Riverpointe is a harbinger of the twenty-first-century West, a mini-example of the rural gentrification that seems to be consuming the land. These will be homes of a sort, of course, and with a stretch of the imagination, even homes below Hells Canyon. But those who build in Riverpointe—like those who run concessionaires where whitewater used to run free—are taking away the very thing they hope to find.

When I was six, my parents bought a house that sat just outside the Seattle city limits. A blacktopped street marked the northern end of the city;

another ill-kept road turned off it and led to our new home. No sidewalks, of course, and very few other houses either. Our backyard was a tangle of vine maple and brambles, the typical remains of an early logging operation. Beyond the unfenced confines stretched an open sesame of second- and third-growth trees to climb, forts to build, sword ferns to throw, plus spiders and garter snakes to torture. Until I was in junior high school, I was the only girl on the block. I learned a lot about the woods, about the creatures who lived there, about how to play outside in the rain without getting cold or wet. In those days before Goretex and thermal underwear, we somehow managed in sweatshirts and scuffed tennis shoes, yellow slickers and rubber galoshes. No one bothered to organize our lives into team sports or ballet lessons; we entertained ourselves.

When I was twelve, everything changed. By then, my own back-yard had been fenced, landscaped, and tamed. Now the woods across the street vanished in a flurry of bulldozing. Look-alike brick houses soon followed, then pavement and sidewalks. Another girl moved into the neighborhood, and her family had a television set. Instead of playing outside with the boys, I sat indoors with Howdy Doody and Red Buttons and the *Ed Sullivan Show*. The suburbs had arrived.

No one looking at the area today would presume the scenes of my youth. Any vacant lot has long since given way to residences built side by side. The streets are more numerous now, square-blocked grids curving narrowly in surprising directions and crowded with too many cars in too little space. Pushing into the area, too, are trendy boutique shops selling breads and bagels, brew pubs, gourmet restaurants, florists with fresh-cut flowers to sell, and coffee that isn't Starbucks. The charm comes from the fact that this city quadrant was completely developed before the words "strip mall" had entered the vocabulary of urban planners.

Not long ago, I drove up the block where I had so happily lived and played out my youth. I hadn't been there since my parents sold their home, fifteen years ago. Some of the houses had stayed the same; others were unbelievably different. In fact, I hardly recognized the one where I spent almost my entire childhood. First of all, it was pale green instead of the off-beige my mother had loved, and the rhododendrons needed pruning. The expansive picture windows had shrunk, the magnificent view prismed by checkerboard panes. A new earthquake code, I later was told. Most surprising, the house itself was bigger, much bigger — Riverpointe-ed, as it were. It extended upward, with a second story replacing the precarious attic I had known, and it hunkered downward, with a full basement now completely habitable. Some family homes appear to shrink with time, but mine had more than doubled in size.

Eying the changes, I couldn't resist. Parking my rental car, I climbed the stairs and knocked on the front door. When I introduced myself, the young woman who answered actually knew my name. "Your family used to live here," she said immediately. "We did all the research before we bought the house." With that said, she gestured me inside and gave me the standard "you can't go home again" tour. My parents' $7,000 starter home, the one my mother would never replace because she loved her yard, her flowers, and the view, had been transformed into a $900,000 showpiece. Same yard, though a bit bedraggled and minus the colorful madrone tree; same sweeping view of the Olympic Mountains. But inside, what a difference. Some of the changes I liked — the livable basement, the expansive master suite upstairs, a substantial new fireplace, the modernized kitchen. Others, like the shrunken windows and the darkened family room, weren't so agreeable to me. And I wondered what my mother would have said had she seen her genteel pastel living room walls transformed to deepest red. Or my own bedroom, currently home to another pre-teen daughter, decorated day-glo pink.

I must admit, however, that I appreciated the enthusiasm of the new owner. She has made the place her own, her own *home*, just as my mother did so many years ago. The home place remains a homeplace and typifies, I think, a naturally evolving urban renaissance, an ongoing reiteration of the entrepreneurial spirit so characteristic of western history. What drew my parents to View Ridge in the 1940s pulls today's families as surely as yesterday's, as inevitably as tomorrow's.

Meanwhile, each of us conjures the details of home in slightly different ways. I am struck by the fact that, when I personally think of home, my childhood dwelling comes first to mind. Neither the home of my adulthood in Reno nor the elegant new Seattle edifice; rather, the homeplace of history, the one that is arrested in time. Home, to me, is still the tiny house at the top of the hill, with the big plate glass windows that opened up the expansive western horizon. It's ironic to note that I cannot recall the names of the new owners of that house on 48th Avenue N.E., as if my own memories simply refuse to acknowledge their presence. Much better, for me, to think of my old Seattle home through the isolated cobwebs of memory. Hearth and home and haven; gossamer, dusty, opaque.

In my imagination, I see a patio crowded with wooden planters carefully tended—every inch of dirt filled with blue lobelia and pink carnations, Dad's sweet cherry tomatoes and Mother's multicolored begonias. I savor the smells of pot roast, Grandma's pepper relish, and lemon meringue pie, the scents of Thanksgiving turkey and gravy and rich plum pudding doused in peach brandy. Even today, when I bring out the Christmas tree ornaments from my mother's childhood, I still think of her indoor jade tree that always sufficed for a more traditional fir. I remember October, too, birthday month and frothy angelfood cake. In the summertime, I recall fierce backyard games of badminton and croquet that honed my competitive skills. I hear Mother shout at us to stay off the rockery, to keep our feet away from her flowers, to be careful of the lawn. At night, Dad is telling his young daughter bedtime stories, an epic sequence of tales about imaginary friends named Tex and the Professor, time travelers whose adventures taught me the sweep of history (and perhaps planted a professorial seed in my own imagination). Or I hear the sounds of bagpipe music playing loudly on the record player whenever my mother left the house. I hear, too, the swelling sounds of laughter and good times. I could go on for pages; we all could, tolling the bells of memory.

But what I remember most about home are the books. Books everywhere; books in bookcases, books lying on tables, books piled in corners. From Aristotle to Betty Friedan, from Jane Austen to Wallace Stegner, from history to biography to poetry to fiction. Magazines, too. *Sunset, Good Housekeeping, Time, Life*. My parents reading constantly. Me, too. Books absolutely everywhere—that's what I remember most about home.

CHAPTER TWO

Cities and Air

Where the air is so pure, the zephyrs so free,
The breezes so balmy and light,
That I would not exchange my home on the range
For all the cities so bright.

Born in a city, raised in a city, I'm not averse to urban places. Unlike the words of the verse that seem to disdain constricted environments, I always find pleasure on city streets and byways. And I enjoy concrete urban stories, too. Where a rural writer of my generation might recall the family pickup sliding on a gumbo-slick road, I can remember the trolley turning a corner too sharply and losing its power when the overhead cables disengaged. Where a rural writer might recall long snowy bus rides to a distant school, I can remember splashing through mud puddles as my friends and I tramped to View Ridge Elementary, six blocks and back, every day. Where a rural writer might recall sagebrush or sand, I can remember pansies and potted begonias. Where a rural writer might recall endless family forays cutting wood, I remember not even the transparency of natural gas heating but an oil truck arriving once a month and pumping its gallons into the underground tank in our front yard.

When my parents wanted a fire in the fireplace, they burned pressed sawdust presto logs.

Where a rural writer of my generation might recall a feast at harvest time—fried chicken, roasts and mashed potatoes and gravy, endless apple pies—I can remember fresh lettuce and tomatoes from the Farmer's Market, chops cut to order by my father's butcher friend, steelhead and salmon caught in the morning and consumed just a few hours later, juicy red huckleberries fresh from the bushes. Where a rural writer might recall farm breakfasts around the kitchen table, I can remember a restaurant called the American Oyster House, where dad and I would order thin plate-sized buttermilk pancakes sprinkled with lemon and powder sugar, then doused in maple syrup, while my mother enjoyed a hangtown fry of scrambled eggs and Willapa oysters. Where a rural writer might recall the taste of fresh-drawn milk, I can remember the look—though I never got the sip—of a frozen daiquiri in a frosty glass. Where a rural writer might recall a barnyard array of hens, roosters, and perhaps a favorite colt, I can remember frequent zoo outings, with imported elephants and giraffes, even lions and tigers and bears.

Last summer I attended a Book Festival in Billings. During one session, a panel of Montana women writers articulated the kinds of memoirs they imagined still need to be written about growing up in the middle years of the twentieth century. I smiled to myself as I listened, for no one mentioned city life at all. Focusing solely on the fading family ranch, they dwelled on variations of their own experiences. Urban adventures were as foreign to them as rural fortitude was alien to me. If an appliance failed at my house, a repairman arrived. If my parents wanted a night out or a week away, they called a babysitter. Indoors, I played with paper dolls, designing ongoing narratives of city life and human relationships and urban complexities. Outdoors, my playmates and I built scrub maple stockades, threw sword ferns at each other, and climbed trees. I knew more about Steller's jays and garter snakes than I did horses and cowboys. To learn about the Wild West, I listened to the radio or went to Saturday matinees. The voices and faces of Roy Rogers and Dale Evans, Gene Autry, the Lone Ranger, Tom Mix, and Hopalong Cassidy comprised a fantasy West, one that had little to do with the West where I actually lived.

My world included Green Lake, a tiny reservoir with a circular paved path. We rented bicycles, rode round and round, then finished off an afternoon by eating hot fresh fish and chips with our fingers. The other nearby lake, Lake Washington, was off limits. Not only did a naval air base impose itself along the shore, but the water was so polluted that swimming was a danger. We never went near Lake Washington, except to cross the floating bridge. At the bottom of our hill, a creek ran past voluminous bushes of blackberries, which we picked and greedily ate every summer. Recalling those early years, I realize that much of my childhood centered around water. Ravenna and Wedgewood creeks, Seattle's numerous lakes, the Pacific Ocean, Hood Canal, Puget Sound. With my parents, I prowled the water's edges everywhere. Rather than riding round ups and branding cattle, we dug geoeducs, cleaned crabs, or roasted oysters on an open fire—activities surely restricted today. I think I subconsciously equate 'downtown' with waterfront property, as if a city like Cheyenne or Denver hardly counts. Downtown demands plentiful seafood restaurants, a fleet of ferries shuttling back and forth, the waft of salt air on the breeze, the seagulls' lonesome cries. And where a rural writer might recall the height of a hayloft, I can remember riding an open-sided freight elevator to the top of the Space Needle, then stepping across a sickening foot or two of open space to stand on the unfinished framework of the soon-to-be-symbolic structure. A high-rise adventure in a high-rise city, where my father and his friends worked in tall buildings and always wore coats and ties.

But suburban life is modulating, too, as surely as the rural world has changed. Where Montana's isolation was compromised by electric power, telephones, television, and snowmobiles, my city exploded with people and plans for progress. In fact, tolling Seattle's best-known businesses is a twentieth-century litany of entrepreneurial success. Boeing started in a garage not far from my grandmother's Kent home. Nordstrom's was a shoe store when I went to grade school with the three Nordstrom boys. Starbuck's and Microsoft and Amazon.com came after my time, but they too transformed the Seattle–Kent–Bellevue–Edmonds quadrangle in extraordinary ways. I hardly recognize the city any more, its hourglass shape and single north-south freeway squeezed by extensive suburbs and strip malls in every direction. When I was a young quasi-adult, however, Seattle seemed like the end of the earth. I couldn't wait to leave. I wanted to see the world, to escape what seemed perpetually mundane and to find glamour elsewhere. Even today, I can't for the life of me figure out anything fascinating about my childhood or isolate a single neurosis that might enliven the printed page. A mid-twentieth-century middle-class urban upbringing—absolutely unromantic—no cattle trails at all.

The nineteenth-century notion of urbanity must have been quite different from mine. What might the verse-maker have meant by a "city so bright?" Perhaps Cheyenne, with its downtown train depot all lit up at night. Or Denver, with its elegant Brown Palace Hotel. Or even Miles City, Montana, whose very name—like all communities called "something City"—suggests its importance. Named for a general, Miles City initially was just a makeshift log hut where the soldiers could buy whiskey. After Nelson A. Miles and his men built a cantonment at the confluence of the Tongue and the Yellowstone rivers in 1876, a town quickly grew nearby. Later, Miles City became the commercial center for widespread cattle operations on the Great Plains. Today it thrives amid developing energy resources. Nannie Alderson, writing in the late nineteenth century, recalls her first glimpse of its central district. "I had been prepared for Miles City ahead of time, so I was not surprised by the horses hitched to the rails along the store fronts, the wooden sidewalks and unpaved streets, nor was I surprised that every other building was a saloon. Mr. Alderson had told me it was a pretty hoorah place." When I saw Miles City many decades later, the downtown area didn't seem very "hoorah" to me, although the city's official website still boasts of its "hoorah" status.

Following Interstate 94 en route from Seattle to Chicago and back again, I always picked Miles City as a stopping point because it was a convenient spot in the midst of what seemed at the time a dreary stretch of highway (my Pacific Northwest sensibility had not yet learned to appreciate the tree-free open spaces). I liked one particular pinkish-painted motel that boasted a large swimming pool and juicy, homegrown hamburgers. Subsequent visits taught me the value of a cowboy bar with a decent jukebox—an updated version of Mrs. Alderson's saloons—but that's another story. In the late '60s, I only equated Miles City with whistle stop, a place to gas up the car and me.

Since I never pictured myself writing about the place, I never made any notes about its sights and scenes. This leaves my imagination totally free. I can recall the length and breadth of the apparently flat horizons, the smells of fresh-cut hay, the cattle fattened for fall. I also can re-envision where the Tongue River rolls into the Yellowstone, and the spot where I once unfortunately camped alongside a family of skunks. The downtown hotel—I've forgotten its name—prominently displays a sign saying "Gus McCrae slept here." In my dreams, the cowboy bar serves microbrews instead of Bud; the jukebox blares Tricia Yearwood instead of Patsy Cline; and I'm thirty again. In reality, though, a long strip mall now shoulders the secondary road out of town, wearing a Wal-Mart as its crown. I wonder if the presence of a Wal-Mart in fact designates a city; the absence of Wal-Mart, barely a town. Perhaps so. But Wal-Mart, as a non-native invasive species, is not a distinguishing western characteristic. Rather, it's just a twenty-first-century Miles City focal point that would astonish Nannie Alderson.

My fondest memory of Miles City centers in a city park where, more than a decade ago, a gathering of citizens epitomized, for me, the social ambience of a rural western community. Fanning out from the Western Heritage Center in Billings to visit distant cities and towns, Mary Clearman Blew and I were talking about our writing with groups of interested people. A dozen men and women in Livingston, a handful in Crow Agency, a fair number in Billings. In contrast, Miles City attracted standing room only. And they wouldn't let us go. Ten o'clock, eleven o'clock, nearly midnight before everyone finally stopped talking. I'm not exaggerating when I say that of all the places I've gone to talk about my books, the Miles City audience was the liveliest, the most perceptive and provocative, the most engaging. I know I was only seeing a narrow slice of the total population, but I, a naïve city gal, was astonished by their eagerness to share their ideas and by their profound sense of community. If I might invert the cowboy's lament about city lights so bright, I would say those lights can attract as well as repel. In Miles City, Montana, they draw the community together.

In Page, Arizona, they do the same. Here my memory is much clearer than the gauzy dream of Miles City, for I recently returned to Page. The lights were dazzling. On Saturday morning at 8 a.m., exactly a week before Christmas, every siren in town exploded with sound. A parade of police cars and fire trucks rumbled down Lake Powell Boulevard, turned left along Highway 89, turned left again to go past Wal-Mart and back onto Lake Powell Boulevard. Lights flashing, horns honking, sirens blasting, the fleet rang in the holiday season. For just a moment, I wondered if Glen Canyon dam might be in danger, then realized the vehicles were moving much too slowly for a genuine emergency and the drivers were waving gregariously at anyone out on the streets. As a holiday celebration, that was only the beginning.

Ten hours later, the real Festival of Lights got underway. Again, the route circled downtown, although the perimeter was somewhat more circumscribed because it omitted the Wal-Mart leg. Forty-plus floats, wildly decorated with lights and bright colors, came past parking lots lined with pickup trucks and cars and filled with cheering crowds. With a police car and a fire truck leading the way, more sirens rang out. An ambulance followed, with its driver, its passenger, and a cowering cocker spaniel all wearing Santa caps. The high school band came next, solemnly alternating between "Jingle Bells" and "Joy to the World." A Pepsi float, borrowed from the Fiesta Bowl parade, showed off the only professional design, though it was pulled along by an undecorated tow truck. Mrs. Page and Mrs. Arizona passed by, and from the mayor's float another woman sang more "Jingle Bells" into a microphone. Two decorated houseboats, several versions of Rainbow Bridge, a couple of ATVs strewn with tinsel, a handful of red and green motorcycles, a VW bug carrying a huge red-nosed Rudolph on top, more frustrated dogs wearing red-blinking collars and golden wreaths, and everywhere people laughing and throwing candy to the crowd.

Standing in the Safeway parking lot, I was reminded of a gargantuan tailgate party. Every vehicle faced the parade, while men and women sat in lawn chairs and youngsters dashed off the curbs and gathered up candy. I saw one elderly woman with her oxygen tank tucked by her side, another with an afghan folded over her lap, an old man bent over his cane. One family was barbecuing hamburgers; another quartet, eating popcorn. Children, too many to count, scattered everywhere. I found myself caught by the moment, as I had been in Miles City, a fleeting part of a community so far from Reno. The energy, the emotion, the enthusiasm crowned the start of the holiday season for me, and I'll never again think of Page in quite the same way.

Until December 18, 2004, I only considered Page—if I thought about Page at all—as a peripheral bystander to engineering accomplishment and to symbolic environmental outrage. Three "monuments to progress" adjoin this hydra-headed company town. Glen Canyon Dam stands on one side of the community, the Navajo Generating Station on another, and Lake Powell dominates the view. Or, in a drought-defined year like 2004, what remains of Lake Powell nestles below a sweeping panorama of red rock canyon walls. Currently, the lake sits at its lowest level since 1969, one hundred and thirty-five feet below full pool. When I last saw its turquoise waters, it was nearly at capacity, so I wanted to see the now-diminished lake. Hence, the trip to distant Page in deep December. I also wanted to see how the community was coping with its losses, for the disappearance of the water was accelerating an economic evaporation, too.

The displays at the Glen Canyon Dam Visitors Center set the tone. "The system is laboring," I learned from the only exhibit that even acknowledged the difficulties of drought. But when I moved to the next panel, I found the water fluctuations justified. "The system is designed this way, and is working well." Such blind rhetoric of pride sharply contrasted with what I saw at the newly constructed Antelope Point Marina, where the lake lapped some fifty feet below the empty boat ramp and where a poorly drained dirt road provided the only water access. Clearly the architects expected the marina, at its grand opening in 2004, to be located near lake level, not sitting high and dry and empty. But no hint of environmental controversy appeared either in the Visitors Center or in the John Wesley Powell Museum in nearby Page. Neither place addressed the ongoing debate about the efficacy of the dam or mentioned its attendant problems. I soon discovered, in fact, that in this community I had best not say aloud the names of the two chief entities—the Sierra Club and the Glen Canyon Institute—that advocate draining the lake and returning the Colorado River to a free-flowing wildness, or argue that at least drawing down the lake level should be a matter of policy. If I wanted to learn more about the alternative point of view, I needed to exercise discretion in Page places of business.

At the Powell Museum, which once housed the cement testing lab and which still demonstrates its original design of "little cubicles, and little cubbyholes," I found a tiny room devoted to "Page: Construction Camp to Vacation Destination." In 1957, Camp Page—soon to be Page, never Page City—grew out of Manson Mesa, a piece of desert that was part of the Navajo Indian Reservation until the federal government orchestrated a land swap. The Bureau of Reclamation cut and graded roads, while Merritt-Chapman and Scott built housing for their engineers and dormitories for the other workers and bladed a flat area for trailers. A school in a Quonset hut opened almost immediately. The early days were rough ones, with few amenities and many difficulties. Doris Knight, whose husband developed the airport from a "makeshift dirt strip," remembers they rolled big red rocks "around to tie the airplanes to." A 1960 aerial view shows mostly barracks, plus a few mobile home tracts, a Babbitt Brothers Trading Company, and little else. By comparison, Page in 2004 has a permanent population of nearly 7,000, many middle-class neighborhoods, a few rather elegant enclaves, additional modular housing, and a good-sized Wal-Mart. Where Lake Powell Boulevard crests above the southeast side of town, several substantial schools, a fancy new library, and nearly a dozen churches stand on blocks of land furnished by the government for municipal purposes. In heritage and by design, Page is a western city in miniature.

In the pages of A Story That Stands Like a Dam, Russell Martin writes at length of the government camp that grew almost overnight. He describes a "booming, brawling, hardscrabble, sandy Page" that soon teemed with mosquitoes and biting flies. Lines at the Post Office often stretched for three blocks or more, as did queues for gasoline and food. But Page was on a roller-coaster ride. Like so many western cities with boom and bust economies, this community saw both good times and bad. Martin explains that in 1963 Page had called itself the "drinkingest, gamblingest, churchiest town in Arizona." But in five short years, it changed from a "camp that never slept, carefree and hearty and irrepressible as an eight-year-old, which it was," to something else. By 1968, he facetiously observes, "you could take a nap in the middle of Seventh Avenue (now Lake Powell Boulevard) . . . and know you'd wake up alive."

Projections of a burgeoning tourist-based economy turned out to be accurate, but in the meantime community leaders sought less volatility. While the dam was being completed, lengthy negotiations also were taking place between the Navajos living on the adjacent reservation and several private out-of-state corporations. Between 1970 and 1974, a separate coal-fired power generation station was added to the scenery. With a 2,250,000 kilowatt maximum output from the three units, the plant is a construction as immense as the dam, and as intrusive. The noise, an ongoing robotic rumble, never ceases. From the stacks, each 775 feet high, particulate emissions spew high into the air in variegated clouds of white, mauve, even green. In wintertime, an inversion captures much of the pollution, so that a low-lying fog often discolors the red rock scenery. Although I could readily determine that the plant is designed to consume 24,000 tons of coal per day, I could never extricate an exact figure for the contaminants pumped into the atmosphere. The power plant apparently has been retrofitted so that its emissions of sulpher dioxide have been reduced by ninety percent, but the sky still looked grimy to me. The city of Page definitely does not resemble a place where "the air is so pure, the zephyrs so free, / The breezes so balmy and light."

The city is, however, a place conducive to poetry. In 1957, Marie and Roger Golliard established the Glen Canyon Trading Post in Page. They eventually became the old-timers, early supporters of the museum and enthusiastic spokespersons for the community. Marie, along with another long-time Arizonan, A. I. Moon, penned a poem that graces one of the John Wesley Powell Museum crannies. I quote "My Desert Home" not only because it conveys the spirit of those who settled Page but because it thematically echoes Idaho's poetry of home.

> In the evening when the sunset casts a crimson glow,
> Across the desert wasteland, there's a place I want to go.
> It's a new town in Arizona in a land that's harsh and rough.

Struggling for recognition out among the sandstone bluff.
It's the home of some hearty people, the sons of the last pioneers.
They are taming the Colorado after a million unbridled years.
There's no place for the weak or timid in this bare and desolate land.
Scorched by the heat of summer and blasted by rolling sand.
But there is a special kind of freedom in this place of hills and stone,
And I guess that's the reason I'll make Page my home.

Neither weak nor timid, these "sons of the last pioneers" may have encountered a hotter climate than did Idaho's settlers, but like their compatriots to the north, they were founding—against difficult odds—a close-knit community. The Golliards and the Moons, like the Jordans and Wilsons, were establishing a place to call home.

Both literally and metaphorically, the lights drew people to Page. While such a place might not be to a cowboy's liking, it sufficed for a generation of workers. Now, however, in a twenty-first-century replication of the late 1960s, events beyond their control are shifting Page's economics. After the parade, I ate dinner at Zapata's, a Mexican restaurant serving excellent food. There, on a Saturday night following popular festivities less than a block away, only two parties came to dine. Zapata's planned to close at 8 p.m. A few doors away, the Beale Outlet store was closed, too, but earlier that afternoon it had been—next to Wal-Mart—the most popular spot in town. I could barely negotiate Beale's aisles, crowded with shopping carts and bargain hunters. For the locals, wintertime calls for curtailed and careful spending.

Much lonelier than the city were the empty shores of Lake Powell. At Lone Rock, a popular primitive camping spot just beyond the Wahweap Marina, I left my truck in the parking lot, then walked for twenty minutes before reaching the water. "Swim at Own Risk" proclaimed several signs, but the shallow murky water looked dangerously uninviting. Alongside the truck, another sign asked visitors to consider their environment. "Think of Lake Powell as a city—a city without water or sewage treatment facilities and without garbage pickup. Now think of 2 million people spending the night each year on Lake Powell beaches. The same beaches are used over and over each night by different boats. How can Lake Powell and surrounding lands stay clean?" Good question, I thought to myself while noting the sign gave no explicit answer. But I found the analogy a curious one. Might a campground be analogous to a city? Is this a modern dimension of a cowboy's nightmare?

Yosemite has always been a mecca for tourists, and Tuolumne Meadows in Yosemite's high country has always attracted campers. Elizabeth Stone O'Neill, in *Meadow in the Sky*, quotes a late-nineteenth-century description of an Indian compound "out on the rocky moraines" where "the breezes blew strongest" to "minimize winged pests," and where "their colored blankets and clothes and teepees made a gala appearance. Here they traded skins and acorns for pine nuts and obsidian," then fashioned arrowheads from the volcanic glass flakes. Meanwhile, Euro-Americans were finding Tuolumne Meadows an equally attractive place to camp and explore. In 1863, cartographer William Brewer enthusiastically praised "a flat nearly a mile wide, green and grassy," with its delicious, "highly tonic," mineral springs. Joseph LeConte, a decade later, sounded even more enthusiastic about the "beautiful grassy plain of great extent, thickly enameled with flowers." Such untrammeled scenery was not to last, however, for sheepherders soon found the meadows to their liking. A few years of overgrazing, and the green grassy expanses quickly turned to dust.

After the area gained national park status, recreationists discovered the meadows. Sierra Club members, among the most enthusiastic, planned their treks with almost military precision. Animals, packers, cooks, and ninety-six participants came to Tuolumne Meadows for the first Sierra Club outing in 1901, toting cots and bedding and enough food for an army. Every summer after that, more and more outdoor enthusiasts found the surroundings appealing. Before long, campers had done almost as much damage as sheep. When automobiles joined the parade to the meadows, the fragile meadows began turning even browner. Helter-skelter along the river, campers set up their tents. Without fees and without time limits, some stayed all summer long. During the 1920s, "the campground was gloriously informal, more an idea than a thing." Many families returned year after year. For them, for their children, and for their grandchildren, the meadows became a second home, and their adventures, retold from one generation to the next, are part of the place's lore.

As long as the roads were narrow, poorly surfaced, sometimes impassable, and often terrifying to negotiate, not too many casual visitors joined the Tuolumne Meadows regulars. After World War II, however, a new and improved Tioga Pass Road attracted more and more people to the park. In time, Tuolumne Meadows became almost too popular. First the Park Service disallowed open camping alongside the river, then sanitation problems forced them to disband the old campground near the soda springs. Today, overnight stays are legal only in a single circumscribed area that can best be characterized as a veritable city of tents. In midsummer, hopeful campers gather at dawn and wait patiently in line to settle into one of the 314 sites available in Tuolumne Meadows. Although most spots are reserved in advance, an occasional drop-in can sometimes secure a space. Those campsites, however, are so close together that there's little privacy and no sense of wilderness at all.

The encampment resembles any urban community, especially one where the neighbors sit outside and the children play on the curbs. A heavy pall of woodsmoke—the campground version of smog—sits heavily in the hollows. Laundry and wet towels hang on rope lines strung from tree to tree. Sounds of music and laughter blend with the smells of cooking and accumulated garbage. With no trash removal during the course of a long weekend, the recycle stations overflow with beer bottles and fuel canisters. Chipmunks and squirrels, the campground equivalent of big city rats, scamper in and out of the trash. Smells of oriental soup, hamburgers, hot dogs, and tacos fill the air. With tents jammed together like tenements, only the bright nylon colors signify campground instead of slum. Almost within spitting distance, I count nine tents, four tent trailers, two netted kiosks set up over picnic tables, and one enclosed plastic shower. That's just on my side of the road.

A few hundred yards away, the highway hums with a steady stream of traffic buzzing from one viewpoint to the next. Every so often, the Park Patrol sirens past. Inside the campground, a handful of helmeted eight-year-olds pedal up and down the side streets, dodging potholes here and there. When they pause, they discuss the relative merits of bicycle manufacturers. They might as well be standing outside a sporting goods store in downtown San Jose. Beyond them, a noisy volleyball game continues with shouts of spikes and misses. A car alarm goes off, rings fifteen times before the owner masters the bells and whistles. I seem to be the only person sitting in a camp chair, watching the action. Everyone else is busy somehow, on task to pursue and enjoy a nine-to-five vacation as if it were a consequential job.

Essentially inaccessible for eight months of the year, the Tuolumne Meadows campground in August is an international city of sorts, a temporary one where citizenship changes nightly. Close by, a dozen Korean neighbors struggle with their tents. Laying out the many pieces, they read the instructions in English and then discuss the meaning in Korean. This all takes awhile. I hear a lot of Spanglish, too, plus the Macarena sounds of someone's CD player. On Sunday night, a loud male voice shouts "Bear!" Other voices heighten in pitch, until everyone realizes he's only joking. In truth, I think I'm more likely to see a bear on the outskirts of Reno. Here, heavy bear-proof containers keep campers' food secure, and the rogue bears have long since been evacuated. Such containers, first developed in Yosemite, have become a high-country standard in the park's campgrounds. Before their advent, Tuolumne Meadows was a haven for hungry bears. I remember a story told by a friend of mine. Thirty years ago, while he was sleeping on the ground not far from his Volkswagen bug, a bear lumbered up to the car, circled it, then opened the hood to retrieve the cooler inside. So experienced was the bear, that he (or she) knew which end to attack. Today, it's hard to imagine sharing an inner-city-type campsite with any wild creature except those foraging garbage-mouthed chipmunks and squirrels.

On a nearby trail, I did see a single doe wander down to the river, but for the most part this place is a natural cocoon from nature. Even the stars are obscured by smoke, if not by the encroaching lodgepole pine. I understand the meadow once was larger, that natural succession is taking place—the grasses giving way to the trees. Drought has affected the area, too. Wherever I hiked this past summer, I found lakes with receding shorelines and evergreens dry-needled and drooping. One of my favorite routes climbs nine miles to the Vogelsang. Located at 12,000 feet, this is one of the five high mountain camps constructed in the 1920s. Each provides food and shelter—at a price—for the hiker who chooses not to carry overnight gear. The Vogelsang High Sierra Camp, like its lower counterpart in Tuolumne Meadows, is another kind of tent city. With water running from a fountain, hot showers, fancy outhouses, and almost all the amenities of home, the hiker need not suffer. At least the tents are real—made of white canvas, pulled down and stored away at the end of every season. One Fourth of July, when I backpacked there, snow still covered much of the trail and the tents were nowhere to be seen. This August, however, a steady stream of hikers flowed to and from the camp. When I stopped at the desk of the High Sierra Camp in the meadows, I found little information about lodging there. A bored clerk glared at me when I asked for a brochure. "You'll have to get on the Internet," she shrugged. Her indifference not only reminded me of big-city life, but also indicated how far we have come from the days when neighborly campers made themselves at home all along the Tuolumne River.

Elizabeth Stone O'Neill suggests several reasons for today's lack of connection with the meadows. New equipment, like the tents and showers sported by my neighbors, makes camping so much easier. So do the elephantine motor homes that now can negotiate a trans-Sierra route. "Many of these new visitors," she writes,

> saw the mountains as a park in the conventional sense, a recreational area, rather than as a wilderness. The meadows sprouted with such hitherto unfamiliar gear as volley and beach balls, baseball bats, air mattresses to float on the river and rafts to run it, and Frisbees. The staccato barking of motor scooters as well as the blaring of radios, electric generators, and tapes often drowned out chattering chickarees and hammering woodpeckers.

Her words concur with my own Tuolumne Meadows experience last summer. This is the plight of parks in contemporary times, an aggregate of campers creating a kind of city unimaginable in the nineteenth century but all too common in today's West.

In 1996, Yosemite attracted 1,030,368 overnight lodging visitors—
larger than the city population of San Francisco. If I were to add an
unknown number of overnight campers to that total, the sum might
well equal the population of the entire Bay Area. Garbage proliferation,
sewage back-ups, air and noise pollution, overcrowding—all the negatives
of big-city life—necessarily follow. A 1980 congressional report, *State of
the Parks*, analyzed "no fewer than 4,345 individual threats to the system's
integrity," and predicted dire consequences if changes were not made.
Twenty-five years later, many of those unfortunate predictions have
come true. However Bob R. O'Brien, in a fascinating book titled *Our
National Parks and the Search for Sustainability*, argues that the campgrounds are under control and that they will continue to be adequate
throughout the century ahead. Those of us who remember "the good
old days" may not agree. Sitting in the midst of a tent city, surrounded by
cars, huge mobile homes, radios, people and dogs, I find myself longing
for more open space and solitude. A modern campground is just too
civilized for my tastes.

In truth, Tuolumne Meadows is as much a company town as Page,
two places predicated by the federal government, powered by urban
urgencies, driven more by economics than by ecology. In many ways,
these two places symbolize the ironies of western urban development—
not a "Home on the Range" stereotype but a more complicated modern
evolution. The American mind-set necessarily hammers wilderness into
community, yet we rarely stop to envision what might actually result
from our constructions. Thus the wilderness-less Yosemite, the Seattle
suburban sprawl, the Wal-Mart-ized Miles City, the Page so dependent
on reservoir fluctuations, the thousands of other western cities scattered
across the plains, against the mountains, and alongside the sea. Each
began as a figment of someone's strike-it-rich imagination; each thrives
because other men and women pursued their dreams as well; each labors
today under the weight of its own success. They're crowded with people
like you and me.

Just as the cities of the American West have grown beyond the ballad's
imaginative scope, so the skies are no longer "so pure" and "so balmy

and light." I thought about writing painful descriptions of Denver smog or the wintertime Salt Lake City air, but decided instead to consider emissions of a more natural sort—the smoke that hovers on our horizons when the zephyrs blow forest fires out of control.

The Coal Seam fire almost burned Glenwood Springs, Colorado, out of existence in mid-June, 2002. Less than a week later the scene had returned to normal, with traffic jammed together where trucks and cars exit the interstate, fast food outlets thriving, and eager tourists clamoring for the popular vapor baths. If those hurried visitors had looked more closely, though, they would have seen where fire had jumped the high-speed highway, where strands of red retardant and blackened charcoal wove along the roadways and between structures as if the scene were an ocean shoreline instead of a mountain retreat, where ashes and mud ebbed and flowed together. They might have imagined the exclamations made and exhortations shouted while the denizens of Glenwood Springs watched in horror when the flames came closer and closer.

Walking along one such scalloped seam of slurry red and black, I watched a golden-mantled ground squirrel carefully make its way into the charred terrain. It came out from behind a log cabin that firefighters had protected, stepped cautiously away from the safety of an unburned patch of tiny white flowers and into the "sterile" burn. This was a squirrel on a mission, its busy nose and mouth and paws seeking "invisible" nuts and seeds that had been popped open by the force of the flames. A Vulcan indicator, its presence showed that despite apparent catastrophe the business of regeneration was beginning almost immediately.

Such is the perennial cycle of wildfires in the American West. What we see on television—an orange-red wall of flame, intense smoke, trees and brush on fire, dwellings destroyed, worried faces, exhausted firefighters, acreage consumed—is almost immediately followed by a natural process of renewal. Even though the visual devastation may remain for years, flora and fauna soon cope with the changed habitat and surroundings. Many trees and plants actually thrive after severe fires, as do certain birds and mammals. Nevertheless, when looking at a fresh consumptive burn, it is hard to believe that fire is beneficial to the environment.

I watched the foraging squirrel for awhile, not only trying to discover what it was unearthing but also trying to imagine the fiery scene earlier that week. Flames tend to burn hotter and to flare more quickly when traveling uphill, so this particular canyon fingering deep into the mountains should have been secure. "It was okay with the crick right here," drawled a workman, who wandered over to see what I was doing. "Except if that tree caught on fire," he added, dipping his blue-billed cap toward the singed pine that shaded my truck. Despite his sanguine tone, the surroundings clearly had been under seige. Although none of the log buildings of the Glenwood Springs Fish Hatchery had actually caught on fire, many were charred on their backsides. And the smell, unlike the romantic aroma of an embered campfire, was an onerous, lung-filling odor oppressively heavy with hanging smoke.

Indeed, this fire was not yet extinguished. Overhead, helicopters plied back and forth, scooping water from the Colorado River into hanging buckets, then disappearing behind mountains to the north, a processional for squelching those flames still threatening distant acres of roadless forest. This rugged terrain was familiar fire-ravaged territory. In 1994, another fire in the same vicinity broke loose with drastic consequences. Trying to outrun what is called a "blowup," fourteen men and women firefighters lost their lives in a matter of moments. John Maclean describes the catastrophic events that day, when a canyon wildfire "burning in debris and litter" transitioned instantly into "one involving all available fuel, from the ground to the tops of the trees." Reconstructing the horror of an entire canyon instantaneously exploding in "suffocating flame and smoke," he details the crew's instinctive reactions and scrutinizes their utter inability to escape the all-consuming conflagration.

Fire on the Mountain tells that story of the Storm King Mountain tragedy. Particularly poignant are the events leading up to the holocaust, for this was a fire that could have been squelched in its earliest stages. A combination of drought and lightning should have alerted both local and regional officials to the potential for a disastrous flare-up, but instead a series of bureaucrats made incrementally bad decisions. While various supervisors hesitated to deploy the necessary firefighters, the fire grew larger and larger until, with disastrous consequences, the situation finally

exploded out of control. The same sort of bureaucratic vacillation fanned
the flames of the Coal Seam Fire eight years later. An underground fire
had smoldered for years in a dormant coal seam near Glenwood Springs,
but the two-million-dollar bid to extinguish the potential problem was
too steep for the locals. When the Coal Seam Fire blazed to the surface,
the attendant cost was astronomically greater. Even though no lives were
lost, the destruction to property was exorbitant. So, too, was the damage
to scenery and wildlife and natural resources, all important ingredients
of the local economy.

As I write those lines, I remember that squirrel tiptoeing out into the
ashes. Perhaps its life had been temporarily disrupted, but the squirrel
itself not only was surviving nicely but also was helping the local economy
as it were by spreading freshly opened seeds and nuts. Already the land
was beginning to regenerate itself.

"Regeneration through violence" is the phrase coined by scholar
Richard Slotkin to define the process by which the American Dream has
manifested itself over and over again. The pattern recurs from generation to generation, as the American people justify their own aggression.
For several centuries, our leaders have reasoned that force ultimately will
bring about good, that conflict will lead to peace. A democratic kind of
ritual cleansing is this regeneration through violence. We easily might
use the same logic to talk about the natural violence of fires. After the
powerful maelstrom of a firestorm, the ecological landscape is reborn in
healthy positive ways. The cycle, ultimately, is a good one. Mostly, though,
we focus on the negatives—the violence, the collateral damage, the human
costs of big burns.

A friend of mine, who works for Nevada's Desert Research Institute,
owns a summertime retreat on a flank of Storm King Mountain. The
firefighters saved his cabin in 1994, but they saved nothing else in sight.
"As far as we can see in any direction," Bill reported, "nothing but burnt
stumps, powdered ash, and debris." Since nothing happened to the cabin
itself, Bill's insurance wasn't applicable. "So we own this cabin in the
middle of burnt-out desolation, with no view worth having any more."
Bill shrugged as he told me about the ruined vista. "They should've let
it burn," he said of his family's second home. "I wish they'd let it burn."

But there is another side to the haphazard nature of pyrotechnic violence. The *High Country News* issue of May 26, 2003, recounts the story of Greg Tilford and his wife, Mary, who lost their cabin in a Montana fire in 2000. They wish fervently that the firefighters had saved their "dream" home. Instead, the flames leveled it to the ground. They and their neighbors lost far more than vacation retreats. They lost everything. The result? A lawsuit against the federal government for its incompetent fire-fighting practices.

Modern fires seem to have engulfed more and more homes and businesses in recent years. Not only the Bitterroots suffered in 2000. That year, too, the Cerro Grande Fire burned more than two hundred houses in Los Alamos, New Mexico. Two years later, Colorado's Hayman Fire covered 137,000 acres and destroyed 132 homes. Meanwhile, in the opposite corner of the state, citizens of Durango were terrified by the steady march of flames that approached their city. Reno is no safer, with sizzling sagebrush that burned dangerously close to my neighborhood just five years ago. A few miles away, another aggressive Nevada fire engulfed Sierra foothill residences, causing several of my friends to spend an uneasy night watering down their roofs. A list of the damages caused by incendiary wildfires could go on and on. Each fire with its own characteristics, its own narrative, its own particular conclusions.

But it is incorrect to suppose that destruction of property is a contemporary phenomenon or that disagreements about how to control such volatility are anything new. Arguments have proceeded for generations. Politicians, forestry officials, ranchers, lumbermen, smoke-jumpers, on-the-spot firefighters, and vocal homeowners in western communities have long debated how fire might best be "managed." We've all heard stories about the ways the Plains Indians set fires to drive game in desirable directions. So did the Paiute people, long before the arrival of the pioneers. In the mountains and forests of the West, too, lightning caused burns at regular intervals almost everywhere. Because these fires recurred so often, excess underbrush rarely accumulated in disastrous amounts. When the pioneers began populating the West, however, they understandably took measures to prevent conflagrations near their settlements. Slowly but surely, without really thinking through the consequences, westerners began a trend that has accelerated over the years: extinguishing small fires preordains the existence of large ones.

According to Stephen J. Pyne, the best-known fire historian of our generation, massive fires in 1910 proved to be the fulcrum on which United States fire policy turned. No single account accurately quantifies the massive amount of western landscape burned that year. One official record says two and a half million acres, but that counts only the national forests. Adding together the decimated national parks, the charred Indian reservations, plus other private and public lands that burned, Pyne suggests the total acreage might well be double or triple that number. One massive blowup alone, which lasted two days, conflagrated the Idaho/Montana border into a burn the size of the state of New Jersey. Seventy-eight fire-fighters died in that particular holocaust, and subsequent headlines savaged those in charge. "The Big Blowup," writes Pyne, "altered the bureaucratic and political landscape as fully as it did the dynamics of Northern Rockies larch and white pine."

Until that headline-making catastrophe, American scientists and politicians had politely been debating the efficacy of allowing fires to go unchecked if they didn't threaten human habitat directly. Men such as John Wesley Powell were rethinking the options and were beginning to believe that the Indians' fire management procedures were the most efficient. After 1910, a year when whole communities were endangered and when smoke was visible everywhere from the Pacific Coast to the upper Midwest, officeholders needed no public opinion polls to tell them that "let it burn" decisions were politically unpalatable. Thus began a half-century of enforced fire suppression, decades when every fire was put out as quickly as possible and when underbrush and under-story trees grew unchecked. Those of us who grew up with Smokey Bear, that Forest Service wannabe who intoned "Only *you* can prevent forest fires" over and over again, learned nothing about the necessity of allowing nature to take its course. Rather, we were taught only the importance of stopping every fire in its tracks.

And while trees were being throttled with increasingly volatile fuel beneath the forest canopies, rangelands were becoming more conducive to big conflagrations, too. Grazing cattle—too many in one place at one time—were chewing up the native grasses, just as exotic grasses from Europe and Asia were opportunistically taking hold in the promised land. Cheat grass burns the hottest of all. Most of the literature I've read focuses on the more "glamorous" forest fires, those that burn in scenic areas where the devastation is obvious to the human eye and those that take a human toll either in lives lost or property destroyed. But anyone who has seen a range fire knows that its onslaught of flames is every bit as heart-stopping as a tree-fed conflagration. Having seen both, I can say they are equally stupefying.

As a child, I was more aware of Smokey Bear than of actual fire. I'm sure that palls of smoke must occasionally have hung on the familiar silhouettes of the Olympic and Cascade mountains, but I don't recall hearing many details. Once I was in college, however, and a counselor at a camp that hugged the western shore of Hood Canal, I quickly learned that fire conditions dictated the ways we organized our excursions into the woods. A red alert—the highest point on a color system coined long before the days of homeland security—meant "do not enter." Almost constant red alerts characterized the summer after I graduated from college, which was particularly hot and dry. Five of us wanted to go backpacking in late August anyway. By then, because we had taken our campers on so many outings and because the bar in Hoodsport was conducive to fraternization on Saturday nights, the local rangers were friends. "Keep an eye on the sky," one said as we waved good-bye. "If you see a small plane waggling its wings, get yourself to a lake or get the hell outta there," he ordered. We laughed, and thought he was kidding.

This is not a story with a horrific climax. A forest fire did indeed burn a large swath through the southern Olympics that week, but it never crept dangerously near our route. We could see it; we could smell it; we never encountered it directly. One night, intrigued, we hauled our sleeping bags up to the crest of Mount Gladys. From there, we watched the flames race up the ridgeline across the valley, crowning explosively from tree to tree—a better fireworks show than I have witnessed before or since. A few days later, our trail finally intersected the route of the firefighters returning to their staging area. I don't recall ever seeing men— only male firefighters were on the scene in those days, no women allowed—

more exhausted than these. Eyebrows singed, smears of charcoal across their clothes, boots alternately ashen and muddy, the men were too tired to even look our way. I remember remarking at the time—"imagine, a handful of twenty-one-year-old single females, sun-tanned, healthy, wearing skimpy shorts, and no one even bothered to smile or say hello." That's when I fathomed the tremendous physical toll exacted by fighting a forest fire.

Eyeball to eyeball with range fires has been less romantic. In fact, my experiences with grass fires and sagebrush fires all have happened dangerously close to suburbia, which presents another western issue. We're building ourselves into niches quite close to potential fire hazards. The farther we extend our homes into fire-prone regions, the more apt we are to see fires surrounding—if not engulfing—our communities. When I was on sabbatical, living east of San Diego at the base of Cowles Mountain Regional Park, I watched two different California wildfires blaze dangerously near my condominium. The first edged down the hill, and expired perhaps a hundred yards away. Meanwhile, I had packed my car with my half-written Edward Abbey manuscript, a few treasures, and a lot of trepidation. I need not have worried. The fire-fighters did their jobs.

A month later, fire approached from the other side. I watched it flash along the far hillside, then blaze down a grass and brush-choked wash. In a dry season, the wash provided a natural conduit for flame. Never did the fire cross the four-lane highway that I hoped protected my housing complex, so the experience wasn't especially traumatic. As a matter of fact, I found it great sport to settle back with a beer while focusing the telescope on all the excitement. I write this not because I have a cavalier attitude toward fire but because I think the ordinary westerner doesn't quite believe that fire will ever consume his or her particular house. A NIMBY sort of attitude, I fear. Surely the residents of Los Alamos never imagined that a controlled burn set miles away would get so out of control that their entire city was threatened. Nor did our local Animal Ark expect flames to shoot overhead across the parking lot while everyone struggled to keep the animals safe in the midst of burning sage. Not in my backyard.

In the West, however, many of us choose to live in close proximity to the natural world. Increasingly, we are building in locations almost impossible to defend from fire. Too many trees, too much sagebrush, too few modes of access, too little defensible space. That's the current buzzword—defensible space—as if my friends with their hoses and their lawns could actually defend their houses against the omnipotence of a fire burning out of control. Of course today's firefighters are much more skilled than in the early decades of the twentieth century. With better training and better equipment, and with history and experience to tell them about the vagaries of unchecked burns, the smoke jumpers and on-the-line crew members sometimes render miracles. Planes dropping slurry and helicopters sloshing water perform heroically, too.

Another book by Stephen J. Pyne, *Fire on the Rim, A Firefighter's Season at the Grand Canyon*, articulates the actualities of firefighting in colorful detail. First he sets the scene: "The horizon is aglow. Flame soars like miniature solar flares, and it seems as though the whole of Hindu Ampitheater has erupted into fire. The slop-over did not die out, but crept silently under the brush, desiccating the overstory, and now races upslope through the canopy. . . . Of its source I can see nothing, but I know that the fire emerges from the Canyon depths, full of instinctive fury at once ancient and unquenchable. . . . It is the fire we dread yet anticipate, at once both a nightmare and a privilege." Then Pyne plunges into the "frenzy," detailing the actions of men and machines. Reading his words, I am especially struck by the juxtaposition between nightmare and privilege. Those two opposites, I think, get at the heart of why fire fascinates us all.

Other authors with first-hand experience are just as graphic. Norman Maclean, who fought fires as a young man, explores the big blowup that caused the Mann Gulch fire in 1944. He speculates about the whirling intensity, "the rotating action . . . of a giant vortex" that may reach temperatures of two thousand degrees, the downdrafts of deadly gases, and the updrafts of heat "sometimes reaching the edge of the atmosphere." A fire whirl, he concludes, "can go almost as fast as the wind." Faster than the dozen smokejumpers, who were caught by the conflagration that August day. Maclean's picture of a blowup resembles Pyne's 1910 "vast

tsunami of flame" that seemed as if the very air were on fire. Ivan Doig,
also writing of the historic past, fictionalizes the front lines of defense.

> Orange flames were a dancing tribe amid the trees, and the
> firefighters were a rippling line of shovelers and axmen and
> sawyers as they tried to clear anything combustible from in
> front of the fire. But then when you got over being transfixed
> by the motions of flame and men, the sense of char hit you.
> A smell like charcoal, the black smudge of the burned forest
> behind the flames. And amid the commotion of the fireline
> work, the sounds of char, too—flames crackling, and continual
> snap of branches breaking as they burned, and every so often
> a big roar of flame as a tree crowned out.

Those of us who are simply onlookers at the fires of the American
West cannot replicate eyewitness accounts written by those who actually
have experienced the ferocity. What we can do, however, is speculate
about the politics of fire. Right now, our officials are trying to manage
both process and outcome. Because the West has suffered immensely
from the ravages of fire during the past ten or fifteen years, we—and they—
are keenly aware of what can happen while wildfires burn out of control.
Newspapers and newscasters lead us to believe that such devastation is
unusual, the result of drought, a lack of sufficient logging, human care-
lessness, or overbuilding too close to volatile timber and grasses. In
truth, the West has always been prone to fire. Humans, however, have
exacerbated the natural problems, have, as Pyne suggests, placed themselves "into the cauldron."

Fire-suppression policies have changed over the years. We no longer
suppose we must extinguish every single forest or rangeland blaze, although
the protection of property is as important as ever. A United States Department of Agriculture brochure touts the current thinking. It looks at the
cycle of life of a western forest, and explains the necessity of fire—"the
ignition key that starts the cycle again." It argues particularly for the
importance of prescribed burns to increase sunlight, help springs flow
more freely, reduce insects and disease, maintain healthy stands of trees,
and enhance the habitat for game, birds, and livestock. If we were to

believe its captions, we would be convinced that "we are becoming increasingly skilled," that "man has learned to control fire." The brochure, titled *Fire and the Changing Land,* was published in 1989; today's residents of Los Alamos or southern California might not be persuaded of its veracity.

With every calamitous fire, officials seek new ways to keep people and property safe—an increasingly difficult task as more and more of us move to more rural western locations. Just this morning, my local newspaper contained an article about a more aggressive fire-control policy that the government intends to put in place. By eliminating the need for environmental assessment or for studying the impact on endangered species, Secretary of Agriculture Ann Veneman recently argued, the "new tools will reduce the layers of unnecessary red tape and procedural delay that prevent agency experts from acting quickly to protect communities and our natural resources from devastating wildfires." What she doesn't say is that the new tools will give carte blanche to loggers, or so angry environmentalists claim. As with every such volatile issue, the truth may lie somewhere in between.

Forests do need to be thinned, and prescribed burns—the current euphemism replaces "controlled burns," which occasionally have turned out to be anything but—can be effective procedures. So Secretary Veneman is correct in insisting that regulations must allow for such activities. What is misleading, however, is the scope of what she advocates. Without local oversight, without ecological review, without any input from citizens who want what is best for their communities, corporate decisions will dictate how our forests look. Two different summers I've spent volunteer days at Lake Tahoe, cleaning up the underbrush left behind by a logging operation. We thinned tiny understory trees, too, using a chipper to turn the wood into mulch. When we finished, the forest looked much safer. And the big ponderosa pines remained intact. What we did, however, is not particularly feasible on a larger scale.

In order to make thinning economically viable, a logging company must take big trees as well as small. Corey Lewis worked one summer at Lake Tahoe, watchdogging the cut. The contract for thinning that area stated clearly that trees larger than thirty-four inches in diameter must be left standing, yet the fine for cutting them was less than the potential profit. As we might surmise, Corey found many violations—121 trees illegally taken in a single 113-acre parcel, with excess ladder fuels left behind. But prescribed burns would be problematic, too, in a thickly populated area like the north shore of Lake Tahoe. I've seen them on the less densely inhabited southwest side, near Desolation Wilderness, but I've never observed them close to homes and businesses. Any sort of fire on the loose in the Lake Tahoe Basin would be an unmitigated disaster.

I find, as I write this chapter, that I'm falling into the same trap that so many authors do when they focus on fire. Forests, rather than sage-brush and cheat grass, have more drawing power. That's partly a function of the way we look at scenery—we put our houses in those places we find most attractive, in among the trees rather than out on the open range. Thus, forest fires threaten more human structures than do range fires. In 1999, 1.6 *million* acres burned in northern and central Nevada. Hardly anyone noticed, except for the ranchers adversely affected. With a rural population of less than one person per square mile, humans were in little danger. The national news paid scant attention to the burns, even though the fires were economically devastating. In contrast, a minor brushfire lit up a dozen acres or so just outside Reno's city limits last week. The *CBS Evening News* highlighted the conflagration, as did NBC's *Today Show* the next morning.

What inevitably makes headlines are those stories about whichever communities are stricken, about wherever humans and fires interact. Fire is a natural phenomenon in the West. We can't expect it to disappear. In many ways, it is a normal part of our lives—the oppressive summer thunderstorm with perhaps hundreds of lightning strikes in a single hour, the column of smoke that bursts upward in shades of orange and beige and ruddy brown, the blood-red sun tinged by particulates we cannot see, the heavy scent of burning sage or pine or fir, the afternoon winds that stir the mix, the darkened sky. Sometimes I look out my Reno window and can barely see a hundred yards. Hiking years ago in the Hoover Wilderness, or just last summer in western Colorado, I remember individual campsites where the smoke dropped visibility down to almost nothing.

Smoke from the famous 1988 fires in Yellowstone spiraled all the way to Reno. I don't recall an unusual smell, but I remember that the sun hung like an orange pendant in the pallid sky. Almost one and a half million acres burned that summer, thirty-six percent of the park plus a significant amount of National Forest lands outside the park. Now, fifteen years later, the burn sites are recovering nicely. That is, Yellowstone is regenerating from the violent episode. Mary Ann Franke's *Yellowstone in the Afterglow: Lessons from the Fires*, published by the Yellowstone Center for Resources, details such changes as dense lodgepole pine seedlings, new clusters of aspen, and large areas of herbaceous vegetation. Even the dead matchstick trees, although I thought them unsightly when I drove through Yellowstone later, provide both food and shelter to large numbers of nesting birds and small mammals in a flourishing ecosystem. Surprisingly few large animals were killed by the massive fires. Bears actually were seen foraging quite close to the flames, apparently oblivious to potential danger. Helicopter crews, assessing the visible body count soon after the flames died down, spotted only 261 carcasses—almost all elk, far fewer wapiti than die each winter from the weather.

Perhaps the most important point made in *Yellowstone in the Afterglow* is the fact that fire has not specifically returned Yellowstone to its ecological past. Rather, the events of 1988 propelled the park and its surroundings into an ecological future that is shaping itself in innovative ways. This "long-term process of renewal" is wholly natural, an "intrinsic" element of the ecology of place, an inherent aspect of evolution. Renewal, neither taking the landscape backwards nor replicating the dispersion of the past, propels the process forward. Some species prosper; others struggle. Some multiply; others disappear. Multiple kinds of woodpeckers, for example, are thriving on the beetles infesting the snags. Large numbers of hummingbirds are relishing the post-fire blossoms that flower abundantly in the open areas. Trout, on the other hand, have not fared as well. Moose seem to be diminishing, too, because of the decreased groundcover that once provided food and safety. As might be expected, though, the coyotes are flourishing.

In truth, the greater Yellowstone landscape is healthy, and getting healthier every day. This is the real lesson of fire today in the American West. Not only is wildfire natural, but it is most containable and efficacious when we work with it in natural ways. Complete suppression is neither good for the environment nor effective as a means of control. As a matter of fact, exploding out of control is natural for fire, too, as evidenced by the many books and articles describing the horrendous blowups of the past. But those printed materials tell us that we perpetually think and behave as if fire were strictly a human phenomenon. *Yellowstone in the Afterglow* reports the ways in which the media portrayed the park as a "national barbecue pit." Conrad Smith, a journalism professor at Ohio State University, determined that almost none of the print or broadcast news touched on any ecological aspects of what was happening. In the heat of the action, this might be expected, but even the follow-up assessments focused primarily on the human interface. Of 589 major pieces published between 1989 and 1993, he "counted only 29 reports that included ecological information in the first three paragraphs." Only five articles discussed environmental impact at all. So the media is not helping us understand the cycle so important in the process of fire.

The interface between wildfires and human beings poses problems without easy solutions. To live in the West is to daily confront difficulties caused by natural forces such as lightning and unnatural causes such as abandoned campfires and reckless children at play. Possible catastrophe cannot be predicted, but fire will most certainly be prevalent every summer throughout all the states west of the Missouri River. David Carle, in *Burning Questions: America's Fight with Nature's Fire*, argues for a "peaceful coexistence," one which responsibly manages what can be controlled—prescribed burns, for example, thinning that puts safety before economics, and intelligent firefighting procedures—and one which accepts the fact that we must become a "fire-adapted species," like the rest of the ecological world. Easy enough to say, in the pages of a book; much much more difficult when a wildfire rages out of control near your house or mine.

The siren sounds of Sunday morning suggest a fire somewhere. In the city, where noises reverberate off buildings and echo down the crowded streets, a forest fire is less likely than a terrorist attack. I'm cognizant of such things, here in San Francisco, just a day after the London Metro bombings of 2004. Almost three years ago, I remember being here in late September, when I climbed to Coit Tower and watched the fog drift over the bay. I stood on Telegraph Hill in the early morning light, imagining how I would feel if the symbols of this city—the Golden Gate Bridge, the TransAmerica Tower, the Oakland Bay Bridge—were eradicated in a single morning. At that moment, this westerner understood how viscerally New Yorkers were grieving. I've never forgotten my empathy, watching the fog connect and disconnect the city's arteries, obliterating the blood red spires and then revealing lifelines across the water again.

If Seattle is the anchor of my childhood and adolescence, San Francisco is the yacht basin of my todays and tomorrows. "I left my heart in San Francisco," Tony Bennett sighs, and it's true. An easy drive via interstate unless blizzards invade Donner Pass or a fifty-minute hop-over flight by air, the city is my goal whenever I fancy a real downtown. I enjoy the street-steep canyons and bay-view vistas almost as often as I seek desert playas or mountain meadows or a sagebrush sea. Because San Francisco is so circumscribed by water, and because the city itself clings to impossible hillsides, the effect is magical, like Dorothy's Emerald City or the home of Harry Potter's Hogwarts School for Witchcraft and Wizardry. Long ago I lost count of the many times I've visited there.

Mostly, I walk the San Francisco avenues. In springtime, when the corner kiosks are awash in fresh flowers—five dollars for yellow daffodils, ten for red tulips—I'll be there. Up stair-step sidewalks to the top of Nob Hill, I'll listen for the Grace Cathedral chimes on Easter Sunday. I'm always struck by its Gothic Renaissance look, as if two architects had quarreled. One afternoon—high tea at the Fairmont Hotel, nibbling tiny berried scones while sipping an imported black brew from Ceylon. Or perhaps a more distant walk through Pacific Heights, studying the iron-gated mansions, pacing the angular streets, and counting the tri-colors of refurbished Victorian facades. I imagine living here, but I couldn't afford the prices and the parking problems would drive me crazy.

In the cool of summer, escaping from Nevada desert heat, I might prowl the Embarcadero, wandering in and out of shops and stores, stopping by the Saturday morning Farmer's Market and tasting the best blackberries I've had since I was a child. A few blocks away, Nordstrom's tops a spiral staircase mall filled with stores that can be found anywhere. Yet their San Francisco shapes and sizes are different somehow, their gray silk dresses more sophisticated, their paisley scarves more elegant. Later in the day, I might play rubber-necked tourist, jamming onto a crowded cable car while hanging on for dear life, or maybe hopping on a boat for a lazy cruise to Alcatraz. Back on the mainland, there's Fisherman's Wharf— the cries of the fishmongers, the crush of customers along the pier, the sweet sharp smells of crab and saltwater taffy. Alongside the wharf, as the city finds new economic focus, more and more tourist vessels tie up to the slips while fewer and fewer fishing boats can be seen. Turning my back on the changes, I head for Union Street, with Anchor Steam on tap.

In the toasted days of early autumn, I like Chinatown the best. Not the Grant Street of tourist traps plying their cheap luggage and T-shirts and oriental gadgets, but the backways where the business of food dominates the scene. Knobby vegetables with unpronounceable names. Scaly fish, their vacant eyes staring up from icy tubs. Inside the cluttered shops, row upon row of condiments and spices with undecipherable uses, plus an unbelievable odor of saltwater and seaweed. I can't understand a word the storekeepers or their customers are saying, but I wish someone would invite me home for dinner. Since that won't happen, the next best option is The Oriental Pearl, an upstairs hole-in-the-wall with the best pork potstickers I've ever eaten. Half the customers speak no English there, either.

In winter rain, I trip over the homeless huddled in empty doorways. A bearded man with an aging black retriever holds a tattered sign that reads "help me, please." An elderly woman swathed in damp sweaters, leans against a corner wall and smokes a stale cigarette. She has sad eyes. Meanwhile, a harsh January wind whirls in the city canyons, turning my soggy umbrella inside out. Undaunted, I slog to David's for a pastrami sandwich before I settle in my seat to watch one more Swan Lake ballet. When darkness closes in, the heights of the buildings as well as the shortness of the days exacerbates the shadows. Daytime will be better, with fresh bagels and hot coffee and another brisk morning walk.

Sometimes, I wander away from the city's core. On BART, to Noe Valley, for example, where a nondescript house on a street that looks like a hundred others holds an enormous collection of mystery paperbacks for sale. Or to Haight Ashbury, where so many tie-dyed flower children, long-haired and free, once frolicked carelessly. I saw the players in the early 1970s, when McArthur's Park had already begun to fade, but never knew San Francisco in its hippie heyday. Not so the Castro district, however, host to the most outrageous Halloween peacock parade I might fancy. I recall marching once in that stream of feathered humanity, laughing uproariously at the scandalous ensembles, and lack thereof. Once I trailed the Bay-to-Breakers run, checking the costumes of those who churned out the miles from the back of the pack. Out to Golden Gate Park they went—caterpillars, locomotives, TeleTubbies, Spider men, Cat women, and of course more peacocks.

At the Presidio, when it was still an army post, I remember visiting a friend from college days whose husband, freshly back from Vietnam, no longer relished his military career. They and their children lived in a brick row house, counting the days until Larry would finish his tour. We couldn't afford the Cliff House for dinner, though I can enjoy it now. Back then, I might drift toward the DeYoung Museum, or wander the carved paths of the Japanese Tea Garden, its square trees and flowering quince shading the way. And on to the Marina District, moving among more trembling memories, this time of earthquakes and quivering landfill. For awhile, after 1989, many of the pastel houses were boarded over, awaiting inspections, expensive repairs, or possible demolitions. That's part of San Francisco, too—stories of the ground shaking in horrific waves.

I recall Seattle earthquakes—the 1949 one when I danced in my grandmother's billowing backyard while my mother shouted from the porch, the 1963 one when my father was caught on a catwalk high above a Union Oil Company tank farm—but I've never been in San Francisco when the earth moved. My mother used to have an older friend I called Aunt Jessie, who stayed with me sometimes when my parents were away. Aunt Jessie was thirteen when the big quake of 1906 hit San Francisco. She would tell stories of fleeing down city streets, of flames and fear and falling bricks. Then she would remember isolated weeks in Oakland, where her family sought refuge and wondered when they might return to the city and what they might find in the rubble. She never regretted leaving San Francisco, always trembling at the terror of the earthquake and never missing the city's cosmopolitan airs. I had a more romantic view, perhaps because my father often went there on business and sent me cable-car postcards that I loved.

Even today, it's hard for me to think of San Francisco in words other than picturesque ones. Lying on my bed on the eleventh floor of the Chancellor Hotel—I always stay at the Chancellor, just around the corner from Union Square—I listen to the siren music that overlays jackhammer sounds of garbage trucks in the early morning air. Outside my window, fog shrouds the tallest buildings as if they were mountaintops tipped in clouds. Yesterday I watched an Indian wedding celebration, with the men dressed alike in cream-colored garb and the women in multi-hued saris of magenta and purple. Everyone was laughing and clapping to the beating of a drum and the jangle of a tambourine, while we onlookers swayed to the rhythms we heard. That's how I think of San Francisco, a multi-ethnic enclave of garrulous voices and exotic scents and high-rise scenery and euphonious sounds. It's a "city so bright" of the twenty-first century, foolishly disdained by the balladeer but a welcome home to so many cosmopolitan aficionados, their lives undimmed by the fog and undaunted by the sounds of sirens.

CHAPTER THREE

Pressed from the West

The red man was pressed from this part of the West,
He's likely no more to return
To the banks of Red River where seldom if ever
Their flickering campfires burn.

Blue jeans; red and white checked shirt; high-topped mocs; faded cowboy hat. Around and around the perimeter of the Medicine Wheel, a thirty-something woman paces in a clockwise direction. In her hands, a bundle of sweet grass, which she tilts in different attitudes as she moves east to south to west to north. Parallel, horizontal, aslant. Her eyes expressionless, her stride intent, her face cast slightly down, around and around she goes.

A couple, hand in hand, arrive and stand silently in front of a rock cairn. She points toward the mementos strung along the protective fence. A tiny dream catcher the size of a silver dollar, sand-gray with topaz beads. Rawhide rattle, tied with bundles. Clam shells. Miniature ears of corn. An intricate set of feathers, lashed together with string. Faded bandanas shifting in the wind. Shredded cigarettes, crushed and scattered. A thread of tiny bones. She points again. Nodding his head, he puts his left arm around her shoulder, and squeezes.

A white-haired man in shorts walks up to the Medicine Wheel signage. Camcorder in hand, he photographs the words. His grandson, an overweight twelve-year-old, asks him, "What's it for?" The grandfather, talking into his recording, doesn't answer the unanswerable. The father joins them. Together, the three without a glance stroll past a marker that reads STAY ON THE WALKWAY and amble toward a distant view, camcorder focused on the horizon. When they're finished with the picture-taking, they walk away. Not one of the three circumnavigates the Medicine Wheel, or even walks to the fence to examine the design. Although the grandfather thought the informational sign contextualizing the scene's history was worth filming, he apparently found the artifact itself much less compelling. When he shows his pictures to the rest of the family, the sign will suffice for the substance.

Getting there took everyone a bit of effort, though. The Bighorn Medicine Wheel sits 9,640 feet above sea level. It rests on a high flank of Wyoming's Medicine Mountain; an FAA communications station with attached year-round underground living quarters lies buried at the top of the peak. Strobe lights blink in the distance. Although the archaeological site has been a popular destination for generations, Forest Service and tribal representatives finally have succeeded in closing the access road to tourists. On June 15, 1995, a fairly stringent set of occupancy and use regulations were put into place. Twenty-first-century visitors now must hike the final mile and a half. Others, however, like the scientists who man the high-tech equipment nearby, can still use machines.

A pair of ORVs throbs into view. The lead driver, a hefty bearded man with reflector sunglasses, is closely followed by a helmeted figure so anonymous she might belong in a Star Trek film. They cruise past the Medicine Wheel, a swath of dust rising heavily behind them. Dustier still—and noisier—is the air surrounding an empty diesel stock truck that bumps up the road from the opposite direction. Surprised at the traffic, I wonder aloud at all the vehicles using a road I thought was closed. A nearby ranger answers without irony, "Because this is a road, we can't stop access. But through traffic isn't allowed to stop. To actually visit the Medicine Wheel, you have to walk." I can hardly keep from observing, "Wasn't the Medicine Wheel here first?" I keep my mouth shut, as four

people on horseback arrive—one wrangler, three dudes. Tying their horses
to a fence, they step across a cattle guard, pass a sign that reads FOR
ALL PEOPLE, and walk to the sacred site.

High in the Bighorn Mountains and far from the banks of Oklahoma's Red River, this ancient artifact signals aboriginal longevity—past,
present, and future. No one knows exactly who built the sanctum, or when,
but most archaeologists agree that construction began several hundred
years ago, and continued from one generation to the next. Aligned with
the sun, moon, and stars, twenty-eight spokes of rock extend from a middle
cairn. Approximately forty-five feet in length, each spoke radiates somewhat irregularly. Around the uneven outside circumference, five smaller
cairns sit in no apparent pattern. No one, in fact, knows either the
provenance or the purpose of the Medicine Wheel. Speculations range
widely. A burial ground, or a memorial for fallen chiefs? Probably not,
since archeological digs have unearthed no human remains. An astro-
nomical observatory, used to mark events such as the summer and winter
solstices? Unlikely, since the site is unapproachable during the winter
snows. A giant compass? Perhaps, but its out-of-the-way location renders
it somewhat useless for normal navigation. Religious site? Quite possibly,
and yet no one can ascertain exactly what rites and rituals might have
been conducted here. The outside cairns may have been shelters for
men on vision quests, or they may have been something else. No one
really knows. Perhaps that's part of the magic of this place, a new world
Stonehenge in the sky.

Comparative photographs show the Medicine Wheel larger than it
is today. In a 1922 picture, the center piece was nearly seven feet high.
Now it's only a two-foot mound of stones. Tourists and treasure-seekers
over the years have helped themselves to the rocks, so the current protection plan, cooperatively worked out by the National Park Service and
local tribes, is crucial to prevent further desecration. A sturdy rope and
post fence now circles the site—easy to see past, not so easy to climb over—
and visitors are not supposed to wander off the designated paths. Some
do, of course, but most tourists are content to walk to the site, study it for
awhile, take a few pictures, and then return to their cars. Nothing tells
them that there's a smaller Medicine Wheel, too, plus an articulated

rock arrow that points to the larger circumference. Off-limits to non-Natives, these nearby, less dramatic configurations are just as puzzling.

I spent some time walking northwest across the high tundra beyond the Medicine Wheel, outside the preservation boundaries where I was free to hike anywhere I chose. The deep snows of winter had just melted, baring stunted spruce with tiny thumb-sized cones, alpine aster, violet shooting stars, and fluffy white American bistort. A July carpet of colors in what must be an extremely harsh January terrain. Deep rifts with limestone overhangs cut crevices into the dirt. So convoluted and dark and deep that I couldn't see inside, these sinkholes seemed nature's architectural counterpoint to the indigenous design a mile or two away. Ten feet, twenty feet deep, and more, the caves are as unfathomable as the spiraling wheel. A few old two-tracks cut the tundra, too, plus other leftovers from sheep and grazing, but no vehicles recently had ventured across the turf and I saw animals only in the distance. The ranger said that various tribes occasionally hold ceremonies along the eastern edges of the cliff, but I found only a few footprints in the mud and no indication at all of any rituals from the past. Still, mystery was underfoot and in the air.

A sign commemorating the Medicine Wheel as a national historic landmark calls it "The Place Where the Eagle Lands." This phrase makes sense to me. The views are spectacular in every direction, with distant snow-capped peaks and summer flowers close at hand. Pikas call to each other from beneath and behind the weathered limestone rocks, which are themselves embedded with ancient shells and fish scale fossils, while marmots climb up and down the shale. One cynical archaeologist has speculated that the Natives chose the site because the stones were the right sizes and shapes to pick up and move easily. But I prefer the more esoteric attitude of an eagle landing on high. Under my feet, flax shades from lavender to baby blue and tiny forget-me-nots cluster together, while inside the ring itself I see mountain death camas and deep purple Indian lousewort. Overhead, summer thunderheads, faintly mauve and building steeply in the sky.

"Eventually one gets to the Medicine Wheel to fulfill one's life," pronounced an Arikara named Old Mouse.

His words, etched nearby, compel most viewers to circle the wheel in silence. I did so, time after time, watching the superficial visitors, watching those who bowed their heads, watching the woman with her sweet-grass bundle, watching the sweep of the sky. If one waits long enough, silence can prevail. The occasional lowing of cattle wafts up from Five Springs Basin; a raven or two croak now and then. A hawk screams; I can imagine an eagle. More silence. Or is that a drumbeat I hear in the wind?

The cowboy songwriter of "Home on the Range" insinuated that Indian peoples effectively had been ousted from the West, but the original Dr. Brewster Higley version—written before the battles of the Bighorn and Wounded Knee—contains no such verse. Neither does the subsequent Goodwin Colorado rewrite of the song. Only after the 1910 Lomax collection does the pejorative red man was "pressed from this part of the West" appear anywhere in print, which may reveal something about twentieth-century attitudes after the conclusion of the Sioux Wars.

At the Five Springs Basin overlook, partway down the mountain, a Park Service marker quotes Buffalo Bird Woman, a Hidatsu whose life must have spanned crucial generations in the late nineteenth century. Reading her words, I realize Buffalo Bird Woman would have agreed that her tribal future looked dire.

> I am an old woman now. The buffalo and black tail deer are gone, and our Indian ways are almost gone. Sometimes I find it hard to believe that I ever lived then. We no longer live in an earth lodge or teepee, but in a house with chimneys; and my son's wife cooks by a stove. Often I rise at daybreak, and steal out to the cornfields. As I hoe the corn I sing to it, as I did when I was young. No one cares for our corn song now. Sometimes at evening I sit, looking out over the river. The sunsets [sic], and dusk steals over the water. In the shadows, I seem again to see our Indian villages with smoke curling upward from the lodges. But it is an old woman's dream. Our Indian way of life, I know, is gone forever.

Both the cowboy and this Hidatsu elder were wrong. Facing the Medicine Wheel, following its spirals, listening to the wind, I know the Native spirits have never totally been eliminated from the West. Traversing the twentieth-century West, I admit that I often found the old woman's dream denied. In the New West of the twenty-first century, however, in many tribal circles, the "Indian way of life" is prospering in unexpected ways.

First, a vignette from the past. While hiking across the mesa that extends northeast of Canyon de Chelly, our group stopped for a late lunch at a Navajo hogan. Mutton stew, fry bread, watermelon. It wasn't just my backpacker's appetite that made me appreciate the meal, for the mutton turned out to be tender young lamb, the fry bread, simultaneously moist and crisp, and the watermelon, a cool counterpoint to the hot food. While I was eating, I chatted with the Navajo woman who was hosting our visit. When she found out I lived in Nevada, she groaned. She'd gone to "away school" in Nevada, and had detested the experience. "No one else spoke Navajo," she said sharply. "I had no one to talk to at all." Her voice lower, she went on to tell me more about the Stewart School, where boys and girls were forbidden to speak their native languages and where the discipline and academics ran counter to their childhood teachings. "I hated it," the woman repeated. "I absolutely hated it."

Later that afternoon, as we hiked farther east, I thought about her words and about the intensity of her voice. At the same time, the sky was filling with thunderheads. The sun disappeared into clouds of black and blue, and a low rumble grew increasingly more guttural. When the storm arrived in full force, the lightning felt as if it were coming from directly overhead. One of my friends carried a hiking staff with a metal tip. We made him walk apart from the rest of us, isolating him as one bolt struck closer than I dare remember. We acted as if Charles didn't exist, as if we didn't speak his language. But only for an hour; not for years.

Meanwhile, I kept looking for shelter—hard to find on a red sand mesquite-topped mesa without trees. Only after the winds had dissipated did our route drop into junipers and a jumble of boulders. Trusting that there would be no more rain, we set up our tents in an arroyo with a seep of potable water. Then our Navajo guide, Alvin, led us another

mile or so, out to the rim where we looked down on Canyon de Chelly.
Backlit by sunset, the scene was stunning. More shades of purple and
mauve and pink than I would have believed possible. Shapes and shadows
worthy of fairytale monsters and ogres and witches. And there was Spider
Rock, the dominating tower of red-stained stone that has always been
sacred to the Navajos of Canyon de Chelly.

For the past several days a dozen of us had been hiking down
Canyon del Muerto, the other arm of the area now known generically as
Canyon de Chelly National Monument. There we had encountered
sacred sites, too, but of a sadly different sort. Massacre Cave, for example.
In 1805, Lieutenant Antonio Narbona led his Sonoran troops, a cadre of
Opata Indian auxiliaries, and a part of the New Mexico militia into Canyon del Muerto. Hunting what they called "renegades," the Spaniards
totally overwhelmed the Indians who were hiding from the invaders in
what later would be remembered as Massacre Cave. Navajo narratives
tell only of women and children and elderly men secreted in the cave,
while Spanish accounts insist that dozens of warriors hid there, too. No
matter, the outcome was grim, with almost all the Indians slaughtered
and many of the troops wounded as well. Lieutenant Narbona's report
says his men fired nearly ten thousand bullets at the enemy, an amazing
statistic given the fact that the Indians were responding with rocks and arrows.

Although the Spaniards eventually managed to capture or kill everyone harbored there, the cave was practically impregnable. The hideaway
sits about six hundred feet above the canyon floor. Scrambling up the
slippery talus was not an easy task; I could not conceive of scaling it
while firing a weapon and dodging arrows from above. Once the troops
reached the top of the talus, the soldiers still had to negotiate a series of
hand and toe-holes that lead perpendicularly up a final, almost vertical,
slope to the cave. My mild acrophobia made the ascent absolutely terrifying. Relieved and somewhat out of breath when I got to the ledge, I sat
and looked out on peaceful red rock canyon scenery. In contrast, beside me
and behind me, were hundreds and hundreds of bullet-hole indentations,
rock chips and fragments, testimony to the Spanish determination. As
recently as 1970, I'm told, scattered bones of the victims could still be
found in Massacre Cave, making the site even more horrific. For religious

reasons, the Navajo people refused to deal with the remains, but early unrestrained Anglo visitors felt free to collect whatever artifacts they might find. By the time I clamored up the cliffside, however, no transportable traces of the encounter were left for us to see. Frankly, I was glad.

As I inspected the bullet gouges, I thought about the timing. January 17, 1805. While the lieutenant and his troops were massacring one tribe, Lewis and Clark—who imagined themselves in a West untrammeled by white men—were enjoying the hospitality of another. Camped beside the Mandan villages on the Missouri River, Clark pens a rather benign January 17, 1805, entry in his journal: "a verry windey morning hard from the North Thermometer at 0, Several Indians here to day." When Lieutenant Narbona paused a week later, he wrote a report that describes his January 17th accomplishments, how his men "dislodged" the Indians, how "our arms succeeded in killing ninety warriors, twenty-five women and children, and taking as prisoners, three warriors, eight women, and twenty-two boys and girls, capturing three hundred and fifty head of sheep and thirty riding horses," how the "Corporal Baltasar is bringing eighty-four pairs of ears of as many warriors" to demonstrate their mission's ultimate success to Chihuahuan Governor Chacón. And while Narbona was writing his bloody account, Clark was noting "a fine day, our inturpeters appear to understand each others better than a fiew days past."

Trained historians have always known better, but I was taught in grade school that Lewis and Clark were the first to explore the western part of what would become the United States. Unbeknownst to me, the American Southwest had already been invaded by Europeans. The Spanish had been there for centuries and, by the early nineteenth century, were intent upon solidifying their holdings. The Canyon del Muerto raid was part of an organized plan to beat the Navajos into submission and slavery. "The red man was pressed from this part of the West," indeed.

Not far from Massacre Cave, rock art tells the story of invasion, too. Where older pictographs and petroglyphs depict handprints, animals, and geometric designs, another patina-stained wall carries the shapes of horsemen wearing winter capes and carrying rifles. Our guide suggested that these were replicas of Kit Carson's troops, but later research tells me we probably were looking at drawings of Lieutenant Narbona and his men. The Kit Carson story, however, is important to Canyon del Muerto, too. His foray in the fall of 1863, widely known as the "scorched earth campaign," was characterized by the wholesale burning of everything in sight. Homes, livestock, clothing, food. Those Navajos who survived the harsh winter took refuge in Canyon del Muerto, where Carson and his men found them in August 1864. More burning ensued, including the destruction of more than three thousand precious mature peach trees and all of the planted corn. As a result, the Indians had to leave the canyon and walk to Bosque Redondo—"the place of despair," located at Fort Sumner in eastern New Mexico some 375 miles away.

I've camped near Fort Sumner, but by choice, not by force. Long since abandoned as a military outpost, turned into a state preserve and later into a national monument, the fort was a focal point for Navajo distress. A "place where they would be put to death eventually," said one deportee, though in truth the government would reverse itself four years later and send the Navajos back to a reservation carved out of their native territory. The time spent at Bosque Redondo, however, was a nightmare for the Indians, with minimal rations, rampant disease, extreme infant morality, and terrible living conditions. Today, none of these egregious details is visible. Most visitors, in fact, head for Sumner Lake, a reservoir oasis in the middle of aridity, a reserve of water that wasn't there when tribal members were suffering so terribly. Sitting beside my truck on a grassy knoll above the "lake," I kept comparing the plight of the Navajos in this dry land with the contemporary cacophony of motor boats and motor homes. Sometimes it's better not to know the history.

When I was backpacking in Canyon del Muerto and Canyon de Chelly, I had not yet seen southeastern New Mexico. I had no idea of the distance trod on the Long Walk that forced the Navajo people out of their homelands, no notion of the hardships inflicted by the soldiers and caused by our governmental policy. Instead, my friends and I blithely meandered down-canyon past peach trees that some say are related to the original orchards Kit Carson thought he had burned absolutely. We splashed in shallow waters and left footprints in the sand. We played at survival skills, capturing water from a makeshift tin cup and bandana apparatus. We climbed up to Massacre Cave because it was the thing to do, in those days before park rules prohibited such forays.

At Mummy Cave, we paused for another look at history. There we examined a complex of dwellings that archaeologists think was perhaps the last pre-Navajo construction in the canyon. Although its massive tower is the primary focal point now, the ruin is called Mummy Cave because of the Indian burials uncovered there. In 1923, under the auspices of the American Museum of Natural History and financed by patron Charles L. Bernheimer, Earl Morris began the excavation. He and his workers not only found such everyday artifacts as sandals and coiled baskets but they also unearthed intact mummies buried with their prized possessions. Later, in the library, I read descriptions of the atlatls, flutes, pipes, jewelry, baskets, fur and feather robes, and various cooking and hunting devices that Morris found in the cave. If Massacre Cave stands for flagrant inhumanity, Mummy Cave does so in a corollary way. Originally a place of respect, with tradition dating as far back as the Basketmaker culture, a place of homage to the ancient people, it too was desecrated by non-Indian invaders. Not with bullets but with shovels. I know anthropologists would disagree, but when I remember all the skeletons held for years in the basement of the Smithsonian, I think my observation is correct. Canyon del Muerto remained a canyon of death until well into the twentieth century.

Beyond Mummy Cave, our tiny group climbed up and out of the canyon, sometimes hand over hand, sometimes wobbling along a narrow pathway to the top. I remember tripping and falling, with my backpack flattening me like a turtle. Better than rolling precipitously off the trail, I guess. As we reached the rim, the first in what would be a series of thunderstorms crescendoed in our ears. Hide in a sheltering cave? Climb the last hundred feet to the rim and sit in the juniper? I didn't know what to do, and our guide wasn't much help. I finally ended up in the cave—at least it was dry—thinking once more about the victims of Lieutenant Narbona's demolition. The pounding rain and the crash of thunder in a way replicated the sounds of the staccato bullets, random and haphazard, and potentially lethal.

The week-long trip down the sands of Canyon del Muerto, across the broad mesa with its hogan hospitality, and on to colors of Canyon de Chelly happened more than twenty-five years ago, yet I've forgotten neither the incredible storms that recurred almost every single late afternoon nor the amazing sunset we watched from our perch across-canyon from Spider Rock. In the West, there always are sunsets. This was one of the finest, at least in my rainbow of memory. In fact, I was on only my second backpacking adventure in the Southwest, so the constant play of colors at the purple end of the spectrum was new to me. I was astonished. I also was struck, as are most people, by the imposing spire of the Spider.

The next day we clamored on down into Canyon de Chelly, a far less precipitous route than our ascent out of Canyon del Muerto, and for two nights we camped as close to the Spider as we dared. Like the stories of the canyons, the invasions and the fertile orchards, the pandemonium of battle and present peaceful calm, the Spider Woman's story is twofold, too. She casts her web to snare evil as well as good. Some say she captures disobedient children, and that the white coloring on top of Spider Rock signifies the bones of her prey. Some say she is impatient, with a temper that may bring unexpected harm. Others say she is benevolent, that she aided the Twins who were the offspring of Changing Woman and the Sun, that she gave them the sacred hoops, and that she helped them defeat the Monsters of the Fifth World in order to save the people. Some say she taught the Navajo people how to weave, thus giving them both warmth and a valuable commodity for trade. Whichever story one believes, even an Anglo can feel the power of her presence.

Na'ashje'ii 'Asdzaa watched while I circled the base of her towering home. Avoiding my friends, as well as the watchful eye of our Navajo guide, I made my pilgrimage alone. Away from our campsite, with its nylon tents and colored bits of clothing hanging up to dry, I walked slowly. Around and around, perhaps three or four times, I circled Spider Rock. Tipping my head back, I could look up at the sun-tipped tower of rock. Another sunset was turning Canyon de Chelly into another kaleidoscope of color, though the prism modulated as my perspective changed. Alongside the canyon walls, shadows darkened the purples and lavenders, muted the pinks and mauves, intimated a darkness reminiscent of the stories of Canyon del Muerto. Yet I found Canyon de Chelly to be a happy counterpoint to the tragic tales of Lieutenant Narbona and Kit Carson. Perhaps it was Na'ashje'ii 'Asdzaa looking down on me and my group. I realized my good fortune to see this special place without hoards of other tourists. Wading up Chinle Wash, strolling past tiny orchards and milling herds of sheep, yodeling to hear an echo from the narrowness of Bat Canyon, exploring Monument Canyon, too, I felt an ambience quite at odds with a canyon of death. This place, indeed, was enchanted. My Spider Woman, if I might borrow her for a moment or two, spins Elysian reminiscences.

Years later, I read the painful lines of "Home on the Range," and wonder if we have come far enough from the politically incorrect lines of that mournful dirge. "The red man was pressed" from these canyons as well as from the Red River Valley of the song. He has long since returned, but to a world with National Park Service oversight and a steady stream of visitors. Indians still farm on the canyon floors, to be sure, but the invasion continues to surround them. First cavalrymen, then anthropologists, now tourists. Open trucks drive up and down the lower washes, daily shepherding visitors to such sites as Antelope House and White House ruins. Our backpacking group, I confess, even made use of these vehicles, for we hiked down-canyon only as far as White House, then caught a truck-ride the rest of the way back to our cars.

Years later, I tramped to White House ruin once again, taking a well-maintained trail that snakes off the rim and heads directly for the old structures. It's the only route in the Monument where tourists are allowed without a guide, the only ruin that unescorted visitors can approach. As I made the trek, I kept looking off toward Spider Rock in the middle distance, longing to go back to its base and circle its perimeter once again, knowing that such an invasion was forbidden by Park Service rules. Too far away to encounter directly the powerful enchantment of Na'ashje'ii 'Asdzaa, I nonetheless could recall the magic of that earlier trip. The legends of Massacre Cave and the stories of the "scorched earth campaign," the secret pictographs and petroglyphs, the happy splashing in the water that courses downstream before it seeps underground near

Spider Rock, the resignation in the voice of my Navajo hostess, the incessant afternoon thunderstorms and the ensuing calm each evening, the sunsets, the incredible indescribable sunsets. In the West, there always are sunsets. Sometimes they drop a red ball of fire behind a silhouetted butte. Sometimes they turn the landscape into an R. C. Gorman painting. Sometimes, they decimate a people, but only for awhile.

At the same time the Arizona lightning storm reverberates in my imagination, a cacaphony of California thunder intrudes. The drone of slot machines. The cascade of falling coins. An occasional shout from a nearby baccarat table. The ring of jackpot signal bells. An elongated jangle of nickels and quarters and dimes, accompanied by a computer voice that intones "Wheel . . . of . . . Fortune." Not the landscape of Canyon de Chelly, but a declivity of another sort. Thunder Valley. The Sacramento Valley's largest Indian casino is home to 1,900 slots, 94 tables, and a 500-seat bingo room. An example of twenty-first-century Indian scenery, Thunder Valley is a canyon carefully constructed, totally artificial, and extremely lucrative.

The United Auburn Indian Community was not always so fortunate in its terrain. For eighty-six years, fewer than three hundred Maidu and Miwok—tribes that had been devastated by the California Gold Rush—struggled to survive on a tiny parcel of useless, rocky land called the Auburn Rancheria. With no designated water supply and no appreciable way to earn livelihoods, the tribe members lived in severe poverty. Steve Wiegand, a reporter for the *Sacramento Bee*, described a typical dwelling in the pre casino years. The house of an elderly woman called Aunt Maxine was a wooden shack with tarps covering the roof and protecting one open side from the elements. Her water came from a hose attached to an outdoor spigot; her electricity from an extension cord running from a neighbor's house. A well for the rancheria finally was drilled in 1946, but because it produced a minimal amount of water that tasted acrid and bitter from excess minerals, it was useless. "We live in slum conditions," one tribal member told another *Sacramento Bee* reporter in 1947. I myself have driven through Auburn perhaps two hundred times, going from Reno to Sacramento or to Davis or to San Francisco and back again. It never occurred to me to look for a tribe or for such abject destitution.

In 1991, these Indians gave themselves a name—the United Auburn Indian Community (UAIC)—and organized formally so they might be in a better position to receive federal aid. Given their long history of neglect by the United States government, however, some of the tribe argued that they should take charge of their own destiny. Three of the four members of the tribal council wanted to build a coffee shop; Jessica Tavares and her followers thought a casino would be a better bet. Leading a successful recall election and ousting the obstructionists, Tavares was chosen as tribal chair and immediately began negotiations with government entities and financial backers. In 1999, the state of California agreed to their formal proposal to build a casino. While a series of subsequent lawsuits kept the tribe's plans in legal limbo, Tavares and her colleagues kept the conceptual project moving forward.

They negotiated with the county to secure a suitable site, finally settling on a forty-nine-acre parcel located in the Sunset Industrial area in southern Placer County. The tribe worked closely with country planners, agreeing to support specific infrastructure improvements, to build a fire station, and to pay for additional sheriff's deputies and fire fighters. Using nothing but their potential earnings for collateral, they borrowed $200 million from Bank of America and Wells Fargo. They chose Station Casinos, Inc., to run the new business for the first seven years of operation. A corporation that owns eleven casinos in and around Las Vegas and caters to local gamblers rather than tourists, Station Inc., then put up nearly $47 million to jumpstart the operation.

Not everyone in the neighborhood was so enthusiastic about a nearby casino. Officials of Rocklin and Roseville set aside litigation dollars and filed a series of lawsuits to try and stop the tribe's plans. In fact, these local opponents were not the only Californians dismayed by a trend toward large-scale Native American gaming operations. Since the late 1980s, when Indian casinos began to proliferate, court cases and subsequent election propositions and then more legal machinations had been the rule. California tribes tried to negotiate with the state, hoping to expand their operations beyond bingo and lotteries, but those negotiations went nowhere.

Finally, a number of tribes and their backers qualified Proposition 5, "The Tribal Government Gaming and Economic Self-Sufficiency Act of 1998," for the November 1998 ballot. Interested parties spent $90 million to pass the initiative, which lowered the gambling age to eighteen and placed no limits on the number of casinos or the number of machines and tables any tribe could operate. Moreover, Prop 5 allowed tribal gaming to be self-regulated, governed only by a tribal-appointed gaming board with no state oversight at all, while the governor would be required to approve every tribal casino licensing proposal. The proposition passed, but less than a year later the California State Supreme Court voided it, saying Prop 5 was unconstitutional because it conflicted with a 1984 state Lottery Act that prohibited the type of gaming played in Nevada and Atlantic City casinos.

Gaming advocates quickly introduced another initiative. Proposition 1A offered a constitutional amendment that would solve the dilemma. That measure passed in March 2000, with sixty-seven per cent of the voters favoring the change. More legal machinations followed, until the Ninth U.S. Circuit Court of Appeals, in *Artichoke Joe's California Grand Casino, et al. v. Gale A. Norton, Secretary of the Interior, et al.*, upheld Prop 1A. Meanwhile, the United Auburn Indian Community was fighting for its sovereign rights in court, too. Placer County supervisor Robert Weygandt, one of the leaders of the opposition, "soon learned that in the face of tribal sovereignty and federal law, their options were limited." A group called "Citizens for Safer Communities" persevered, but in September 2002 a federal judge dismissed the last remaining lawsuit. Immediately the United States Department of the Interior took the casino site in Sunset Park into trust for the tribe, and construction crews began work a month later.

Just eight months after that, Thunder Valley opened with much fanfare. Advertised as "the most exciting entertainment destination in Northern California," Thunder Valley aims to provide "Las Vegas excitement, glamour and action," with "thousands of the newest games." Though this Reno resident rarely ventures inside a local casino, I thought I was prepared for the ambience and the atmosphere. One foggy winter afternoon I drove over the mountains to Lincoln, California, home of Thunder Valley, home of a new breed of emancipation and tribal sovereignty.

The casino sits northeast of Sacramento in the midst of once-profitable but now abandoned agricultural lands, a quick seven and a half miles north of Interstate 80. Those seven-plus miles pass a landscape of new construction and the flat leftover undulations of overgrazed pastures. Fields of dreams, perhaps. Although many cars turned off at the new Galleria shopping mall and its Nordstrom's anchor store, as many more went on to Thunder Valley. The new casino complex sits at the corner of Athens Avenue, a name that reminds me of a European past and of consequent dreams of perfection, and Industrial Boulevard, an American twenty-first-century economic appellation with a very different set of connotations. I followed a white Plymouth Gallant, with a license plate holder that read "Outta My Way, I'm Going to Reno." Clearly, the middle-aged couple inside were not going to Reno at all, but were set to spend their Saturday afternoon and evening in fog-shrouded California. Signs directed us toward the new casino parking lot, a huge affair lined with pipe-stem trees and striped with enough parking places to accommodate three thousand vehicles. From every light post and in every aisle, Musak throbbed an anticipatory beat.

My Aunt Ruth loved to gamble. She and my uncle often visited me in Nevada. They would park their fifth-wheel trailer at a mobile home village in nearby Sparks, and then spend countless hours downtown. I remember going with them to the piano bar in the old Mapes Hotel, before urban rehabilitation directed its implosion, where Uncle Irv's bold baritone voice sang for hours along with the keyboard music and where Aunt Ruth, between drinks, drifted away to the slots. After Uncle Irv died, Aunt Ruth stepped up her gambling enthusiasm, choosing bus tours that took her on weekend junkets to the nearest play. When she died, I inherited her coins. I stashed the leather purse filled with nickels, dimes, and quarters in a cupboard, and forgot about them. In the guise of research, however, I dug them out and carried them off to Thunder Valley, hoping for a string of luck that Aunt Ruth would have adored.

There, in the parking lot, I sorted through her treasure trove. Nickels in one pocket; dimes in another; quarters in my belt pack, which sagged under the weight. There's a unique smell to a heap of coins, a pungent and tangible aroma of money that spells out casino as surely as Marcel

Proust's madeleine cakes helped his narrator remember the past. Memories of good times with Aunt Ruth and Uncle Irv mingled with a recollection of the night I parlayed a five-dollar Nevada State Fair coupon into a hundred bucks. I detect a pattern here—I gamble only with someone else's money. But I was ready to try my Indian luck. I marched across the parking lot, my steps in time with the drumbeat Musak, and I got ready to enjoy. Already my hands smelled like slots.

Thunder Valley itself is a squarish building of stucco, tile roofs, and shale rockwork pillars. Potted palms cluster around the doors. Faux California, I think, as I look around for any sign of Indian ownership and find none. As far as I could see, no signification for the United Auburn Indian Community appears anywhere on the building. Station Casinos, Inc., doesn't advertise its presence, either. At the entrance, I paused to fill out a slip of paper for the daily drawing. Raley's, a California and Nevada supermarket chain, was offering $500 worth of free groceries that day. Every twenty-four hours, a new drawing. I didn't win, but I did get my name on a Thunder Valley mailing list. More about that later.

Inside the casino, I was struck immediately by the hum and hubbub of slot machines, the carefully textured movement of warm air at just the right temperature, the bustle of players searching the aisles for just the right play. Since I was looking for a modern kind of tribal landscape, I focused first on the indigenous animals available. Lobster Mania. Fox and Hounds. The Great Turkey Shoot. Rich Little Piggies. Whales of Cash. Wild Bear Salmon Run. Roamin' Rhinos. Double Dolphin. Leopard Spots. The geographical biology of slot machine appellations was a bit mixed, I'm afraid, and occasionally intertwined with the fanciful. Double Dragons. Enchanted Unicorn. Pink Panther. The Munsters. I liked the names, each one designed to attract a willing player. Milk Money. Hexbreaker. She's a Rich Girl. Just my cup of tea.

But when I stepped up to the face of She's a Rich Girl, I was utterly stymied. There was no handle to pull, and the machine wouldn't accept coins at all. Aunt Ruth's money was useless here. Looking around, I saw no one with a paper cup full of dimes, no one with an ash tray of nickels, no one's pocket sagging with quarters. Instead, the gamers clutched squares of plastic that looked just like debit or credit cards, while brightly colored umbilical cords tethered the players to their cards and to their machines. Insert plastic; touch screen; watch the spin of digitized reels; count the poker faces of digitized cards. Sherman Alexie of the Spokane/Coeur d'Alene tribe depicted the interior of Washington state's Tulalip casino in his 1996 novel, *Indian Killer.* "Bright lights, flashing bulbs, sirens announcing wins. The *whirr-whirr-whirr* of the slots spinning, the *thuk-thuk-thuk* of the jackpot-jackpot-apple, a loser, falling into place." In California less than a decade later, listening to the noises of jackpots ringing and pseudo-coins falling, I realized I was hearing all digitized sounds. No personal interaction; no smell of money anywhere. This was not my aunt and uncle's Oldsmobile.

Scanning across the casino floor, looking for help and explanations, I spotted a long line of middle-aged gamblers snaking circuitously back and forth in front of a counter lined with computers. At one end, a Rewards Center assistant manager was entering data into her machine. Fortunately, Nita turned out to be someone who can input data and talk simultaneously. I learned a lot. "No coins in Indian casinos," she said. "I don't think there are any slot machines that take coins anywhere in California. Certainly not in any of the newer places." She went on to explain that most of the people in line had just arrived by the bus load. Apparently, everyone who comes by bus receives a five dollar coupon that must be redeemed at the Rewards Center. The coupon becomes a debit card, to which a player can add money of his or her own. The old-timers took all this for granted, but several newcomers were puzzled by the technological transfer. The Aunt Ruth-look-alikes asked a lot of questions.

"I don't give you anything," said one of the workers behind the counter. "I just load it on your card." Three elderly Korean women looked uneasy. Shaking their heads, they exchanged rapid-fire conversation. "Automatically loaded on your card," the attendant repeated. "Your pin number is your year of birth." The coinless operation reminded me of a Monopoly game, where the paper dollars, the rents, the hotels on Park Place bear little resemblance to actual economics. Indeed, this must be the point, to lull the players into a false sense of nonreality, as if the money were unreal. Insert plastic; touch screen; play again and again. I saw one "nickel" machine advertising "play 75 credits." You do the math.

"No coins," repeats Nita. "It just makes sense." She explains the Players Exchange, where tickets can be redeemed for cash. When a ticket prints, in fact, the sounds of dropping coins accompany the process. While Nita talks, a nearby machine blares again, "Wheel . . . of . . . Fortune," and more acoustic noncoinage falls. What Nita didn't explain was the more draconian benefit from a coinless operation. RFID (radio frequency identification) chips, embedded in the plastic cards, allow a casino to track the players and their playing habits. Mark Pilarski, a syndicated gaming writer, explains: "With the swipe of your slot club card, onboard software knows your name, address, interests, denominations of play, favorite machines, how much you have invested and your winnings at any given hour." Casino managers now can trace every slot machine bet whenever anyone uses his or her card. On the plus side, this means accurate "comping" for high rollers; on the negative, it entirely eliminates anonymity. I must say that I personally prefer the weight of Aunt Ruth's coins, but apparently I no longer have that option.

An interior casino has a landscape all its own, so in that respect Thunder Valley seemed familiar. Like all the other gaming establishments across my adopted state, it's a maze, with short-stubbed aisles that run into one another and almost force a potential player to weave in and out among tables or machines. Just as the outside is faux California stucco, the inside is carpeted in faux Oriental rugs, the walls are painted in soothing earth tones, and Tuscany paintings hang inside the restrooms. Shale on the inside pillars mimics the shale on the outside. The staff moves crisply through the maze, while the players meander to and fro, pausing here and there to play. One man, I think, is asleep, his blue baseball cap tipped down on his forehead, his body slumped against the back of his chair. Then I spot the tightening of his jaw and the movement of his fingers on his screen. An elderly woman pushes past in her wheelchair; another nudges her oxygen tank between the stools. A heavy-set man wearing a kewpie hat limps from one machine to the next, while his wife obediently traces his movements. Another balding fellow in a faded green coat moves his walker toward the door. This is not a young crowd, not at all.

"But you should be here at night," Nita insists. "No buses and a very different clientele." She wrinkles her nose but smiles. Nita makes nighttime sound distasteful, with younger customers, much more alcohol, and not a few scuffles. She prefers the day shift, sanitized. In fact, she loves her casino job. "Excellent benefits," she exclaims. "And a nice break room, with a restaurant." She smiles again, radiating the sunny attitude that characterizes all her behavior. Patient with the impatient customers, she finishes every transaction with a "Good Luck" wish. I ask her about the management and ownership, and about the Indians. How do they fit in? "I don't really know any Indians," Nita responds.

Some ethnic distinctions are clear at Thunder Valley, however. Certain Boarding Passes—a plastic euphemism if I've ever heard one— work in the slot machines; others, at the tables. A customer must choose, and it appears to me as if most of the Asian clientele chooses the tables while almost everyone else seems to select the slots. "Right," said Nita, adding more data into her computer. Over her head, the Thunder Strike jackpot adds to its potential winnings. $92,729.64 and counting. Meanwhile, Nita fills a drawer with more red and pink and orange tether cords, and nods to another set of customers. "Good luck to you guys; have fun!" One edgy woman wearing a white sweatshirt is less sanguine. "She has to get in line," she says sharply to a Japanese gambler, "all the way to the end." The would-be player understands little English, and ignores the woman's imperial commands. Nita continues smiling. "Have fun!"

When a chorus of enthusiastic shouts punctuates her words, I decide to leave Nita and the Rewards Center and follow the noise. I cross over to the Falls Bar, a casino centerpiece with flat-paned artificial waterfalls coursing down the sides of the enclosure. It's a symbolic slap, I think, at the waterless milieu of the rancheria. Not much business yet, even in the late afternoon of a foggy winter Saturday. In front of the bar I find a mechanized roulette table, the first I've ever seen. Its players are tethered, too, tied to their positions with those colored umbilical cords that hook onto pockets or wrists and attach to the machines. Lights flash, the wheel spins, a computer debits or credits the cards while keeping track of the play. No one speaks to anyone else; everyone concentrates fully on the programmed roulette. I remember the first time I ever visited Reno with my parents, and I recall how fascinated I was by the women I called the "bag ladies." Gray-haired, stooped, shopping bags by their sides, they pulled the arms of the one-armed bandits over and over again. I was too young to go inside a casino, but the women were almost on the sidewalks, just inside the open doors, feeding their sweaty coins into the slots, caressing the handles and cajoling the machines. Anonymous to each other, they nonetheless were interacting with their games in ways quite distinct from the bloodless Thunder Valley players two generations later. I shift the weight of Aunt Ruth's coins in my pockets, and feel no temptation to change them into plastic.

The tables turn out to be different, too, not much blackjack as I know it but mostly baccarat and Pai Gow poker. Each carries a $25 minimum wager, with either a $1,000 or $2,000 limit. I can't imagine placing a $2,000 bet on anything, but Asian players surround every table and in some cases line up behind the seats. As many as three or four deep are watching the action. I don't have a clue about what's going on, although a series of lights glows on and off under the neon letters *P* and *T* and *B*. A slender Asian woman deals cards with fingers fast as lightning. Watching her, I think of an ex-graduate student of mine who proudly announced that he earned more dealing baccarat than I made as a college professor. When I wondered why he was bothering with a graduate degree, he opined that working in the stifling surroundings of an indoor casino didn't seem much like a lifelong career. Unlike Nita, many casino workers eagerly seek other jobs. But she is correct, Thunder Valley pays quite well. A floor supervisor earns an annual salary of nearly $50,000, with "a medical and dental plan, a 401(k) plan, access to tuition assistance and even a card that lets him buy gasoline at the commercial fueling station the casino's vehicles use." Thomas Dean, interviewed by *Bee* reporter Steve Wiegand, likes his job.

Most dealers, however, look bored, their expressions tight-lipped and closed. Slapping the cards, scooping the chips, shuffling and slapping and scooping, they keep the play moving as quickly as possible. Hovering behind them, the pit bosses watch every move made by players and workers alike. Dressed in dark suits, poker-faced with hooded eyes, these overseers lurk catlike, ready to pounce should anyone make a false move. Everyone—players, dealers, pit bosses—concentrates fully. "Gaming" seems almost a euphemism for the serious strategic action. In fact, the entire process moves along with military precision. If this is battle, it's analogous to twenty-first century warfare as seen on the evening television news. Bloodless, digitized, sanitized, impersonal. A bleached-blonde cocktail waitress, wearing high heels and a skimpy black costume, clicks past. For the Asian clientele, bottled water and an occasional juice. If this is war, it's serious and sober business.

I still haven't spent any of Aunt Ruth's money. I walk away from the tables, back past Nita's counter—she must be on her break—and glance toward two other giant progressive machines set away from the wall. One is Monopoly, so I pause and count the mechanized increments. $3,351,284.92 soon becomes $3,351,341.97 soon becomes $3,351,474.45. I calculate that the pot grows by approximately $30 every minute, by $.50 every second. An overdressed woman, wearing a mauve suit, matching scarf, and button heels plays over and over again. She neither glances my way nor looks up at the increasing totals. She just clutches her purse, and plays and plays.

A food court, rather like one I might find in a shopping mall, stretches along the north end of the building. I have four choices—hamburgers, Mexican food, pizza, and a Panda Express. I choose the "Gourmet Chinese Food," mostly because it's the only station with a long line and I naively assume that this indicates the best food. I soon figure out that the Panda Express line exists because all the Asian customers received food coupons on their buses, along with their five-dollar chits for gambling, and that hardly anyone speaks English. The buffet moves slowly, as Koreans, Japanese, Chinese, and Thais point and choose. My egg roll turns out to be soggy, and my fortune cookie sounds an odd note. "Saturdays are good days for taking care of chores," reads the tiny scrap of white paper. No chores for me on this gaming Saturday, unless I count note-taking as a chore, but at least I got to use a few of Aunt Ruth's coins on my oriental repast.

If I were to go back to Thunder Valley now, I could flash my own coupon. A week after my weekend sojourn, I began receiving mail from the casino. "Dear Ann," each letter begins. "Welcome and thank you for visiting the BEST casino around." The first letter is worth five dollars in complimentary dining, as long as I bring it to the casino within the next six weeks. I learn that the brochure I picked up on site is wrong. Not a mere 1,900 slots, but over 2,700 now. "That's more than any casino in California, Reno or Tahoe!" the letter boasts. "With the new additions, it's like we've added a second casino!" Lots of exclamation points. A Thunder Valley News Flash! is included with the letter. It opens by asking, "HAVE YOU BEEN THUNDER STRUCK YET?" If I hurry—and I must, because supplies are limited—I can earn points toward "some terrific gifts." A Thunder Strike mug; a Thunder Strike T-shirt; a Thunder Strike cap; a lightweight jacket or even a suede one. "YOU COULD BE THE NEXT LUCKY WINNER. Just ask Bill from Merced, California, how easy it was to win his $64,206." I wonder if he got a T-shirt or a ball cap.

Between three and four million visitors came to Thunder Valley in its first year of operation. That's an average daily attendance of nearly ten thousand people. The amount bet totaled more than five billion dollars, with net profits of more than three hundred million. The tribe already has repaid its loan from Station Casinos, Inc., is repaying the construction loans, and has money left over for tribal benefits. Individual income is a closely guarded secret, but has been described as "between healthy and hefty." Every member now receives free medical, dental and vision care, plus free tuition and tutoring for education at any level. The tribe recently bought a 1,100-acre tract at Camp Far West Reservoir, where members can build new homes on an upscale version of Indian lands. Grants of $40,000 apiece will be available for down payments.

Greg Baker, tribal administrator, showed me a mock-up design of the planned Sheridan community, with a day-care center, a place for senior citizens, recreational fields, ponds, walkways, and five-acre "envelope" lots that will remain unfenced. A school and health-care facilities will be located there, too. Sheridan, a twenty-first-century version of a "reservation," will negate the old connotations of poverty and deprivation and will be a place where tribal members can enjoy all the benefits of their new wealth. Greg also showed me an up-to-date map of the traditional rancheria, with property owned partially by individual tribal members, partially by outsiders, and partially the tribe itself. One day the UAIC hopes to regain all of the old land, which is situated in the midst of a growing suburbia.

Later, Greg drove me to that Maidu/Miwok patch of ground so I could see the few remaining double-wide trailer homes, the abandoned derelict cars, the old mattresses tossed aside, the digger pines, and the incendiary grasses for myself. It looked like a firetrap, mostly abandoned, though a couple of places were occupied and a couple more were being refurbished. Immediately next door, however, an enclave of trophy homes lined the ridge-top, their flame-retardant rooftops visible from everywhere in the rancheria. Oakview, Southridge, Grand Oaks, Diamond Ridge, and then the rancheria. Close by, on the western edge of the rancheria property, some of the youngsters have put up a red, white, and blue skeletal teepee to remind those who live in the nearby upscale subdivisions that "This is Indian country." Since neither the Maidu nor Miwok peoples lived in tepees, this seems a rather ironic gesture, but the Indians say that the teepee reminds them of their heritage and their pride. Also a mark of their ancestral past is the tribal cemetery, which abuts a fancy new Health Club and a row of professional offices. "MAIDU burial site," reads a modest wooden sign. Plans for the future prevail here, too, including landscaping, an iron gate, and a more elaborate sign.

While taking care of themselves, the UAIC are also looking after the local community. Shortly before the first anniversary of Thunder Valley's opening, the tribe gave $225,000 to Placer County nonprofit groups. Ironically, many beneficiaries are the same groups that so vehemently fought the casino location in the first place. The UAIC plans to make further donations, expecting to spend more than $30 million on various neighborhood improvements. A spokesman also calculates that the casino locally spent $82 million in its first year of operation, purchasing food and beverages and products like light bulbs and toilet paper, while paying its employees decent wages. Clearly, the impact is extraordinary, and perhaps more positive than the "Citizens for Safer Communities" might have foreseen.

Economically, this operation is a coup, employing nearly two thousand workers, with an annual payroll of $44 million. The 247 tribal members call it "a miracle." In 2001, ninety-six percent of them were earning at below-poverty levels, with no health insurance and with enormous economic and social problems. They survived primarily on United States government grants of various sorts. Before Thunder Valley, two-thirds of them owned neither checking accounts nor credit cards, an unbelievable statistic in today's world. After Thunder Valley, the tribal outlook is considerably brighter. When I asked Greg how many Indians were employed at the casino, he grinned at my naiveté. "No need," he smiled.

The Indians take their responsibilities seriously. A bulletin posted in the tribal administration building announced the latest tribal election results. Nearly eighty-six percent of the eligible General Council adults had voted, a rate of participation that would put most Americans to shame. Overall, the UAIC is organized exactly like a democracy—a formal governmental structure with representative committees overseeing every facet of operations. Right now, most of the tribal energy is going into training this generation and educating their children so everyone has the skills to manage a multimillion-dollar business. The learning center model is "an enormous financial commitment," says Greg, and a "testament to the tribe" and its priorities. Important, too, is the health and wellness component, which is compounding rapidly.

As much as I enjoyed my conversations and e-mails with Greg Baker, and with Doug Elmets, the tribal public relations director, I was frustrated by the fact that I hadn't talked to any tribal members. Neither man seemed inclined to introduce me to anyone else—in fact, when Greg drove me through the rancheria he never stopped the car. Too intrusive, he implied. Maybe Thunder Valley is just too corporate; maybe I should look at a smaller, more hands-on operation. I wanted to ask, for example, about another bulletin posted on the board, the one offering landscaping advice and fiscal information for the installation of in-ground pools. That seemed to me emblematic of the gargantuan overnight success for members of the UAIC—from no running water to swimming pools in just a few years. I wondered, too, if every Indian gaming operation was as profitable as Thunder Valley. And I wanted to hear Indian voices define their own landscapes, changed by the advent of casino designs.

Nineteen miles north of Klamath Falls, Oregon, near the tiny town of Chiloquin and far from any large population center, the Kla-Mo-Ya landscape differs distinctly from look-alike Las Vegas casinos. Walking past the waterfall that graces the entrance, I stroll into a single smoke-filled room. Sherman Alexie wrote that "the most dangerous thing in the [Tulalip] casino was the thick cloud of cigarette smoke." I'll have to agree; unlike Thunder Valley, Kla-Mo-Ya's air smelled stale. The two restaurants—the Rapids Deli and the Still Water Buffet—implied a fresh, outdoors orientation, however. And like Thunder Valley, wild animals were populating the slot machines—Whales of Cash, Golden Goose, Frog Wild, Wild Bear Salmon Run, Buzzard Bucks, and more. There weren't as many of them, though. In fact, Kla-Mo-Ya's maximum occupancy allows only 1,068 gamblers, while Thunder Valley boasts three times as many machines and draws ten times as many people every day. Of Kla-Mo-Ya's six blackjack tables, only three were in use on a sunny summer afternoon. No keno; no poker; no bingo; no alcohol; no coins anywhere. The gamblers looked familiar, though, mostly middle-aged and mostly tethered to the slot (a misnomer, now, in this coinless age) machines.

I sensed that Kla-Mo-Ya (a composite name signifying the members of the Klamath Tribes—the Klamath, the Modoc, and the Yahooskin Band of the Snake Indians) is an Al's Diner kind of operation, a blue-plate-special casino that purposely attracts the local loggers, farmers and ranchers, plus Winnebago vacationers passing through. It is, after all, the second largest tourist draw in the county, surpassed only by Crater Lake. And its parking lot has plenty of room for eighteen-wheelers—I counted twelve that day—pausing along Highway 97. Not only is the scale smaller than a Thunder Valley operation, but the scope is more localized. The general manager, Donnie Wright, is a Modoc; two-thirds of the employees are tribal members, too. The tribe, wholly self-financed at this point and operating independently, fully manages its own property and already has paid off one set of casino bonds.

After failing to meet any Thunder Valley Indians, here I was able to talk with several Klamath and Modoc people. As expected, I was unable to determine any dollar amounts of the casino's success, for the financial details are closely guarded, but clearly the operation is profitable. Like the UAIC, this tribe contributes a fair portion of their earnings—$20 million annually—to the community in goods, services, and payroll, and also provides grants to local agencies. Obviously, Kla-Mo-Ya is thriving, with a master plan for future expansion that includes a truck stop, a golf course, a hotel, more amenities, and expanded gaming. I managed to learn that 2004 was a "record year"; 2005 projections are even higher.

Right now, the profits are being returned to the casino operation, a fact that troubles and frustrates some of the tribal members. I saw no evidence of "in-ground swimming pools" and 5,000-square-foot up-scale homes with landscaped lawns; the nearby town of Chiloquin—once a part of the reservation, now privately owned—looked weighted down by poverty. The Klamath Tribes, originally cobbled together by the United States government in 1864, is notoriously poor. It has a troubled history with the government, exacerbated by the Modoc War of 1873 when a band of Modoc people tried to return to their original Tule Lake homelands and were thwarted by the United States Army. Unfortunate years of exploitation followed, plus another broken treaty and an incessant shrinkage of reservation lands. All this antagonism culminated in a 1954 Termination decree that abolished the reservation and all federal responsibility to the tribe. Along the way, 23 million acres of "peak to peak" tribal lands shrunk to zero.

In August 1986, after lengthy negotiations and a significant ruling by the courts, the United States government restored federal status to the Klamath Tribes. Now all tribal members of one-quarter blood and over eighteen years of age belong to the General Council that oversees the sovereign nation. A smaller Tribal Council of ten elected members speaks for the tribe and makes day-to-day decisions. So the governmental design resembles that of the UAIC, although this particular Tribal Council is larger than theirs. Actually, this tribal group is larger, too, with more than twice as many enrolled members. So I set out to learn exactly what they thought of their gaming operation.

First, I talked with Elwood Miller, Jr., director of the Natural Resources Department, who detailed many of the land-use issues still troubling the Klamath Basin. He saw the casino as a useful means by which the tribe is gaining financial stability. His focus, however, was on the ancient tribal lands that were lost throughout the twentieth century rather than on the

modern money-making machine. His holistic words were firm as he spoke
of the ways that the settlers took from the system, whereas "we take the
products of the system." For Elwood, the casino is only one aspect of
economic independence. Even more important, to him, is future land
and timber and salmon restoration. "I hope the Creator will intervene,"
he specifically said.

His words echo what I later read in the March 2005 issue of
Klamath News, the official publication of the Klamath Tribes. There,
the tribal chairman carefully articulates, "We have always had a connection to the land and believe that we were placed here as stewards of the
land." Allen Foreman's words were spoken at a c'waam ceremony, which
is a spiritual time "to express and reaffirm our covenant to the Creator
and his to us." Clearly, the tribal focus is far more profound than blackjack and bingo.

After speaking with Elwood, I spent several hours with Taylor
David, the tribal public information specialist. She echoed this point of
view. If I learned nothing more from my conversations with Klamath
tribal members and from reading their printed materials, I gleaned the
strength of their reliance on their Creator and the powerful optimism
with which they view the future. Taylor—a descendant of the Captain
Jack who led the Modoc band during the 1873 war and who was executed
for his efforts, and granddaughter of a college saddle-bronc champion—
spoke eloquently of tribal spirituality and of their absolute insistence on
serving the community. Elwood actually chastised me for using the word
"quarrel" when I spoke of the Klamath Basin irrigation and wildlife
issues, preferring that we talk about parity instead. Taylor agreed that
understanding divergent points of view and consequent cooperation was
critical to solving the problems and aspirations of all the people who live
in the area. Negotiating with the United States government, the newly
energized tribe fought successfully for sufficient twenty-first-century water
for salmon habitat. Now they hope to recover 600,000 acres from the
Fremont and Winema National Forests. Currently, the tribe owns slightly
more than 500 scattered acres in trust. The casino, the tribal administra-
tive offices, the health and dental buildings, and the cemetery sit on the
largest blocks.

The admin building, in fact, is located atop an ancient flint-gathering place. The area behind the structure remains as a park to honor tribal ancestors. In 2002, Ivan Jackson handcrafted a Modoc winter house, replicating the old methods of construction as closely as possible. Taylor and I walked out to see the finished structure. Thirty feet wide by four feet deep by fourteen feet high, it is made of five layers of materials— eighty-eight lodgepole beams, split cedar and yellow pine slats, fifty-five handwoven tule mats for insulation, grass sod to cover the mats, and a layer of dirt overall. Just as the casino seemed to me more personalized than Thunder Valley's, so the Modoc winter house was more natural than the Auburn tepee. Maybe I just liked the high desert wind blowing on a hot afternoon more than I liked the Sacramento traffic, but here I felt much more connection to the land. As Taylor and I were walking toward the pine and tule and sod winter house, her nephew jumped out from behind a sagebrush and pretended to shoot an arrow in our direction. "Still wild Indians around here," she said, laughing. Indians who care deeply about their heritage, I might add.

Hanging on the wall of Taylor's office is a Cree Indian Prophecy. "It could be Modoc," she explained.

> Only after the last tree
>   has been cut down.
> Only after the last river
>   has been poisoned.
> Only after the last fish
>   has been caught.
>   Only then
>   will you find that
> Money cannot be eaten.

Taylor smiled as she watched me copy the words, commenting that too many outsiders don't understand them. I thought the saying was particularly appropriate in this tribal setting, where everyone pulls together both monetarily and metaphysically. Even as the Klamath peoples enjoy their new-found economic status, they retain their old priorities. "Things come full circle," Taylor repeated. "If not in my lifetime, in a future generation," the land will be returned to those who originally honored it. Then, as Elwood said, we will "feel culturally and spiritually whole again." The casino, as I understand it, is just a single step on the way to that end.

This, of course, is another way of saying "home" and the Klamath Tribes in a single breath. After the horrors of Termination, when their sovereign status was dissolved and when every eligible tribal member subsequently received $43,000 in return for their lands (although the tribe retained hunting, fishing, gathering and senior water rights, a fact that now enables them to bargain for water sufficient for salmon rehabilitation), the concept of home disappeared as quickly as the money. But now, symbolized in part by the casino, in part by the new tribal administrative building—with its fine collection of native baskets and native sculptures—and in part by the Modoc winter house, a reestablished sense of home seems possible. A handout produced by the tribal Culture and Heritage Department states very clearly that "The Klamath and Modoc creation legend begins in this area. The Klamath and Modoc people do not believe that they migrated from another area." *Here* is home.

Still musing about their heritage and ancestral tribal pride, I thought about contradictions I had seen in the casino itself. The internal blare of a popular country and western song, "Cadillac Cowboy," contrasted sharply with a new novel most Klamath people despise. Rick Stever's *Buy the Chief a Cadillac* underscores all the Indian stereotypes while sugarcoating the terrible pain of Termination. I found the Klamath Muzak even more oddly out of place than the sounds of the Thunder Valley parking lot. Also out of place was the internal Kla-Mo-Ya décor. Each seat at the blackjack tables, for example, is marked by a Plains Indian dream catcher insignia, while the chairs are covered with a Zuni zig-zag pattern. I guess the ploy is to use "Indian-ness" that tourists might like, while keeping the genuine heritage just below the radar. When remodeling and expanding, however, I trust the tribe will discard superficial borrowings and make the landscape its own. Already the logo announces proudly, "This is our home. This is where we were born. . . This is our world, where we were formed, where we come from, who we are." So say the voices of a sovereign nation emerging behind and beyond a casino landscape; so say the voices that proudly nullify the fearful prediction of Buffalo Bird Woman.

A June 28, 2005, piece in *Indian Country Today* reports that "American Indian gaming grew at a fairly robust rate of 12 percent and grossed a total of $19 billion in the past year." A month later, The Reno *Gazette-Journal* upped the ante, calculating revenues at $19.4 billion and saying that "revenues at 367 tribal casinos and gambling outlets rose about 15 percent, from 16.8 billion in 2003." Slot machine-tethered tourists do indeed bring money into starving economies. Culturally, however, non-Native visitors may be a mixed blessing. Mary Louise Pratt uses the phrase "imperial eyes" for the ways in which visitors inadvertently denigrate the very culture they purport to enjoy. Renato Rosaldo takes her concept one step further, defining "imperialist nostalgia" as the burden of tourists who mourn the passing of what they themselves have transformed by their presence. The archaeologists digging in Canyon de Chelly fit Pratt's category, while my own sojourn mirrors Rosaldo's. Just as the archaeologists dug up in order to preserve, I and thousands just like me have inundated the vista points to such an extent that the historic significance is almost lost. In our own ways, with imperialistic fervor if not imperialistic intent, we forever altered the ruins.

Is it any wonder that groups like the United Auburn Indian Community and the Klamath Tribes want to appreciably alter their ruined terrain as well? Everywhere throughout the West, in fact, tourism and gaming have become critical ingredients of twenty-first-century tribal life. From the American Southwest to the Pacific Northwest, from the curio shops of Colorado to the casinos of California, visitors are seeking out what the tribes have to offer. Thunder Valley, in effect, is a replacement reservation for the rancheria that failed. As if their tribe were recolonizing California, the small group of Maidu and Miwok natives took a page from the imperialist handbook, and revolutionized their surroundings. Likewise, Kla-Mo-Ya became a post-Termination landscape of renewal, as if the Klamath Tribes were reestablishing a claim on south-central Oregon, and effectively capitalizing on tourist capital. The tepee and the zigzag décor and the casinos themselves may be out of place in a literal sense, but metaphorically they indicate that sovereignty has its benefits after all. So does imperialism; so does taking advantage of the locals, the Aunt Ruths and the Uncle Irvs and their plastic placebos.

CHAPTER FOUR

Glittering Stars

How often at night when the heavens are bright
With the light of the glittering stars,
Have I stood here amazed and asked as I gazed
If their glory exceeds that of ours.

Thanks to A. B. Guthrie, Jr., and to the efforts of the Helena and Bozeman Chambers of Commerce, Montana lays claim to the title "Big Sky Country." Originally, the phrase was coined—probably in *Sunset Magazine*, although the precise provenance is unclear—to describe almost any firmament in the interior American West. From Montana to New Mexico and from Nevada to Colorado, big sky prevails. Big sky—bold, without subtlety, aggressive, a blue umbrella tinctured with clouds of varying shapes and sizes and shades, a black overlay of sullen weather. Big sky defines the West. Or at least some of the West. It doesn't characterize Seattle, where incessant winter rain lowers the ceiling in flat tones of gray. Nor does it apply to San Francisco or San Diego, where fogs can choke the city skylines. Nor does it appear in Phoenix, although big sky might have been there fifty years ago, or in sprawling Denver, where present-day smog yellows the mountains.

When I lived in Colorado during the mid-1960s, hints of a vaporous horizon already were visible. Sometimes the sun, a round red eyeball with a hangover, glared at the landscape before dropping behind the mountains. Sometimes Denver's downtown faded into a shadowy nether-world haze. Sometimes the details blurred. The residents wondered if unsightly automobile smog and layers of dust might be harbingers of things to come. Old-timers spoke of the pure mountain air that suddenly didn't seem so clean after all, and watched a dark thickness of pollutants grow right along with the city. Politicians eager for new businesses, urban development, and extended city limits ignored the signs of "progress" and encouraged further growth. In time, "bright heavens" became an illusion from the past.

When I moved to a smaller Reno, I thought little about particulates. Living in the northwest quadrant of town, I never noticed any smog at all. Then I moved a bit higher on the mountain, and found that I looked across a faint stratum of tans and browns. Visiting friends who lived on the valley floor, I could smell both the smoke of winter wood fires and the throttling whiffs of exhaust. When the congealed air caught up with my house, I moved to the other end of town and higher still. Now I survey an expanse sometimes so tarnished that the skyline dulls and the downtown casinos almost disappear. Even though Reno enforces a fireplace "no burn" code on the unhealthiest days, the City Council does nothing to curb the fumes from traffic exhaust pipes or the clouds from commercial effluvium. Such is the fate of urban big sky today; such seems to be an unfortunate future.

"Home on the Range" describes an unclouded Edenic panorama that the twentieth century gradually dissipated. Subsequent decades of pollutants have darkened not only the cities of the American West but the distant vistas as well. The best-known desecration comes from three Southwest coal-fired energy plants—the Four Corners Power Plant outside of Shiprock, New Mexico, the Navajo Generating Station to the east of Page, Arizona, and the Mohave Power Plant in Laughlin, Nevada. Two hundred miles ought to be the normal visibility at the Grand Canyon; a twenty-to-fifty-mile range is more likely when the closest behemoths spew a full complement of sulfur dioxide, nitrogen oxide,

and mercury. At the Page operation, "state-of-the-art electrostatic precipi-
tators and wet-lime flue-gas scrubbers" are supposed to eliminate "more
than 90 percent of its air-born contaminants," reports Russell Martin, in
A *Story That Stands Like a Dam*, but he concludes that the "more than
a hundred tons of fly ash and toxic gases a day" nonetheless pollute the
air of the High Plateau. When I drove toward Page in mid-December, I
could see the power plant's clouds from miles away, and the southern
end of Lake Powell was thoroughly shrouded underneath a purplish-blue
cloud of bruised and abused air.

Charles Wilkinson describes the Shiprock operation in more vivid
terms. Steel standards like "praying-mantis" antennae surround boilers
"like gigantic teakettles," which swallow 24,000 tons of coal every day
from a mining operation that uses massive quantities of dynamite and
nitroglycerin. He quotes one Hopi woman who said "the mining and air
pollution were like rape." I know I wouldn't care to live under such
showers of acid rain. The 1970 Clean Air Act supposedly limited the
allowable amounts of pollution, and a 1977 amendment specifically
addressed the air quality of national parks and wilderness areas. Grand-
fathered power plants, however, still emit four to ten times the amount
predicated by those bills passed three decades ago.

Driving back to Reno from Arizona, I could see the emissions from
Laughlin, Nevada, where Southern California Edison Company's 1,580-
megawatt plant clouds the air with "nearly 40,000 tons of sulfur dioxide"
each year. Theoretically, those pollutants will be reduced by more than
eighty-five percent, or else will disappear completely. According to the
U.S. Environmental Protection Agency's and the Izaak Walton League's
websites, the installation of a "baghouse (a giant fabric filter)" and new
burners in the plant's two boilers is underway. But this retrofitting is turning out to be prohibitively expensive, and the operator is insisting that
the plant will shut down if fiscal and regulatory relief isn't granted. The
California Public Utilities Commission is debating final action. It now
looks as if either the current "Clean Air" strictures will be relaxed for the
particulate requirements, especially for the mercury, a neurotoxin that
significantly affects the food-chain, or the Mojave Generating Station will
close. Since negotiations are continuing, even as I finish this chapter, I

cannot guarantee one outcome or the other. At this moment, visible clouds of green and gray from excessive lead pollution—the most in the nation—continue to dim the desert skies. To stop that pollution, apparently the plant must be mothballed, putting hundreds of Hopi Indians out of work and decimating the tribal budget. So the stakes are high. Who can say what the sky will look like in another month?

Despite such discernible visual losses, however, big sky still characterizes many parts of the American West. Not everywhere is dimmed by industrial effusions. The stars glitter, even if we can't always see them. And if we get far enough away from city lights, the sky can become a pointillist's canvas. Camping in northern Washoe County, a remote stretch of Nevada desert far distant from electricity, I stare at a summer sky. Awash with the Milky Way, the heavens seem close enough to touch. Or far enough away to imagine worlds populated by "all the fire-folk sitting in the air!" Lying in my sleeping bag and staring upward, I feel upside down, as though I had fallen in a black hole with the sky pulsing all around me. Gerard Manley Hopkins, a late-nineteenth-century Jesuit priest from Great Britain, celebrated the grandeur of the natural world by syncopating unexpected cadences and inventing word combinations that constantly surprise. "The Starlight Night" projects a staccato rendition of star-studded heavens—"circle-citadels," "elves'-eyes," "quickgold," "wind-beat whitebeam," and white poplars "set on a flare!" The anthropocentric poet, believing "it is all a purchase, all is a prize," metaphorically urges environmental consumption, but most of his language and imagery comes straight from a transcendentalist imagination.

Because I myself don't quite see the sky as a giant Wal-Mart, I cannot buy his creative logic. But I like Hopkins's images, the surprising ways he jolts my expectations, the explosions of sound and meaning. Just as Igor Stravinsky's *Rite of Spring* jars my ears or impressionist painters like Claude Monet startle my eyes, so Hopkins creates simultaneous disruption and integration, a melodic dissonance that sounds just right in the desert. I memorized some of Hopkins' poems when I was young, and those lines come back to me whenever I stare at a starstrung sky.

> The world is charged with the grandeur of God.
> It will flame out, like shining from shook foil;
> It gathers to a greatness, like the ooze of oil
> Crushed.

That is how I imagine the stars, "shining from shook foil," as if the twinkling had grown so large that it was crushing all the senses. Watching the Pleiades shower of shooting stars last August, tracing the points of light spinning down to the horizon, I know Hopkins was correct when he concluded, "And for all this, nature is never spent." Most westerners, I suspect, will concur with his priestly pantheistic point of view.

> Glory be to God for dappled things—
>   For skies of couple-colour as a brinded cow
>   For rose-moles all in stipple upon trout that swim;
> Fresh-firecoal chestnut-falls; finches wings;
>   Landscape plotted and pierced.

Hopkins never visited the American West, but when he mused that "the mind has mountains; cliffs of fall / Frightful, sheer, no-man-fathomed," he seemed to be describing not only the poetic imagination but the "no-man-fathomed" natural terrain of Nevada, Montana, and other big sky landscapes. I think of his words whenever I'm in the midst of stippled horizons and wherever I'm wandering through "landscape plotted and pierced." Throughout the West, I am certain, "nature is never spent," although I fret at extractive policies that may hasten its decline. Most of the time, though, I'm optimistic about the "grandeur" of "dappled things" for skies of couple-colour" everywhere, especially in the earthtone landscape that surrounds me.

This past year I've kept track of the Reno sky, noted the colors that come and go with the seasons, sketched out the shapes that predict thunderstorms or snow, followed the weatherman's prognostications, right or wrong. What I've seen belongs on a painter's palette, or in Gerard Manley Hopkins's poetic notebook. Heavy slate-gray clouds that bulk up on the horizon, the ominous precursors of a winter blizzard.

They storm across the sky, lower onto the horizon, obscure the edges of mountains crushed by their imagined weight. The sky outside is gunmetal gray, its shapes washing into ocean waves of water waiting to fall. Or three months later, an Old Man of the Mountains cloud, facing north, blows bubbles with a bubble pipe, puffing stratocumulus tessellations here and there. No inclement weather that day, just the froth of spring. Later in the season, a Sierra Wave cloud that resembles a flying saucer hovers just off the crest of Mount Rose, while the wind batters the valleys below.

John A. Day, in *The Science of Weather*, calls clouds the "billboards of the sky," announcers and advertisers of the weather to come. In midsummer, a vertical rainbow bisects Reno. Angled in the eastern sky; magenta to the north; lime-green to the south. The rainbow signals the end of a storm-flushed day, when quarter-sized raindrops plunked on my deck and nickel-sized hail fell to the south. Or it's October, and the first snowfall of winter may occur in the Sierra tonight. A heady wind was the storm's precursor, followed by sleek fibrous "billboard" clouds and a temperature drop of twenty degrees. Day, who describes these altostratus clouds as "a layer of great horizontal extent," imagines looking through them as if peering through ground glass. Checking out his imagery, I decide he's correct, though I prefer Hopkins's "fresh-firecoal chestnut-falls" to Day's "detached clouds in the form of delicate white filaments of white or mostly white patches or narrow bands."

I also decide that Nevada's cloud formations are every bit as various and as stunning as Montana's. True, Montana's January clouds are more ominous than western Nevada's, the sky more threatening, the weather more severe. But either place can generate bulging summer cumulus clouds that explode summer torrents from a very big sky. The recipe, I think, calls for egg whites, baking soda, yeast, black strap molasses, anise, and a dollop of mud, thickened and tossed against the sky. The less imaginative John Day, on the other hand, imagines cumulus clouds as giant cauliflowers. Somehow that prosaic vegetable doesn't belong in my mix.

Just a few weeks ago, I flew from one big sky to the next, en route with anvil thunderheads both west and east. As the pilot edged the plane alongside the enormous clouds, I could peer into the depths, as if I were

looking into a black and white volcano waiting to explode. From Bozeman to Reno, clouds alternately opened and closed the view—a ski resort,
billows of clouds, Idaho Falls, anvils of clouds, the Wasatch front, pockets
of clouds, the Ruby Mountains, streams of clouds, Pyramid Lake, dashes
of clouds. What caught my attention, though, was that ski resort: The official Big Sky of Montana, the place where catch phrase and cash phase
come together in a glorious combination of heavenly lucre.

Newscaster Chet Huntley was the imaginative force behind corporate
Big Sky. He and his wife, Tippy, often vacationed near Lone Mountain, an
11,166-feet peak less than an hour's drive from Yellowstone's northwest
entrance. In the 1960s, they began shopping for recreational investment
property. In truth, they were looking for a tax shelter. As the Huntleys
investigated the ranching possibilities, they gradually realized the winter
sports potential. In 1969, on a very large scale, their investment dream
finally came true. Through various purchases and a complicated series
of land swaps, the Montana Power Company, Burlington Northern, Conoco,
General Electric Pension Fund 7, Northwest Airlines, Meridian Investment, and Chrysler Realty managed to obtain more than ten thousand
contiguous acres. Development quickly got under way in two different
sectors at once—Meadow Village and Mountain Village. The former,
located where cattle used to graze on Trail Creek Ranch property, was to
include a golf course, restaurants, shops and other amenities, plus numerous condominiums, chalets, and cabins. The latter, 1000 feet higher at
7,500, was to be situated right at the base of potential Lone Mountain
ski runs. More elegant than its lower cousin, Mountain Village would
attract high-end visitors and vacationers to a world-class destination resort.
With special permission from the Montana governor, Huntley and his
colleagues called the operation "Big Sky."

Two years later, Arnold Palmer was laying out an eighteen-hole
championship golf course, condominiums and mountain retreats were
under construction, and ski runs were being cleared. When the gondola
and the newly constructed Triple Chair lift opened on December 15,
1973, the place was in business. A lift ticket cost $7.50. A year later—
March 23, 1974, when Huntley Lodge was completed—the resort officially opened. Unfortunately, Chet Huntley died of lung cancer earlier

that month, so he never saw the enterprise's immensity. If he had lived, however, he would have enjoyed the 5,000 acres of skiable terrain, a 4,350 vertical feet drop, 150 named runs, more than 75 kilometers of groomed trails, and a backcountry that abuts two separate national wilderness areas. Mountain biking, fly fishing, white water rafting, horseback riding, hiking, golf, and an extensive conference center lure summer guests as well. A summary of amenities highlights more than twenty-five restaurants, more than forty shops, diverse music, and full-service spas.

But in the early days, investors struggled to make Big Sky a success. Because the new resort was distant from any major population center and because the Bozeman airport was rather small, getting to Big Sky was not easy. So even though Big Sky quickly developed a reputation for short lift lines—even now the busiest day will draw only 5,200 skiers—it didn't attract enough paying customers. Besides, the road to the mountain was abominable, a slippery slope of red clay. Locals called one section "Cobelt's Million Dollar Corner," because Ken Cobelt would position his wrecker near the worst drop-off, then extricate one vehicle after another. Power outages plagued the new resort, too, especially at the higher village where, until 1988, a single line served the entire area. Rick and Susie Graetz, in a charming booklet about the resort's developing years, describe the candle-lit parties. One New Year's Eve, for example, was celebrated by three thousand revelers partying in absolutely frigid darkness.

Meanwhile, an oil embargo and the ensuing high price of gasoline kept skiers at home. A national recession in the early 1970s caused real-estate sales to stagnate, and one particular development—the Deerlodge Condominiums—turned out to be poorly constructed. Those investors, with the help of a forty-lawyer team, settled with Chrysler, but the resort's reputation suffered. As a result of these multiple problems, bankruptcy loomed. Finally, Everett Kircher, who already ran two successful ski corporations in Michigan, secured Big Sky in 1976, paying approximately forty cents on the dollar for the indebtedness. His family corporation, Boyne USA, still privately holds the resort, and many of his family members remain involved in the day-to-day operations. Under the Kircher tutelage, the resort thrives.

Other accommodations now are opening alongside Big Sky. The most recent, Moonlight Basin Ranch, appeals to upscale buyers with unlimited budgets. The lodge is an immense structure of rock and pine and ostentation. Three stuffed mountain goats appear to amble up the sides of an enormous fireplace. I counted fourteen single malt scotches and twelve premium vodkas behind the bar. The Moonlight Basin developers already have opened new ski runs on the north shoulder of Lone Mountain, so that skiers can ski right to this lodge, too. Or directly to Cowboy Heaven, under construction, where a fully furnished penthouse suite costs $1.5 million. That's a bargain, I soon learned. A handout from the Montana Real Estate Co. of Big Sky, LLC—"The Right People, the Right Team"—itemizes available "Luxury Properties and Fine Homes." For 5.5 million, I could buy a "beautiful lodge" of more than 9,000 square feet. For half that purchase price, I could have four bedrooms, five and a half baths along the "lush banks of the Madison River." Or I might choose from an array of "freestanding ski chalets offering incredible Spanish Peaks vistas, heavy log accents & superb finishes," each for the modest price of a Cowboy Heaven penthouse.

Gates protect many of the properties. Summit View, according to its brochure, is "Big Sky's premier residential community and nature conservancy." I'm told that the gates are there to protect the wildlife, and indeed I saw a moose and her calf hovering near the roadway. I wondered, though, about the wildlife within. Who owns these places anyway? I spoke with one builder who explained that many of the "getaways" are purchased site/sight unseen. He mentioned chatting earlier that day with a couple who bought two unfinished condos off the Internet. One of the two properties already had appreciated from $1.2 million to $1.9, and it's still not ready for occupancy. Such a pattern of paper profits, luring investors into the resort marketplace, propels purchasers toward a new version of the American Dream, although just this morning on the news I heard economists theorize that high-end real estate will be the next dot-com bubbleburst.

Scholars who study the American West agree that a building boom like Big Sky's is a reincarnation of early-twentieth-century historian Frederick Jackson Turner's thesis, one more frontier that juts into the wilderness as surely as did the pioneer trails, one more opportunity for entrepreneurial success. This particular frontier, however, attracts the haves rather than the have-nots, and suggests a rather different kind of speculation. Many of the handouts I picked up from the Big Sky realtors extolled the investment potential of the homes and condos they were selling. One, subtitled "A Blueprint for the Future," noted that "as of April 1, 2004, nearly $50 million of property was in escrow ready to close within 60–90 days." April Fool's Day indeed. These places can be rented out, a Ponzi promise that a condominium in any one of the twenty-four separate condo associations will pay for itself. That's certainly what those Internet shoppers were imagining, and what today's forecasters fear might end soon.

One brochure touted, in bold letters, a "COST RECOVERY PRO-GRAM." Boyne USA "guarantee[s] your rental income over the next five years will be sufficient to cover your owners [sic] fees plus the princi-ple and interest on a 75% loan-to-value ratio." In fact, Boyne USA promises to pay the difference if a shortfall occurs. Such a bargain involves two assumptions—that the purchaser can afford to put twenty-five percent down in cash and that the rental market will remain sustainable during the life of the loan. In other words, Boyne USA picks up at least $100,000 in cash from each purchaser, and is liable only for short-term consequences. The brochure assuages guilt by asking a buyer to "Imagine this being your family legacy." The word "legacy" appears often, sometimes in bold print, as if a Summit condominium were a treasure to be handed down like the family farm. Here, indeed, is a high-rise American Dream of opti-mism and opportunism.

Walking around the complex, I heard frequent warnings to "Look out for bears!" I know the staff means to keep their guests secure from prehibernation major Ursas, but when I heard the words repeated over and over something else came to mind. During the building seasons—summer and fall—a continuous growl of construction reverberates across Mountain Village. Trucks snarl the crossings, workmen hammer inces-santly, realtors ply their trade. Everywhere I strolled, I heard the sounds of dollars. Obviously, I understand that Keynesian economic philosophy and favorable tax laws together have made second and third home investments profitable, leading to more and more construction in various vacation locales. Yet I must muse about the environmental shock waves that ensue from rampant overbuilding.

At Lake Tahoe, for example, building moratoriums tend to fail while lawsuits prevail. The Tahoe Regional Planning Agency does its best, but Bay Area buyers have the cash to hire smart lawyers who can argue effectively in court. Nowadays, the Mom and Pop resorts of the 1950s are few and far between, as new condos and cabins thicken the slopes around Squaw and Heavenly valleys. Construction and contractor association lobbyists would have my head for the heretical thought I'm about to express, and realtors would be aghast. But it has always seemed to me that the elimination of mortgage interest deductions on all but primary dwellings would benefit the western landscape. Fewer individual trophy castles, more centralized resorts, fewer roads to nowhere, less wilderness sprawl. With a deliberately convoluted tax code and so many interest groups powering any real debate, I don't suppose such a radical revision of public policy will ever come to pass. I can dream, though.

And what if the local bull moose turns out to be a bear? What if growth stagnates and stalls? I don't mean to be a pessimist, but I've seen too many abandoned farmhouses in the American West and watched too many marginal ranches fall to the auctioneer's gavel. Should buyers gullibly trust that "gain follows the snow" just as "rain follows the plow?" History suggests that the rational answer should be "no." Yet, as I check the sales sites on the internet six months after drafting this chapter, I discover I would be several thousand dollars richer if I had only put twenty-five percent down before the ski season began. If I had twenty-five percent to put down, that is, or could magically generate it from a stock market sky, or if I hadn't heard the warnings on this morning's news.

Ironically, the enchanting lure of the Big Sky Resort differs little from Gerard Manley Hopkins's rose-colored vision of the natural world. Recalling his phrases of "quickgold," and white poplars "set on a flare," his vision of a "landscape plotted and pierced," I remember his assumption that "it is all a purchase, all is a prize," his exhortation to bid and buy. Surely, this is happening today alongside Montana's Gallatin National Forest and the adjacent Lee Metcalf Wilderness, happening at Lake Tahoe, too, where dreams of "quickgold" ironically invert the balladeer's vision of "glitter" in the sky. If I read the clouds correctly, storms may lie ahead. Inevitably, June turns into January, though just as inevitably January eventually turns into June.

Other glitter guises manifest themselves in the American West, too. Gold and silver, for example, were glittering metals a hundred years ago and remain alluring treasures today. Names from the past, like Pikes Peak, Virginia City, Tonopah, Cripple Creek, Golden, Rhyolite, Silver City, or Leadville are familiar to anyone who has paid attention to the glowing stories of western settlement. Current mining operations draw engineers and investors just as surely as those diggings in the past. But what glitters on the way to the bank may leave behind a landscape far less glamorous. With an outdated 1872 Mining Law still in force, and with a beneficent government enforcing its license, mountains and watersheds through-out the West continue to be at the mercy of an aggressive, though profit-able, industry. Panamint Valley, just a mountain range away from Death Valley National Park, exemplifies the typical extraction pattern.

Surprise Lake glistens on the playa of Panamint Valley. Often dry, alkali-caked, and blowing in the wind, Surprise Lake received an unex-pected amount of spring rain in 2003. So my sense of its normal aridity is tempered by an unusually wet scene, with whitecaps rather than dust devils. Across the expanse, a well-maintained road steers straight and true. Closer to the foothills on the eastern side, a sign announces the road's raison d'etre. "CR BRIGGS LITTER REMOVAL NEXT 12 MILES." "Litter" is an ironic choice of words. Canyon Resources, owner of the Briggs Mine, is responsible for the high-quality litter-free route that leads to an in-progress open-pit, heap leach precious metal operation.

The statistics are staggering. In the first seven years after its con-struction in 1996, the Briggs Mine processed a total of 65.5 million tons of rock, including 43.7 tons of waste, while producing 467,244 ounces of gold and 129,323 ounces of silver. Until 2001, the ore was crushed in three stages to a minus one-quarter-inch size. Now, in a more economical process, the ore is placed on the pad directly. The leach pad, I might add, has just been expanded, bringing its current capacity to 22.7 million tons, and a recirculation system has been newly installed, accelerating the recovery of residual gold. I could cite even more data from Canyon Resources's website, but in truth the numbers don't do justice to the visual impact. Exactly what do millions of tons of rock resemble after being smashed to pieces smaller than a fingernail, then redistributed into an artificially patterned landscape?

"An Aztec ruin," said one of my friends when we gawked at the mine from a distance. The triangular shapes of the terraces do indeed resemble constructs from the past, and the sculpted landscape did remind me of some ancient architectural contrivance. I suppose if I liked "designer scenery," the mine site might even be called spectacular, with its multiple shades of sandy-mauve-apricot-gray and its angular geometric patterns. Alarming, however, is the accompanying spray that shimmers, if not glitters, in the sunlight. Although the sprinkler apparatus looks like a typical park irrigation system, it's actually cyanide that spatters the scene. Unfortunately, cyanide is the most efficient way to leach precious gold from unwanted rock tonnage and terrain. As a sign on the main office building explains, "This area contains chemicals known to the State of California to cause cancer, birth defects, and reproductive harm." So what appears to be water on the terraces is actually deadly poison. And what purports to be an architectural wonder is something quite different. From afar, massive trucks resembling tiny arachnids creep along precariously graded ledges. I can hear the rumbling atonality from miles away. Up close, the prefab mine buildings sit staggered on a bulldozed flat. They, too, are dwarfed by the rearranged land. The magnitude of the disruption is everywhere apparent, as tons give way to ounces.

Actually, a comparison of historic descriptions of the area's pre-mine days with the current gargantuan scene lays bare the pulverization. Redlands Canyon, which the mine swallowed, was the escape route for the Death Valley '49ers, a group of immigrants stymied on their way to the California goldfields. "We came to an almost perpendicular fall of about ten feet," wrote William Lewis Manly, one of the men who sought help for his companions. "The wall on the north side was thousands of feet high and leaned over the canyon; the south side was sloped. The canyon represented a mammoth crevice. Now the question was what to do and how to do it." Once they manuevered past the canyon obstacles—first to go for help, then to return to the stranded pioneers—Manley and John Haney Rogers had to guide the frightened families back over the escape route. "How to get over it and not kill the mule and cattle was the question of vital importance. . . . The rocks on the north side hung over, more than perpendicular, and seemed to be sky high, while those on the south side sloped back a little, but the gorge was so steep and narrow the sun never shone down into its depths." Manly goes on to describe how everyone "hitched along the side of the rough, steep, rocky, cliff, looking only for a place to put their fingers, and feeling out the narrow path for their feet, afraid to tremble lest they lose their hold." They tied ropes to the children, lowering them down to their "anxious" mothers. The men gave "strict injunctions not to look down, lest they become dizzy and fall to the bottom of the canyon, which would surely kill them." The pioneer travelers, ignoring the bodies of the horses lying below, could not have imagined the canyon's current demise.

Leroy and Jean Johnson's book, *Escape from Death Valley*, not only tells the stories of the '49ers woes, but also retraces the pioneers' travels. By car and on foot, the Johnsons meticulously followed the old routes and described how the focal points looked more than a hundred years later. At one point, they interviewed Harry Briggs, who mined the area before Canyon Resources bought his claim, and they also explored the extant Redlands Canyon gash. "The walls were high and almost perpendicular in places," wrote the Johnsons of the landscape in the 1980s. "Small rock falls were smooth from years of gully washers. Clumps of yellow flowers and white Jimson-weed trumpets brightened our way."

None of this exists any longer—not the steep gorge, not the perpendicular rock, not the dizzying heights, not the clumps of yellow flowers. What might have been preserved as a national historic site instead sits in ground up pieces of rock a quarter-inch in diameter. Or rests in someone's bank vault somewhere. Or waits in a scrapings mound facetiously labeled "TOPSOIL STOCKPILE" by Canyon Resources.

Energetic opposition tried to derail CR's Briggs Mine. Permission for the huge operation, however, seems to have been a tacit addendum to the 1994 Desert Protection Act. In a trade-off reminiscent of Echo Park and Glen Canyon on the Colorado River, one pristine area was saved while another was sacrificed for profit. "Just part of the deal," says Eldon Hughes, one of the conservationists most responsible for the accord. A lawsuit filed by the Timbisha Shoshone tribe of Death Valley argued against the mine, but was rejected. A 1998 protest against the mine's expansion was disallowed, too. In 2003, in fact, the Bureau of Land Management granted Canyon Resources an application for further exploratory drilling beyond the northern perimeter of the current dig. The accompanying FONSI—a Finding of No Significant Impact—declared that the collateral damage would be insignificant. Conservationists counter that estimate, however, by calculating that a mere hundred-acre disturbance would generate a road density approaching that of Santa Monica.

Right now, a single razorback dirt road grinds up the ridgeline to the particular bench where a mining extension might be placed. Because the mapping phase is finished and the exploratory drilling is yet to begin, no big equipment currently is visible. On a warm spring day, the ridge is almost pristine, decorated with yellow flowers—bottle bush, bottle brush, bitter bush, bitter brush, all jumbled together up the canyon and onto the hillside. But spiking out from the spiny road are a dozen or more exploratory two-tracks that have flattened the nearby vegetation. So it's quite possible to imagine the magnitude of the potential disruption, the breadth of the plans that would crush this area in a matter of months. Conceivably, this glittering landscape may well become another Aztec ruin, another dissolution of rock tonnage and cyanide and pebbles and ounces of precious gold.

Many, of course, would argue that such a process reflects the course of empire, the very progressive exploration that settled the American West. The William and Mary Goodwin 1904 version of "Home on the Range" contains additional verses that tout the extraction process. For example,

> Oh, give me the hills and the ring of the drills
>   And the rich silver ore in the ground;
> Yes, give me the gulch where the miner can sluice
>   And the bright, yellow gold can be found.

Obviously, the Goodwins didn't foresee the advent of open pits, leach pads, and cyanide sprays. In truth, though, from the California '49ers to the current operators of the Briggs Mine, fortune-seekers have always brought entrepreneurial energy to western mining installations and, tangentially, to attendant cities like San Francisco. Colorado and Denver reflect the same pattern. What a "strike-it-rich" or "jackpot" advocacy ignores, however, is the aftermath. For every mother lode, there follows necessarily a deserted village.

A few miles north of the Briggs Mine, still a part of the Panamint Range, Surprise Canyon cuts downhill from a shoulder of Telescope Peak. Year-round snowmelt and perpetual springs make the creek a surprising oasis in the desert. Where the sides of the canyon look like wizened skins of dried earth, the interior resembles an Eden. Cottonwoods, watercress, flowering catsclaw acacia, waterfalls tumbling from one level to the next. I'm told that desert bighorn sheep occasionally are visible, up on the rocks, amid the juniper and piñon pine. In December 1872, rich silver ore was discovered at the head of Surprise Canyon. Stock worth $61 million was sold. Immediately, a town of two thousand residents sprang into existence, and by July 4, 1876, a new thirty-stamp mill was in operation in Panamint City. The boomtown cycle was on its way.

Twenty days later, Panamint City was only a memory. A flash flood coursed down the canyon, carrying the entire operation—in pieces—out onto the playa below. Even today, the "city" itself still lies buried underneath the muck, the aggregate of mud and rocks and machinery and organic matter and whatever else washed down through the canyon walls. In the early 1980s, another mining operation opened in Surprise Canyon. In 1984, another flash flood washed it out. Dutifully, Inyo County officials tried to keep a jeep track open up-canyon. Just as surely, another flash flood tore down the road. Right now, the upper canyon remains impassable. Although a handful of people live part-way up—an easily drivable road leads to their land—the rest of Surprise Canyon can only be negotiated on foot. Meanwhile, the glitter of silver lies buried under tons of water-swept detritus and rock.

Ballarat, a third kind of mining remnant, sits midway between Surprise Canyon and the Briggs Mine. Closer to the edge of the playa and so less vulnerable to the vagaries of sudden summer floods, Ballarat used to be a supply center for the gold and silver mines on the western slope of the Panamints. In 1897, its population reached five hundred. I'm told that it housed a Wells Fargo station, a post office, a school, a jail, a morgue, three hotels, seven saloons, and no church. Its heyday, however, lasted only a few years. The nearby Ratcliffe mine produced a million dollars' worth of gold, but suspended operations in 1905. By 1917, the U.S. post office had closed, and Ballarat began its full descent into decay.

Now the place is privately owned, with a caretaker on site to keep an eye on the left-over buildings and relics. Some of the adobe and bleached-board ruins are carefully labeled. "JAIL HOUSE 1899," for example. Many are propped up by timbering or held down by cables. Others have fallen over. Some are filled with junk—a dissembled wash basin, old bottles, corrugated tin, a rubber hose, a broken chair, yellow plastic, a punctured oil drum, wire bedsprings. Beside the shack, an ancient green truck plus an old wagon with bent-wood and arched-iron wheels. Donna, the forty-something resident overseer, tends the cemetery even more carefully. She tidily has lined the graves with stones, and the tombstones seem polished not only by the wind but also by human hands. One belongs to the close friend of hard-rock miner and prospector Harry Briggs. "Me lonely? hell, no! I'm half coyote and half wild burro!" reads Charles (Seldom Seen Slim) Ferge's inscription underneath a tattered American flag. Tourists park their SUVs, walk around a bit, then drive off into the dust. Not much glitters, except for the water-soaked playa, occasionally.

As prices fluctuate, so does the profligacy of the mining industry. In 2001, the average price for gold was $271 per ounce, while silver went for $4.36 per ounce. That same year, the Briggs Mine estimated its cash revenues at something higher than $28 million. By 2005, the price of gold had risen higher than $500 per ounce; forecasters predict it will hit $1,000 in less than a decade. For those who extract profit, the glitter tangibly remains. For those who would relish an untarnished landscape, however, the glitter distinctly dulls when an open pit, heap leach cyanide operation ravages a canyon. "It's immoral to tear apart a mountain for so little," insists activist Tom Budlong, who has spent years working to protect the Panamint Valley from further inroads.

Tom took me camping at the south end of the valley, just beyond the playa waters of sporadic Surprise Lake. The dirt road beyond the mine quickly turns to corduroy, but that doesn't stop the tourists. As we drove, we passed motorcycles—their stylishly dressed drivers glittering in the sunlight—and dune buggies and an assortment of SUVs. No one else was spending the night, however, so we finally had the valley to ourselves. I parked my truck near a garden of shotgun shells. Red, orange, yellow, blue, green, black—there must have been hundreds of them, forming a rainbow pallette in the sand. More Edenic were the flowers, just coming into bloom. From a distance, the Mojave always looks sterile and stark; up close, especially in late March when tiny blossoms boldly color the desert floor, the Mojave is awash with white and yellow hues.

Wandering around the edge of the playa, peeking and poking at the spring flower display, I found a clump of dodder, or witches hair, as it's sometimes called. Dodder is a parasite, a golden globe that looks as though a ball of yellow-orange steel wool had wound itself around a young creosote bush, or as if a Grimms' fairy tale doll had lost her head. Any plant, attacked by witches hair, doesn't have a chance. From a distance, the dodder was lovely, glittering beside the road. Up close, its parasitic growth looked much more like an evil freeloader that sponges off the native plants, squeezing the life away. Too obvious, I thought, to compare witches hair to extractive mining. And yet I saw two unnatural entities attach themselves that day to a landscape otherwise thriving without their presences. I saw what that kind of freakish consumption can do. Gold glitters, to be sure, just as does dodder from a distance. But, in my opinion at least, more glory exudes from a Surprise Valley and a Panamint Range where nature remains natural, rather than stifled, crushed, and rearranged.

When I drafted this section of *Oh, Give Me a Home*, conservationists feared further expansion of the Briggs mining operation. From my brief sojourn on the flagged slope north of the current incursion, I assumed development was imminent and so did the activists who were trying to protect the area. After that week in the desert, I signed onto Tom Budlong's e-mail list serve, "Friends of the Panamints." As a result, for the past two years I've been getting an education in the vagaries of modern mining law. The 1872 decree remains the gold standard, freely allowing exploration wherever and whenever minerals might be unearthed on public land. The law pronounces mining as "the best use of the land," relegating all other commodifications to inferior status. And while the coal, oil, and gas industries pay royalties for their mining practices, the metal extractors do not. A company like Canyon Resources can patent a mineral claim on public land for less than five dollars an acre. Moreover, the law makes no mention of potential environmental destruction. Written long before the days of our current gargantuan practices, it says nothing about protecting communities from subsequent degradation and pollution. The Environmental Protection Agency, in fact, estimates a cost of more than $7.8 billion to clean up mining Superfund sites, a projection that includes only the most poisonous of places, not another half-million lesser hardrock mines across the country that have been abandoned. Taxpayers, not mining companies, foot the bill (although twenty-first-century regulators insist on bonding, which may or may not be sufficient to cover the costs of recovering the land). And the EPA says nothing about visual pollution. In 1872, no one thought much about the potential eyesore of a Briggs operation at the end of an empty desert playa, let alone what could happen to the groundwater nearby. In 2005, many people acknowledge not only that invasive mines can be quite ugly but that their practices may be physically harmful to all of us.

Some states have been receptive to conservationist concerns, taking direct aim at the most outrageous ills of current mining law. Montana and New Mexico boast the strongest standards to keep mineral extraction in line; Arizona and Nevada, the weakest. California law lies somewhere in between. For example, a 1998 Montana initiative outlawed open pit heap leach mining. Six years later, Canyon Resources—the corporate owners of the Briggs Mine are active in Montana, too—introduced a counter-initiative that would have granted a special permit for their Montana operation. After spending more than $3 million dollars in promotional ads, CR's exception was defeated by Montana voters, fifty-nine to forty-one percent. The problems associated with previously polluted sites, such as Butte's Berkeley Pit, a polluted aftermath of Anaconda Copper, and Dillon's W. R. Grace vermiculite mine and its resulting asbestos fiasco, apparently persuaded the Montana electorate that not every mining operation is desirable.

Meanwhile, in 2003, the California State Mining and Geology Board (the SMGB) issued a new Backfill Regulation, ordering that new open pit mines must be filled after the mining operation is finished. In effect, this meant restoration, which is to return a site to its prior state, rather than reclamation, which is to make a site somehow reusable. The former turns out to be much more costly than the latter, so expansion of the Briggs Mine in the Panamints, at least for the time being, is no longer economically feasible. The hillside of yellow flowers still blossoms this spring. Given its setbacks in Montana and California, Canyon Resources stock slid appreciably downward, but the company's president, Richard De Voto, remains optimistic.

Conservationists cannot relax their vigilance because more politics have intervened. California governor Arnold Schwarzenegger just recommended elimination of the SMGB. Observers were surprised by his sudden move, until watchdog Tom read a Canyon Resources shareholder communication report. "Conversations are underway with the staff of the current Governor," the communiqué brags, "with the hope of modifying that rule" requiring backfilling of any new metal mines. Clearly the glitter of politics, the sparkle of money, and the lucrative glow of lobbyists are having an impact in California. Just as clear is the fact that extractive practices across the country remain in a perpetual state of flux.

As I write these words, I'm acutely aware that the political climate could change overnight, but right now the federal government seems to be enthusiastically endorsing mineral exploration everywhere. Just last week, the United States Congress approved oil exploration in the Arctic National Wildlife Refuge. Drilling will effectively eliminate the last pristine tract of wilderness in the fifty states. Last year, Phelps Dodge Corp paid the United States government only $875 for 155 acres on Mount Emmons in Colorado. The land is within sight of the Crested Butte ski area, where resort property is selling for $100,000 a lot, or a million dollars an acre. Since the proposed molybdenum mine is unlikely to be built, and the property is likely to become another Big Sky, cynics suggest that the deal is calculated speculation. Reporter Jim Spencer of the *Denver Post* characterizes the scheme as "statutory herpes." BLM officials disagree. No one yet has overturned the Mount Emmons land giveaway.

Closer to home, another specific application of the 1872 Mining Law recently put Reno residents in sharp conflict with the particular legalities. An Illinois-based corporation proposed a mineral operation just north of the city limits. Oil-Dri manufactures kitty litter. Hungry Valley, which is home to the Reno-Sparks Indian Colony, contains clay that would make excellent kitty litter. Under the auspices of the 1872 Mining Law, Oil-Dri applied for a special use permit. If granted, two open-pit mines would blossom in the desert, with twenty-four-hour lights and ongoing noise in an otherwise quiet area. Analysts predict that arsenic-laden water would leach into the regional water table, while mining trucks would utilize residential streets as haul roads. After a great many legal machinations and heart-wrenching public hearings, the Washoe County Commission denied the special permit. At least for now, no kitty litter excavation will take place in Hungry Valley. Under the auspices of the infamous old law, however, Oil-Dri has sued for damages in federal district court. Ironically, the corporation is arguing its case based on an abstraction of those "best use" property rights emphatically guaranteed in 1872.

Two years ago I went to a local fundraiser for Great Basin Mine Watch, a Nevada outfit that pairs environmentalists with Native Americans in order to further issues of environmental and social justice. Valerie Cohen, a local painter and activist, donated one of her watercolors to be raffled off that evening. I won. Hanging in my family room, now, is a constant reminder of an artist's view of an unadulterated Hungry Valley, the blues and whites of winter contrasting sharply with the yellows and browns of the landscape itself. The overall effect is poignant, a desert rainbow rendition of what is all too fragile. That, of course, is the obvious problem with all ongoing environmental battles. Once loss is incurred—a mine built, a pristine region defiled, a Hungry Valley turned into an open pit—time cannot be turned back. The damage is done. After that, all that glitters does so in corporate bank accounts, not under the wide-open western sky.

The Donners and their infamous companions could not have imagined the extent of modern mining. Neither could they have envisioned the expanse of mountain ski resorts nor the necessity of generating bad weather on purpose. The snow piled around them seemed more than sufficient. Like Mark Twain, who observed that "everybody talks about the weather all the time, but nobody does anything about it," early westerners assumed that clouds dropped a finite and unassailable amount of precipitation. During the middle years of the twentieth century, however, physicists figured out a way to possibly augment snowfall by burning a solution of silver iodide and sodium iodide in acetone. This releases silver iodide particles which, in turn, can generate additional snow from winter clouds. The Desert Research Institute, affiliated locally with the University and Community College System of Nevada, has used this technique for years.

DRI scientists began at Lake Tahoe in the 1960s, and have since expanded their weather modification operations throughout the state. Tahoe, the Truckee River and Carson River basins, the Walker River, the Ruby Mountains, the Tuscarora Mountains, and the Toiyabes all benefit from DRI cloud-seeding expertise. Either released from aircraft or from remote-controlled generators, the chemicals disperse statically or dynamically. As a result, Nevada mountain ranges receive more annual precipitation than otherwise would fall. Estimates of the DRI program's success vary, but somewhere between 20,000 to 80,000 acre-feet of additional water fell each year for the past ten years, at a cost of somewhere between $7 and $18 per acre-foot.

I love the scientific diction. "Cloud particles" and "plume transport" come together in a "collision/coalescence" to generate "weather modification" such as "precipitation increase" and "visibility improvement" (read fog dispersal) and "hail suppression." "Glaciogenic" and "hygroscoptic" seeding agents do the trick. Cloud seeding can occur either from "the homogeneous nucleation of the ice phase," where something like dry ice cools water drops to temperatures below –80 degrees Centigrade, or more commonly, from "heterogeneous nucleation," where a foreign particle like silver iodide helps freeze a water droplet. Both methods are "highly portable," highly lucrative, and generally successful. Whereas the State essentially funds the process in Nevada as part of a governmental initiative, other places in the West rely on commercial applications. North American Weather Consultants, Inc., advertises their services on the web. "Our projects are never of the cookie cutter variety. We will work closely with you to design and implement a project which is tailored specifically to your circumstances." Weather Modification, Inc., which calls itself "The World's Leader in Weather Modification Technology" and which is one of the largest such businesses in the country, actually contracts its services with the Desert Research Institute in a private-public sector partnership.

Arlen Huggins, the man in charge of the DRI operation, introduced me to Brandon and Jason, who fly for Weather Modification, Inc. We were standing on the tarmac at the Reno airport, and I was watching the two pilots do their preflight visual check of the Cessna 340 that would soon be in the air. When wind gusts blew us sideways as we tried to talk, I wondered about the safety of flying in such weather. But no one seemed concerned. Instead, the men were eager to point out the specialized equipment. Mounted just below each wing tip, a solution-burning generator that looks like a silver bullet was filled with AgI. Behind each engine, a twelve-pack of "ready-to-go" flares was firmly in place, each flare resembling a pyrotechnic "firecracker" waiting to be lit in midair. Two metal attachments on the nose of the plane would measure the weather conditions. Imperative are a temperature of –5 degrees C, or lower, and an atmospheric water content sufficient to make seeding successful. I peeked inside the plane, a two-seater, with no room for passengers. Instead, I saw a boxy generator, a computer programmed for the operation, and not much else. Utilitarian, all the way.

When I was in college, I once flew from Reno to Oakland in the midst of a blizzard. I think that was before any DRI snowfall enhancement programs in the Sierra Nevada mountains. The daughter of Fran Murphy, the man whose company built the Glen Canyon suspension bridge, invited me to spend our winter break skiing at Squaw Valley, and her father's private plane had been placed at our disposal. Disposable is exactly how I felt as we bucked our way through the buffeting winds above Donner Pass. Sitting in the front seat next to the pilot while Jeannie and her father sat strapped in behind us, I could watch the instrument panel, could visually see electronic evidence of the stomach-lurching midair drops. Obviously, we finished the trip safely, but I'll admit that I've never since been totally comfortable within the confines of a small aircraft. In 1980, four DRI researchers were killed in a plane crash while seeding the clouds. One, Peter Wagner, was the husband of a friend.

So in my imagination the difficulties inherent in Sierra Nevada overflights, with or without scientific enhancements, are multiple. But Brandon and Jason seemed focused on their mission rather than on any imminent danger, and Arlen insisted that even though icing is always a concern, aviation practices and modern science have found ways to combat it. If icing—which is rather like pogonip on the wings—occurs, it's relatively easy to head west from the Sierra Crest and to drop down to a lower elevation. "In the Rockies," Arlen said, grimacing, "it's harder to get lower and warmer." So I kept my cowardly thoughts to myself, and waved good-bye as the navy-blue and silver N37356 taxied away from us and headed into a heavy overlay of clouds. For three hours Brandon and Jason would fire their wares just upwind of the Tahoe Basin. With luck, the storm would then sag south, the plane could quickly be refueled, and they could resume seeding over the Walker Basin this afternoon. Best of all, they would be adding to the already considerable snowpack of 2005.

Arlen and I left the storm outside, and sat down in the JetWest pilots' lounge to talk further. Because this particular April storm is a cold one, because there's still room for additional water storage in the Sierra reservoirs, and because the snow itself will hold more water content, today's cloud seeding will be especially fruitful. Better than in a drought year, in fact, when runoff draws down any accumulation. From November until May, DRI oversees the state's cloud-seeding program. The primary purpose is water enhancement, though Arlen explained that cloud seeding could control fog as well. This past winter saw a lot of fog in our valley, fog that might have been dispersed had not the fear of potential lawsuits prevailed. Getting rid of the fog automatically creates snow, and that snow would fall "right along south 395," said Arlen. "The commuters wouldn't like it at all." But air passengers didn't much care for the cancelled flights, either, so future changes in fog abatement may be made. Apparently, Salt Lake City and Boise, two nearby cities with similar topography, seed clouds regularly, but Reno hasn't done so since 1995. "Not since the current population boom began," Arlen pointed out.

Cloud seeding is also used for hail suppression. I learned, in fact, that North Dakota is one of the leading cloud-seeding locales in the country, and that the University of North Dakota actually has a degree program that combines pilot and meteorological training. Later I read that the "total economic benefit-to-cost" ratio of cloud seeding in North Dakota is over 45 to 1. *Atmospheric Weather*, a special issue of *North Dakota Water* that extols the pluses of hail suppression, further detailed an Alberta, Canada, project. From 1982 until 1986, a government-subsidized program kept catastrophic hail losses to $18 million. When the program was abolished, from 1987 until 1990, losses skyrocketed to $113 million, "a 500 percent increase." Needless to say, the project was reimplemented immediately.

Cloud seeding in the West seems to be here to stay, although applications seem somewhat sporadic. Some areas, like Nevada, are committed to its presence and its efficacy—although Arlen must go before the State Legislature every session to request renewed funding. Most places take a more localized approach. Irrigation districts often hire the professionals, either to enhance the water available for crops or to interfere with potential hail storms. I asked Arlen about any watershed projects. Along the Colorado River, for example, upper basin cloud seeding might affect downstream water supplies. He answered by saying that Nevada governor Kenny Guinn had just asked him the same question. Unfortunately, while such a project might be feasible, no one is considering a broad-based application at this time. Perhaps that will occur in the future, but for now the scope is limited.

In fact, Arlen pointed out, these days "not enough dollars are going into weather modification research." Most of the money goes toward operations instead. Where the Bureau of Reclamation was quite involved in weather issues during the 1970s and '80s, it's "no longer interested." Once current technology was perfected, the Bureau engineers went on to other projects. Only in Australia are scientists trying out a new technical methodology. The United States National Academy of Sciences recently issued a report that urges further weather-related research. The report begins, "The impact of human activity on weather and climate has been of increasing national and international concern over the past few decades. In stark contrast, there has been little parallel research directed at understanding the ability of humans to intentionally modify weather." The politically independent Academy wants this deficiency corrected. Calling for a "coordinated national program," the report itemizes microphysics, dynamics, modeling, and seeding issues that need further study. The annual DRI report of Nevada's cloud-seeding program picks up on the Academy's suggestions, and articulates the ways in which Nevada can add to the national conversation.

Arlen's eyes lit up as he talked about the possibilities. We were still sitting in the JetWest pilots' lounge, and I was still listening to the meteorology of the moment. I smiled to myself. A ring of five overstuffed recliners was pulled up in front of a big-screen television set. While Arlen talked, the Weather Channel beamed in the background. He had already shown me a computerized version of the current storm, complete with currents, vectors, and cloud densities, so I knew the pilots were technically attuned. But I still was amused by the centrality of the Weather Channel. A number of men and women filtered in and out of the pilots' lounge while we sat there; no one changed the television station.

Before Arlen and I finished our conversation, I wanted to know about possible health hazards that might ensue from an unhealthy dose of AgI, but apparently the dispersed cloud chemicals are significantly lower than what the U. S. Public Health Services deems acceptable. Specific analysis has determined that snow layers in the impacted drainages contain silver at three or four parts per trillion. Not enough to worry about. I also wondered about global implications. If DRI effectively seeds Nevada clouds, do Utah or Colorado or New Mexico mountains suffer as a result? By seeding clouds, are we stealing precipitation from elsewhere? When Arlen described the proportional impact, however, my concerns were allayed. Perhaps two percent of the total water budget in a single basin at a single moment would be affected by cloud seeding, and before the clouds moved elsewhere they already would be increasing their moisture content. DRI could add many, many more generators and many, many more flights before any appreciable change would be effected. When Arlen asked me to imagine the impact of a single fifteen-degree plume in the middle of a thousand-square-mile watershed, I understood the proportional insignificance. A lot more cloud seeding could occur without noticeable public impact.

Even so, a set of predetermined criteria dictates when seeding is inappropriate. If the avalanche danger is extreme, cloud seeding is suspended. Likewise, when the wintertime temperature soars and flooding seems possible, no seeding occurs. This past winter, for example, excess moisture brought the Sierra snowpack to almost 150 percent of normal and for a week or two scientists worried about the flood potential. Temporarily, DRI had to stop seeding. Also, cloud seeding never occurs during major holidays because the potential traffic problems would be horrendous. Public perception, rather than "sound science," dictates that particular decision. Arlen recalled talking once with a crew of snowplow drivers. At best, cloud seeding might generate one inch out of twelve in a major storm. Hardly a problem for a snowplow with a ten-foot blade. Yet, because someone stuck on Donner Pass might blame cloud seeding going on overhead for his or her woes, operations cease when Interstate 80 is packed with cars.

Tonight I'll listen to the weatherman on television's 5 o'clock newscast. While Mike Alger will talk of chain controls and road closures in the mountains, he probably won't mention the seeding of clouds, a transparent part of weather management that the public for the most part ignores. Most of us, in fact, have little understanding of weather modification. "It often snows more near Washoe Med," Arlen said, laughing. Probably "the oxygen tank vents create local snow" in a chemical interaction similar to that of cloud seeding on a foggy day. It wouldn't occur to any of us, though, to ask that the Washoe Regional Medical Center turn off its oxygen. Most of the time, I think we agree with Mark Twain and presume that weather is out of our control.

This time of year, when the high desert has begun to warm but when cold fronts continue to charge across the Pacific Ocean, the resulting weather seems wild and wanton. Seventy degrees last week; fifty degrees today. (And several months later, I'm proofreading this page on a record-setting day of 104.) One hundred-mile-an-hour gusts across the peaks in the Sierra; forty or fifty miles per hour here in the valleys. My house feels as if it is ricocheting all night long. Mark Twain famously called our wind "the Washoe Zephyr." He made fun of a violence that "blows flimsy houses down, lifts shingle roofs occasionally, rolls up tin ones like sheet music, now and then blows a stagecoach over and spills the passengers." He added a rollicking characterization of the layers of dust created by a Washoe Zephyr's energy—"hats, chickens, and parasols sailing in the remote heavens; blankets, tin signs, sagebrush and shingles a shade lower; doormats and buffalo robes lower still; shovels and coal scuttles on the next grade; glass doors, cat and little children on the next; disrupted lumberyards, light buggies, and wheelbarrows on the next; and down only thirty or forty feet above ground was a scurrying storm of emigrating roof and vacant lots." I've always admired his imagination, but sometimes reality is almost as magnificent.

In December of 2003, Reno experienced the most violent winds ever recorded here. One set of friends lost their power for four days, sitting huddled in front of their fireplace, trying to keep themselves and their fish-filled aquarium warm. Meanwhile, they could look outside and see pieces of their neighbor's roof blowing by. And they could wonder what was happening to their own house, though they were afraid to go outside and see. When I hear about hurricanes and tornados, watch the destruction on TV, I realize that Nevada winds are comparatively benign. Yet I stay inside when impending severe weather looms on the horizon. Of course, cloud seeding has no impact whatsoever on blusterous and rampant gales.

John Haller, another DRI atmospheric physicist, once told me that Reno has more distinctive cloud formations than almost anywhere else in the world. "It's the proximate combination of the ocean, the mountains, and the desert itself," he said. "That's why I live and work here. This is the place to see clouds of every description." After that, I started

GLITTERING STARS 137

paying more attention to the Nevada sky. Yesterday morning, for example, scarlet streaks painted the horizon from one end of the valley to the other, then slowly morphed into pink until daylight finally washed the colors away. Midday sunbreaks flared brightly against clouds on the move, as the storm tried to blow in from San Francisco. By evening, at dusk, the clouds were more threatening, with an early dark descending. Blue wool on black tartan on gray tweed. Characteristic high desert weather, pushing in from the ocean, full speed ahead with only a little help from my friends. No glitter last night, except in ski resort cash registers and the Nevada watermaster's computer.

As Arlen and I were finishing our conversation, we stepped outside and into today's weather. Where Brandon and Jason and the Cessna had taxied off into the wind, now the tarmac was wet with rain and spitting snow. I bent my head into the wind and scurried for the security of my car. Driving away from the airport, I imagined Brandon and Jason generating a mini-blizzard overhead, though I knew better. They were miles away. Heading toward campus, I passed Washoe Med in an even thicker cloud of white and I remembered Arlen's depiction of the oxygen tank vents. Perhaps I was seeing weather modification after all, although the day wasn't foggy. By the time I parked at the university, the surge of moisture already was abating. Two hours later, sunshine poked through the clouds and the temperature began slowly climbing. Like so many spring days in Nevada, this one was schizophrenic, a bulletin board of sky announcements that couldn't seem to decide which season was in charge. I can report that two inches of snow fell later than night at my house, and that today is iffy, and that tomorrow will be warm enough for a golf game. With no help whatsoever from DRI.

If Nevada weather is schizophrenic, so is my twenty-first-century view of western skies. From the glitter of gold to the gutter of pollution, from second-home sprawl to the star-strung distances, I'm all over the map. What remains constant, however, is the panoramic scope of big sky country, the breadth and depth of wind and weather coupled with the energy and intensity of wanton extraction and wild speculation. Big sky country is jackpot country, a landscape "plotted and pierced" that has been gathered to greatness like the "ooze of oil / Crushed." Just as surely, however, it is territory that inherently reflects what Gerard Manley Hopkins has described as "the grandeur of God," what Wallace Stegner considered "the geography of hope," and what I like to call the spirit of space. Metaphorically, if no longer quite literally, western skies are rarely cloudy.

CHAPTER FIVE

Flowers and Flocks

Oh, I love these wild flowers in this dear land of ours;
The curlew I love to hear scream;
And I love the white rocks and the antelope flocks
That graze on the mountain-tops green.

Near the end of her 1927 novel, *Death Comes for the Archbishop*, Willa Cather describes the tamarisks that Father Joseph "had come to love . . . above all trees." She pictures the shapes and colors of one particular row that her two priests "had found growing when they first came,—old, old tamarisks, with twisted trunks." She notes that, like the men themselves, "their trunks had the hardness of cypress. They looked, indeed, like very old posts, well seasoned and polished by time, miraculously endowed with the power to burst into delicate foliage and flowers, to cover themselves with long brooms of lavender-pink blossom." The archbishop, Father Latour, appreciated this special plant as well, remarking on the colorful sprays of bloom and the fibrous trunk "full of gold and lavender tints." As I read this passage, I am convinced that Willa Cather, like her fictional characters and like so many other real-life travelers throughout the American Southwest, assumed tamarisks were native to the region. It probably did not occur to her that this particular plant—now often called by its more common name, the saltcedar—was actually an invasive weed, a precocious raider, a biological terrorist of sorts.

Cather's pictorial passage is an anachronism. What she herself admired in the 1920s was hardly a part of the mid-nineteenth-century landscape she intended to describe. Introduced from Asia in the early 1800s, the tamarisk at first was valued as an ornamental shrub, as a wind-break, as vegetation that could control streambed erosion, as shade. Although the plant adapted readily to the American Southwest, looking lovely while actively competing for available water, saltcedar would have just been taking hold when the Cather's nineteenth-century priests were bringing Catholicism to the arid desert. Their tamarisks would have been sparser, and smaller, and less obtrusive. While the archbishop and his colleague might have seen a few here and there, it is very unlikely that the trees would have been as tall and sturdy as those Cather describes. Most probably she is characterizing the tamarisks of her generation, not of theirs.

Anyone traveling in the American Southwest today might well be mistaken about saltcedars, too. To the untrained eye, they look perfectly natural. So common are these flowering trees, they seem as scenic as saguaros, as native as ocotillo, as everyday as the sand itself. Yet, when John Wesley Powell floated the Colorado River in the 1870s, he never mentioned seeing a saltcedar. In fact, 1938 marks the Grand Canyon's first documentation of a tamarisk's appearance. My old friend Don, among the young archaeologists who catalogued Native American ruins and artifacts in pre–Lake Powell Glen Canyon in the late 1950s and early 1960s, remembers seeing only a little saltcedar in the Glen. His slides reveal nowhere near as many waving fronds as grow so prolifically today. Only half a century later, however, the tree is the dominant riparian growth throughout the Colorado River basin.

The saltcedar is tenacious. One individual tree can produce a half-million tiny seeds per year, seeds that the wind rapidly disperses. With a long taproot efficient at seeking underground water, no dormancy require-ments, and an ability to reproduce in very saline soil, the saltcedar can establish itself anywhere in the desert Southwest, as long as the elevation is lower than 5,400 feet. Not only is this shrubby tree tenacious, but it also is aggressive. It out-competes other desert plants, soon extirpating the natives and colonizing new terrain. Moreover, it does not use water wisely or well. Some scientists say that "saltcedar has the highest known evapo-transpiration rate of any desert phreatophyte," although others have made measurements that cast doubt on the assertion. "Phreatophyte" sounds like "threat-o-phyte" to me. Either way, it's a plant that takes whatever water is available by sinking a deep taproot into the water table or saturation zone. Any unused moisture evaporates quickly into the hot desert air, a physiological process that results in severe water depletion wherever the saltcedar takes over the landscape. What may be lovely to behold becomes a persistent nightmare for the desert ecosystem.

Saltcedar is an equal opportunity plant, attracted both to undisrupted riparian zones and to areas manipulated by man. As soon as southwestern engineers began building dams to control the cycles of natural flooding, saltcedar found favorable new conditions. In fact, saltcedar was more successful in the managed floodplains than were the native species. Scientists estimate that, by 1961, more than 1,400 acres of floodplain had been inundated by saltcedar. Along the Grand Canyon's inner gorge, where dams have not been built but where water fluctuations are carefully managed, pink fronds bedeck almost every nook and cranny. Dominating the sandbars and offering a shady respite from the summer sun, they look as natural and as welcome as can be. Yet they do not naturally belong. I remember hiking down a sandy unnamed wash toward Lake Powell and finding myself in a miniature tamarisk forest of sorts. Even the reservoir's ebb and flow didn't deter their growth. Some, in fact, were knee-deep in muck, thriving in the unnatural oscillating shoreline. But I also recall eating my lunch in the shade of some picturesque fronds and, ruefully, being grateful for their presence.

Even where human activity is discouraged or absent, saltcedar flourishes. It spread aggressively in the 1970s and 1980s, taking over natural springs and ousting the native plants and reeds. For example, when I clamored up and down Utah's Fish Creek and Owl Creek canyons in 1977, the obscure drainages were picture postcards of red rock seeps and fresh green foliage. My friends and I sunned ourselves in pools of clear blue water, prowled in and out of tiny abandoned Anasazi shelters, saw no one else for nearly a week. Even where the mouths of the canyons intersected, where cattle placidly were grazing, the landscape was remarkably pristine. Idyllic, as I recall, partly because of the setting itself and partly because the trip was my first backpack in canyon country. One friend who accompanied me on that hike returned to Fish Creek five years ago. "You wouldn't believe it's the same place," Ellen reported. "Tamarisks surrounding the pools, seeps desiccated and dry, sagebrush encroaching on the dusty flats, overtrodden and overused." She sighed and repeated, "tamarisks everywhere." A federal fact book reports that by 1998 "the weedy saltcedars have successfully invaded nearly every drainage in arid and semiarid areas in the southwestern United States and occupy over 1 million acres." Ellen's recent inspection of Fish and Owl Creeks confirms this governmental analysis.

A month ago, on my way to the Imperial National Wildlife Refuge thirty miles north of Yuma, Arizona, I discovered what I would call an Avenue of Tamarisks. For nearly half a mile, the entrance road steers through an old-growth thicket of enormous saltcedar trees. The sturdy trunks reminded me of Willa Cather's description — "very old posts, well seasoned and polished by time." Each individual tree must have reached thirty or forty feet into the thin blue sky. But the fronds of winter were less picturesque than Cather's "long brooms of lavender-pink blossom." Rather, the foliage appeared brittle-blonde, colorless at road level, lightly lime-green above my head, everywhere dull and lacking life. One spot, perhaps twenty by twenty feet had been burned, charred to ground level either on purpose or by the flick of a tourist's cigarette. Whichever, the burned square gave me access to an inner coagulation of saltcedar, an impenetrable twisting of trunks and fading fronds. For a moment, I felt as though I had been dropped into fairy tale scenery, where evil witches cackled behind every tree. I could almost hear the saltcedar cackle, too, gloating over its easy elimination of competitors. Not a single native plant grew along my Avenue of Tamarisks, only a canopy of darkness belonging more properly in *Hansel and Gretel* than in the American Southwest.

A bit farther along the road, I found another demonstration of how this particular southwestern scenery had transformed itself and was changing still. Near the Refuge headquarters, the saltcedars had been replaced by a tidy cultivated line of cottonwoods. Before the Europeans arrived, cottonwoods grew naturally all along the Colorado River and its tributaries. Because this particular section of the waterway between Imperial and Parker dams—in truth the whole distance from the Gulf of California to Fort Mojave, two hundred miles upriver—was accessible by steamer, and because wood was needed to fuel the riverboats, the available cottonwoods quickly disappeared. At the same time, saltcedar was slowly replacing the natives along the uncultivated bottomland. After the dams were built, the impact was heightened, so that today's cottonwoods are only those recently reintroduced. Ironically now, the native trees must be planted while the invaders proliferate with ease; the natives nurtured while the newcomers run wild.

Ironically, too, the Colorado River is an unnatural reflection of itself. Anyone who saw it four or five generations ago would hardly recognize the streambed anymore. Now it steers a plumb-bob course through a razor-cut shoreline, canal banks shaved absolutely straight and tousled with exotic growth. The channel no more looks like the pre-dam Colorado River than my backyard garden resembles its original sagebrush-covered hillside.

I think about all this on a December day while a pontoon boat motors me up the Colorado. After thirty miles or so, we turn off the engine and drift back down the sluggish, almost lethargic, winter water. Sandbars angle from the banks, so we steer the pontoon boat from side to side, poling wherever the water is particularly shallow. When we get stuck, and occasionally we do, the four passengers rush to the high side, using our collective weight to lift the low side off the river bottom. Is *this* the Colorado River? Hard to believe, with a current that barely moves and a knee-deep riverbed of sand and mud. We float past tamarisks twenty feet high, their dry winter fronds waving brown and beige. We float past rushes and reeds I can't identify, matted clusters of nauseous yellow-green. We float past Styrofoam plates and empty beer cans, a summer's worth of detritus that doesn't disappear in this flood-free zone. This is an unwashed river, I decide, the sad blue rippling remains of what the early pioneers and settlers called "Big Red."

Later, I found an 1874 description of steamer passage on the Colorado. Martha Summerhayes, who accompanied her soldier husband to a number of out-of-the-way army posts in the Old West, wrote about their adventures in a book published in 1908, *Vanished Arizona: Recollections of My Army Life*. One of her earliest frontier experiences took place on Captain Jack Mellon's boat, the *Gila*, which delivered supplies and people up and down the river for years. Steaming from Yuma to Fort Mojave took eleven days; Mrs. Summerhayes did not have a good time. She complains about the "intense heat," "the interminable days," the "insufferable" staterooms, "the intolerable glare," and "the monotony of the scenery."

Along the way, however, she begins to notice certain details. "As the river narrowed," she comments, "the trip began to be enlivened by the constant danger of getting aground on the shifting sand-bars." So my 2004 impression was wrong. Even before any dams were built, this section of the Colorado was prone to shifting sands. Just as my companions and I had to pole our pontoon boat away from the shallows, rocking from side to side whenever we got stuck, so the *Gila's* deckhands "stood ready with long poles, in the bow, to jump overboard, when we struck a bar, and by dint of pushing, and reversing the engine, the boat would swing off." One big difference between my trip and Mrs. Summerhayes's, however, was the texture of the river itself. Where the Colorado today runs blue, the old Colorado was "so very muddy," with banks of "low trees and brushwood." In 1874, "the Rio Colorado deserves its name, for its swift-flowing current sweeps by like a mass of seething red liquid, turbulent and thick and treacherous." Not so, the soft rippling channels of my engineered canal. Not so, the foliage either, for I never spotted any "thick clumps of arrow-weed and willow" as described by the young bride, nor any "clump of low mesquite trees" like the ones that offered her the only shade along the river.

My own companions turned out to be rather indifferent to comments about the altered state of the Colorado. They live nearby, and this revisionist scenery is all they've ever known. For years, they've enjoyed leisurely forays up and down a listless canal-of-a-river. Sometimes the water is higher, sometimes lower, but the river never exceeds its management parameters. What they see is what they get, always. The vegetation, the exotic interlopers are, to them, characteristic of what they've always known.

I suppose the same holds true for my familiar Nevada landscape. The university library contains a book of posters produced by the local Cooperative Extension. "Wanted—Dead, Not Alive!" reads the title. Turning the pages, I examine pictures of invasive plants I thought—if I thought about them at all—were native to our high desert soil. Austrian Peaweed, with a seed the same size, shape, and weight as an alfalfa seed. Dyer's Woad, a yellow mustard flower that colors springtime fields and pastures. Eurasian Water-milfoil, thickening the shallowest waters of Lake Tahoe with millions of "starter stems." White Horsenettle, toxic to grazing cattle. Hounds Tongue, with "prickly nutlets that cling to clothing and animal fur." Klamath Weed, bearing more showy bright yellow flowers that—if we don't know better—we might admire. Diffuse Knapweed, another flowery plant with shades of white and rose and purple. Russian Knapweed, more attractive blossoms of pink and purple and white. I'm not even a third of the way paging through the book, and I haven't been citing every poster.

While the colorful pictures could be nursery advertisements, the reality is much more grim. I read about the toxicity, the threats to horses, sheep, and cattle. I read about the economic impacts, especially when noxious weeds mingle with crops like alfalfa or linger in bales of hay. I read about the "robust, spreading root and numerous seeds" of Tall White-top, a plant I've naively prized. "Do not collect this plant as a dried flower for arrangements," the poster warns, while I suppress my own culpability. I also consider my own aesthetics. Canada Thistle, for example, and a host of other thistles bring color to a high desert spring. Iberian Starthistle, Musk Thistle, Perennial Sowthistle, Scotch Thistle, Yellow Starthistle. "Vicious spines," reports Cooperative Extension; "pretty," I think distantly whenever I step around them. One summer, in fact, I purposely cultivated a yellow starthistle in my backyard, then bird-watched the tiny house finches attracted by its seeds.

Some of the invaders have ugly names. Dalmatian or Yellow Toadflax. Even though their names resonate harshly, I've often enjoyed this perennial that looks like a garden of snapdragons in the desert. Other names sound more romantic. In fact, we westerners are so innocent of the imbalance between noxious and native plants that we memorialized one of the major intruders in a popular cowboy ballad. "See them tumbling down," we hum to the strum of a soft guitar. "Pledging their love to the ground!" the verse continues in an ironic misstatement of invasive prowess. "Lonely, but free, I'll be found / Drifting along with the tumbling tumbleweeds," the Sons of the Pioneers, Perry Como, Hank Snow, Roy Rogers, and others have lulled us with their words. Because of this song, perhaps one person in a thousand today knows the tumbleweed was an uninvited guest.

In fact, the tumbleweed, or Russian thistle, hitched a ride from southeastern Russia and western Siberia, taking over the western landscape even faster than the sons of the pioneers. The Russian thistle, a member of the goosefoot family, was brought to South Dakota in 1873 in contaminated flax seed. Livestock, railroad cars, threshing crews and the wind quickly spread tumbleweeds throughout the West. The balladeer's glamorous high desert traveler is in fact a destructive invader. Not only does it create allergies in people but it takes away moisture from the soil, interferes with farming, and shelters pests and crop diseases. The tumbleweed makes fire-fighting difficult when fiery clusters advance in front of prairie wild fires. It's also a driving hazard, and clogs irrigation ditches throughout the West. Tolerant both to drought and to alkaline soil, the tumbleweed germinates very quickly. When I went to the library to learn about the Russian thistle and the song that has so romanticized its presence, I discovered that the words and tune were written by Bob Nolan in 1934. The timing underscores the fact that the tumbling tumbleweed was never a part of the cattle-drive West at all. Rather, it's an invasive species, one characteristic of the "new world's born at dawn" that the second stanza of the song foreshadows.

If the tumbleweed signifies supposed western glamour, however, cheat grass occupies the opposite end of the spectrum. Native to the Mediterranean region, cheat grass simultaneously arrived in Colorado, probably with packing material, and in the Pacific Northwest, probably with impure seed, in the late 1800s. Now cheat grass grows almost everywhere in the West, with devastating results. In Washington state's Palouse country, for example, the weed reduces wheat yield by twenty-seven percent. The invader is unpopular with ranchers, too, because the mature plant burrows into the mouths of grazing stock and cuts their tongues. Even more problematic is the role cheat grass plays as a volatile fuel for wildfires. We all know that big burns now recur with nightmarish regularity. Unfortunately, flames—perhaps piggybacking on tumbling tumbleweeds—readily leapfrog from one stretch of cheat grass to another. My federal fact book tells me that almost 17.5 million acres are infested in Idaho and Utah alone, a wholesale displacement of sagebrush and native grasses. A wholesale opportunity for fire as well.

Equally responsible for the modern spread of wildfires is another common plant introduced from another continent. *Eucalyptus globulus* came from Australia in 1853. Growing chiefly along the eastern coast of Tasmania, eucalyptus found a similar climate in California. By the 1870s, large scale cultivation was already in place. This quick-growing tree was touted as an important lumber source for railroad ties, shipbuilding, and furnace-making. When its wood proved too soft for such commercial uses, it was hailed as an attractive ornamental. Unfortunately, it proved instead to be an invasive entrepreneur. Eucalyptus thrives on the moisture of summer fog, but becomes dryly dangerous when Santa Ana winds blow east to west. In fact, because of its high volume of forest debris and its extreme flammability, the eucalyptus may be the single most volatile tree in the world. The stringy bark not only bursts into flame but, when carried by the wind, starts random spot fires everywhere it lands. The 1991 Oakland hills fire and the 2003 San Diego and Lake Arrowhead infernos exemplify the difficulties firefighters encounter in regions fueled by blazing eucalyptus.

Like other invasive species, eucalyptus proves difficult to remove. A homeowner can grub a tree out, but unless the stump is ground to pieces to a depth of at least two feet, resprouting will occur. Insects, such as the long-horned borer, may serve as destructive agents but, because many homeowners enjoy the ornamental plant, the introduction of pests is likely to be unpopular among the neighbors. Chemical control probably works best. I regularly teach Rachel Carson's *Silent Spring*, however, so I never can comfortably imagine using toxic herbicides to solve garden problems. When I consider the chemical options outlined in *Invasive Plants of California's Wildlands*, I cringe. Triclopyr, imazapyr, glyphosate, the very words remind me of laboratory experiments. Their popular names, designed to attract buyers, sound repellant to me, too. Garlon, Arsenal, Stalker, Roundup, Rodeo. "Whoopee-ti-ai-oh," a roundup/rodeo cowboy might croon. "Git along, little (botanical) doggie!" But it doesn't quite work that way, when rousting persistent invasive species. Problematic, too, is the way a landscape looks once chemicals have been applied. Poisoned trees, dead and dying, dried and dropping, are ugly. But that doesn't seem as significant to me as the possible impact on human health. Nearly half a century after the publication of *Silent Spring*, people still ignore Carson's apocalyptic warnings and bring Roundup to the rescue.

Clearly, the dilemma of invasive exotics is not easily solved. On the one hand, they not only are dangerous but they often extinguish native plants. On the other, eliminating these botanical terrorists completely turns out to be nearly impossible by any suitable means known today. Because the invaders are so common and so prevalent, non-native species actually dictate how we view the American West. Eucalyptus, cheat grass, tumbleweeds, tamarisks, lombardy poplars, they're everywhere. Just as my friends enjoy the engineered Colorado River and its botanic banks, so we accept these plants as an integral part of the scenery, as natural as can be. When I drive across Nevada, where I've lived and hiked and studied the terrain for more than thirty years, I can't tell what grew here two hundred years ago and what is newly opportunistic. Cheat grass and tumbleweed, unfortunately, look as native as the purple sage.

Dan Flores has written a thoughtful book titled *The Natural West: Environmental History in the Great Plains and Rocky Mountains*. Arguing that the explorers of European descent never saw a pristine West at all, that in fact there never was such an unaltered landscape except in the pioneer imagination, he muses about what we mean when we say we want to restore the West to its original condition. "Original condition" is a meaningless term because the West, like all geological constructs and biological entities, is in constant flux. Yesterday's Ice Age is today's Global Warming is tomorrow's Inevitability, whatever that might be. So, given the inroads made by exotic plants, given the speed with which they arrived and the acceleration with which they reproduce, given the fact that they literally are everywhere, how can we presume to eradicate them? Should we, in fact, even try? Flores concludes, "Now that ecology has discovered history, environmentalists for the first time in this country are being asked to reassess exactly what it is we mean when we say we seek 'to restore wilderness.'" Can we, should we, attempt to turn back the clock? Or should we simply accept the present and its subsequent future? Did my pontoon ride on the Colorado River actually float me past what has come to be a twenty-first-century version of a natural scene?

The saturated sandy river bottom moves in a constant state of flux, even though the river itself is passive right now. Enjoying a new sandbar, two dozen pelicans cluster together in the winter afternoon sun. Occasionally, a handful fly off on a reconnaissance flight, but the birds quickly return to home base, their current refuge of shifting sand. Before the construction of the nearby dams, this part of the Colorado often stretched fifteen miles across, a labyrinth of flooding wetlands, depths and shallows. I wonder if there were pelicans in 1857, when Don Diego Jaeger built a poorly surveyed, poorly constructed irrigation canal that flooded as soon as gully-washers decimated the inadequate culverts and canals. Or in 1912, the year the Yuma Siphon was engineered to "disburse" river water to the Imperial Valley in California and to "deliver" water to the Yuma Valley in Arizona. Are these pelicans a remnant of that West or an embellishment of this one? Do they belong in a natural or an unnatural West?

Where we were floating, the Imperial National Wildlife Refuge fronts the Colorado for nearly thirty miles on either side. Its 25,125 acres provide a stopover for some 235 species of migratory birds. A colorful brochure points to the designer habitat, and tells visitors what they will see. "Wetland wildlife is most abundant in winter," the flyer reports, "when 'snowbirds' such as cinnamon teal and northern pintail use the refuge. During the summer months, look for permanent residents such as great egrets and muskrat." I look, and spot a variety of ducks drifting as lazily as we are. They especially seem to like the bankside water, where the matted vegetation thrives. The brochure continues, telling me that "the refuge surrounds one of the few remaining 'wild' places on the Colorado River. This stretch is valued by boaters," it says, "for its remote scenery." Because the word "wild" is in quotation marks, I assume the anonymous author comprehended irony. But I'm still astonished that a government publication could even remotely call this landscape "wild." Only a few yards from the riverbank, a dirt road ambles parallel to the water. On the hillside beyond, I can see mine tailings and more two-tracks heading cross-country. Here on the river, other boats meander past. My friends tell me that, in summertime, the channel is so overcrowded with water craft of all shapes and sizes that it's hard to find room to maneuver. Perhaps this popular place is emblematic of the now-natural West, a landscape irrevocably changed and changing, a landscape in flux.

This thought takes me back to our point of entry. We pontooned onto the river from a place known as Martinez Lake. Established as a fishing camp in 1955, the resort has been home to human snowbirds for half a century. A Yuma publication boasts that there are "hundreds of miles of shoreline on lakes and channels within a short distance of the lake, serving as home to Bigmouth Bass, Catfish, Bluegill, Tilapia and Striped Bass." A retired person's paradise, I'm sure, analogous to the pelicans' perch, perhaps.

Walking around the resort, I find myself studying another lesson in alien invasion, another paradigm of today's natural unnatural West, another conceptualization of home. I can tell just by looking that many of the tin trailers have been here for almost fifty years. The fraying sides and unpainted frames huddle close together along pot-holed streets that twist and turn in unexpected directions. The layout looks unplanned, as if the residents both permanent and part-time had settled themselves wherever it seemed convenient. Many of the trailers and houses edge quite close to the water, as if zoning were a foreign concept then and now. Boats are tied up helter-skelter, too, as if they were tamarisks trying to claim every available inch of shoreline. No city planner ever worked in this eclectic place, I decide.

In many ways, Martinez Lake mimics the entire West of the twentieth century and now the twenty-first. Early generations of snowbirds arrived slowly, with little disposable income, with an enthusiasm for inexpensive travel or for cheap property, with an opportunistic kind of joie de vivre as they explored receptive locales. My aunt and uncle, those gamblers of Chapter Three, gave up their home in Washington state's dampness and wandered the sunbelt states at will. Content with itinerancy, they spent a week here, a month there, a few days somewhere else, like tumbling tumbleweeds from Seattle instead of Russia. Ill health finally forced them to settle in what's called a "Park Model," a permanent mobile home, an oxymoron abutted by hundreds of others that looked just like it. The attached "Arizona Room" held their excess belongings. More upscale than the early Martinez Lake dwellings, their "trailer" nonetheless was typical of those bought by many of the invaders from cold states to warm. Functional, relatively inexpensive, convenient, minimal upkeep, taprooted into the asphalt in ways just as opportunistic as adaptative alien weeds.

My companions of the river float trip, belonging to a different generation, project for themselves a decidedly rosier future than befell Aunt Ruth and Uncle Irv. In effect, though, they're behaving no more and no less "naturally" or "unnaturally" in their Arizona environment. Bob bought his Martinez Lake property thirty years ago, a two room shack with no particular amenities. "When I retire," he said, "I'll fix it up." Commuting from San Diego, he has done just that, elongating the original shanty by adding a well-designed, well-built adobe structure that stretches massively from one corner of his property to the other. With a sunning deck, a fireplace, a pot-bellied stove, extensive plate glass windows, a modern kitchen, two tiled baths, and a wall of electronic equipment with niches for his art collection, this "vacation" getaway no longer resembles any of the neighboring places. Replicating the amenities of home, fitting architecturally into the landscape while dwarfing the smaller cabins on either side, Bob's place seems to me a harbinger of the next generation's affluent invasion of the West. I might even say it's a "natural" evolution, for it's indicative of what is happening wherever up-scale is extirpating small-scale.

Interspersed all among the shanties and Airstream trailers and pieced-together old vehicles, substantial second homes rear skyward around the lagoons of Martinez Lake. Right now the newer construction looks somewhat out of place—too fashionably designed, too fancy for the neighborhood, too costly. But even as I write these words, the whole neighborhood is transforming itself. While some residents are just trying to hang on to their property as best they can, others are busily planning for future construction. Before long, the snowbirds of the present will extinguish the snowbirds of the past. Bob's neighbors, for example, already have blueprints for a structure that may well dwarf Bob's.

Everything I might say about the saltcedar, the eucalyptus, the tumbling tumbleweed, or even the cheat grass, applies just as fairly to the new denizens of Martinez Lake. We call it progress. Just as Willa Cather's "long brooms of lavender-pink blossom" can turn into an Avenue of Tamarisks with cauterized trunks and pale lemon fronds, so the hospitable summer shade once created by willows and cottonwood now hunkers beneath motor home awnings and trellised patios.

At the Imperial Wildlife Refuge, I picked up a slick flyer. "Have You Seen This Plant?" the lettering boldly asks. In italics, the colorful page announces that *"Giant salvinia, Salvinia molesta, is an aquatic fern prohibited in the United States by Federal law."* I smile at the words. Prohibiting an opportunistic exotic invader is an ecological Sisyphusian exercise in futility. This particular "molesting" plant from South America is already taking hold in Louisiana and Texas. In California, it can be found downstream from Blythe to the Imperial Dam, throughout the All American Canal, and into the Imperial Valley. I suggest that a single flyer is not going to dissuade it from further proliferation. Like the teeming tourists, with their enthusiasm for the desert's winter warmth, this plant will go where it wishes.

The New West, then, is our own creation, a natural outgrowth of opportunism and progress. To see it as a damaged environment is to misunderstand the inevitable presence of an indescribable and unimaginable variety of invasive species, human and nonhuman alike. To fantasize about the past, to point fingers at present practices, to imagine a future free of such interlopers, is to ignore the lessons of history. "Always blow out jet ski intakes and wash boats and equipment land-side before traveling to a new waterway," the flyer demands. "Not likely," I say to myself as we drift past the botanic detritus that lines the Colorado channel. "Not likely," in this twenty-first-century home on the range.

If tamarisks and tumbleweeds aren't exactly "Home on the Range's" beloved "wild flowers in this dear land of ours," neither the song's screaming curlews nor its grazing antelope flocks densely populate the modern West either. Just as invasive species take over a landscape so thoroughly that the interlopers become thoroughly familiar, so the elimination of particular animals disrupts a natural balance. The famous examples of vanished, endangered, or recovering species are well known, of course. Wolves in Yellowstone, grizzlies in the Sierra, steelhead along the Columbia River, passenger pigeons and snail darters and spotted owls—all these have had a fair share of media attention. But what about the less newsworthy creatures? Might their disappearances skew ecological well-being as well?

Marmot Lake, at 11,800 feet, sits high in the Sierra Nevada's Humphreys Basin. Frozen much of the year, stark and treeless, devoid of trout, it invites few visitors other than those who plan to climb nearby Mount Humphreys. What is unusual about Marmot Lake, however, is its trout-free status. Most mountain lakes were planted with game fish in the 1920s, first by packers hauling trout in on horseback, later by planes dropping hundreds of trout from the air. Early federal and state biologists paid casual attention to which lakes they were stocking and kept no survival statistics whatsoever. Their program was successful, though. So accustomed are we to good fishing that most Sierra campers today believe the fish are native to the region. In truth, most of those thriving trout we routinely catch and eat are not native at all.

Meanwhile, a flourishing trout population means that other species are on the decline. At one time, mountain yellow legged frogs abundantly populated those Sierra Nevada lakes and ponds located between 5,000 and 12,000 feet in elevation. Now they are rarely seen. Researchers can count mountain yellow-legged frogs in only about twenty percent of the sites where the amphibians once were prevalent. So in 1995, the Biodiversity Legal Foundation formally petitioned the USFWS to list these frogs as an endangered species. No decision has yet been made, but if the species is to survive, such a listing may be critical. Perhaps more vital, however, are programs to reintroduce the mountain yellow-legged frogs to their original habitat. Ironically, a formal endangered listing might well curtail the current scientific endeavors.

In 1995, the Sierra Nevada Aquatic Research Laboratory began an ambitious research agenda. After surveying 2,200 lakes and ponds in the High Sierra, Roland Knapp and Kathleen Matthews determined that non-native trout played a major role in the frogs' decline. Knapp then devised a way to remove non-native trout by using gill nets with mesh panels. The trout swim through, get caught by their gills, try to back up, and cannot. One of the lakes Knapp purged of trout was Marmot Lake. Once its waters were devoid of trout, he planted twenty adult yellow-legged mountain frogs and ten tadpoles in its waters. Five years later, Marmot Lake has too many frogs to count. Roland Knapp tries, however. On July 28, 2002, for example, he calculated there were 1,481 larvae clustered just off shore.

Sitting alongside Marmot Lake a week later, I find it hard to comprehend the counting procedure. One pile of squirming tadpoles and sub-adults scatters when my shadow gets too near. How many? "Maybe 800," Roland responds in an offhand way. How does he know? "Walk along the shore and count jumps," he teases, though he insists the lake is now home to 110 adults, 750 subadults, and 1800 tadpoles. Roland is so thoroughly caught up in the details of the project that his enthusiasm is almost infectious. Three or four days ago, I had never laid eyes on a mountain yellow-legged frog. Now I eagerly hold one, turn him over to see his mustard color, lean close to smell the strong garlic whiff that characterizes this species. "An Italian Stallion," my friend Cal jokes about the spicy froggy cologne.

Roland caught the frog with a net, much like someone would snare a butterfly. In fact, Roland looks rather like a caricature of a nineteenth-century naturalist, with his yellow shirt billowing and his beige safari hat trailing its protective covering down his back, the way he strides along the shore and drops his net into the water. His is a high-tech operation, however. He carries a Palm Pilot in a waterproof shockproof case plus a backup module so he cannot lose his data. In the past, a year of research involved three months in the field, six months entering data, and three months checking for errors. Now, with Palm Pilot and computer, data entry not only is seamless, but accurate. Technology enables Roland to accomplish a good deal more each summer than he could in the past.

What Roland accomplishes, however, is aided by the frogs' own proclivities. As soon as a lake is trout-free, opportunistic frogs arrive. All they need is connectivity. One kilometer downstream from Marmot Lake, for example, is Cony Lake. Thanks to Roland, it, too, has no trout, and already the frogs are reintroducing themselves. With a frog-hold secured in Marmot Lake, the expanding population is looking for new territory. Both upstream and down, adults and sub-adults are beginning to wander.

As I sit beside Marmot Lake, and listen to Roland talk about his beloved frogs, I think about the information he is sharing. It seems that I've never really seen a High Sierra mountain lake in its pristine condition. When I think of all the trout I've eaten, I realize I've feasted on an invader species. Hybrid trout in the same category as cheat grass? That's a complicated concept to wrap my mind around. Complicated to think about, too, is the fact that none of this research could be done if the mountain yellow-legged frog actually were listed as an endangered species. Handling frogs, as we did and as Roland does so often, would be forbidden. "Much better to use a potential endangered species designation as a club," my conservation biologist friend Peter Brussard insists. "If an animal actually gets listed, science usually goes down the drain."

Humphreys Basin is still a relatively untrammeled part of the Sierra Nevada. The name of its signature body of water, Desolation Lake, suggests what early mountaineers must have thought of its terrain. Most hikers today, intent upon the John Muir Trail or headed over Paiute Pass to circle around toward Evolution Basin, avoid its emptiness. Camped there for a week, our small group saw only a handful of other visitors. In the early-twenty-first century, when lightweight food and gear invite a constant stream of Sierra Nevada hikers and climbers, no one, relatively speaking, chose to camp at a lake called Desolation.

One morning, following a tracery of green, I climbed up to a higher tarn. I sat where I could look out over the entire basin. My friends, trekking off to climb a peak, had left me to myself for the day, left me to the silent sweep of wind that always blows at 11,000 feet, to the thin sun of August that only slightly warms this high elevation. Too many tiny lakes and potholes to count, too many khaki and beige marmots to count, too many buzzing dragonflies to count, and nobody—absolutely nobody—in sight. Directly below was Desolation Lake, its boomerang shape carved into steep and shallow rocky shores. Across and to the east, towering Mount Humphreys, all Class 4 ridges, jagged and steep.

Later in the day, thunderheads would roll behind its distinctive shape, so that Humphreys looked like a white knife piercing blue black clouds. Later still, the peak became a rainbow, its top in the sun, with magenta shadows triangulating down its steepness. Every cloud a different shade of apricot, melon, gray, black, or off-white. John Muir's characteristic Range of Light, as he so accurately described these mountains. The next morning, I would hike to Humphreys Lake, a midsized scoop of water tucked in a bowl, en route up the northwest ridge of its namesake. High above timberline, there were no trees in sight, although vast beds of purple and occasionally white lupine colored the otherwise rockbound landscape. I sat for a long time, and watched the water. The fish were jumping; not a frog in sight.

Dramatic examples of species salvage are occurring throughout the American West, but California seems to be taking a lead role. Or perhaps California is simply taking advantage of large-scale opportunity. If frogs anchor one tiny end of an ecological spectrum, the opposite end is crowned by enormity. The condor is a majestic kind of signature bird, with a wing span nine or nine-and-a-half feet, one of the largest in the world. To see one in the wild is a kind of miracle. Fossils tell us that condors once nested widely across North America, that evolution itself—or at least the extinction of the Pleistocene megafauna—caused a large number of them to disappear except for those that sought refuge in central California. Curious, susceptible to lead poisoning, liable to be shot because they're such visible targets, these already-scarce birds diminished rapidly after European settlers arrived. After awhile, the population became so small that sightings were rare. On March 11, 1967, the nearly extinct California condor was listed under the Endangered Species Act. By 1987, only twenty-seven had survived the rigors of the twentieth century.

In a last-ditch effort to save what was left of the genetic pool, the twenty-seven were preserved in captivity, and biologists began the breeding program that slowly but surely is regenerating the huge bird. By 2002, the total population numbered 202 condors; 78 of those fly free in the wild.

I talked with Curt Mykut, the condor's Roland Knapp. Wearing a condor cap and a gray condor T-shirt, Curt, a field biologist who works for the Ventana Wilderness Society, looked like a bird-man to me. He talked like a dedicated ornithologist, too, with an eager passion for his work that punctuated his words. We were standing on a rounded pinnacle of lichen-covered rock, just a scramble above the popular High Peaks Trail at Pinnacles National Monument. There, not far east of Highway 101, six juvenile condors recently have been released, and two more are in a nearby pen awaiting freedom. Four more will arrive at the site later this year. From our perch, we had a clear view north, south, and east. And we were looking for condors. Curt held a VHF positioning antenna, trying to listen for and locate the collared birds. One condor's collar emitted a steady cheep, cheep, cheep whenever the antenna pointed northeast. "Resting somewhere," Curt assumed. This lazy condor wasn't moving at all. Three other big birds had flown farther southeast the day before. "First time they've ever left the park," the worried biologist said. "Haven't heard a beep for more than twenty-four hours." While we chatted, he continued to flash the antenna, but no more condors flew into range.

Listening to Curt's concerns, I worried, too. As he described the problems the birds might encounter, I wondered how the condor recovery program could ever be successful. Unlike most birds, these don't breed until they're about seven years old. A lot of tragedy can happen in seven years. Also, a pair hatches only one chick per year. Again, a lot of dangers can befall a single baby bird. But the statistics, in this case, don't lie. More than eight times as many condors are alive today than existed in the 1980s, and a few mature pairs are even breeding in the wild. The prognosis for condor success, still somewhat iffy, increases every year.

In fact, the missing Pinnacles juveniles flew into my range that evening, not only easing my fears for their safety, but then putting on an unbelievable acrobatic aerial show above my campsite. Sitting in my camp chair, I watched the four riding the thermals back and forth above a ridgeline, catching an uplift, spinning into a downdraft, drifting up and down and across, combining feathered strength and beauty, soaring through the air. At the Reno Air Races each year, biplanes, MiGs, propeller-driven hand-me-downs, and other relics from the past zip east to west and north and south. Nothing aerial I have ever seen, however, could compare with the grace of these relic birds. I wish I had been closer, close enough to see the wildness in their eyes. But I had to be content with the narrow range of a pair of binoculars.

While I was peering intently, a turkey vulture flew into view. Alongside its condor relatives, it looked like a tiny sparrow. The big birds simply ignored its presence, as if something with a five-and-a-half-foot wingspan were a tiny speck on the horizon. And still the condors soared, for nearly twenty minutes until, one by one, they dipped their wings and silently disappeared over the horizon.

The Pinnacles birds are all young males, sexually immature but already full grown. Curt told me to check out the Ventana Wilderness Society website, where I might learn all sorts of condor facts and figures. A chick is born with its eyes open, taking up to a week to hatch from an egg. Adults, who can weigh as much as twenty-two pounds, will consume two or three pounds at a single feeding. Like their vulture cousins, they eat only carrion, leftovers as it were. They're scaredy-cats, showing their emotions through skin-color changes and throwing up when they're afraid. Since a condor has no vocal cords, it makes hissing and grunting noises by forcing air through its body. Finally, the website reports, condors cool off on hot days by utilizing a process called urohydrosis, defecating on their legs "to reduce their core body temperature." Learning about urohydrosis, I rethink my yearning for an up-close encounter. When I saw the Pinnacles four, the temperature was close to 90 degrees.

Curt tells me that they're often spotted on the High Peaks Trail, which I've hiked more than once without seeing a neighborhood condor. Because they've all been raised in captivity, they're unfortunately curious and appreciate people. "Last week," he said, "one was sitting on the bench by the restroom on Scout Peak. When I got there, a circle of tourists was surrounding it, snapping pictures and oohing and ahing." Curt went on to describe the sinking feeling he has every time one of his charges potentially endangers itself. Not that someone might harm a condor in the Pinnacles preserve, but that the condor will not learn the survival skills necessary to avoid human encounters. The solution? "Easy," laughed Curt. "I pulled out my Super Soaker Squirt gun, and I blasted the bird in the chest!" No doubt the sons of the pioneers never imagined a modern-day biologist shooting an endangered species with a squirt gun. This very contemporary action exemplifies human intervention taken to the nth degree.

In fact, the intercessions of human beings preceded both a lake full of yellow-legged frogs and a sky barely stippled with condors. Without scientists like Roland Knapp and Curt Mykut, I probably wouldn't be able to describe a personal experience with either frogs or condors. Writing about the two, however, I can't help wondering why these particular creatures are being preserved. Nature selects in a random way. That's the nature of evolution, where certain species thrive for awhile, then are extinguished for one reason or another. For the past several centuries, however, humans, consciously and unconsciously, seem to be making the choices. Much has been written about the disproportionate acceleration of today's endangerment and loss. Norman Myers, in his "Foreword" to *Protecting Endangered Species in the United States*, cites troubling statistics. Approximately 10 million species live on earth today, comprised of perhaps 2.2 billion populations. Those populations are disappearing at a rate of 43,000 per day! On the other hand, little has been written about why we try to retain certain animals while we let others slip away.

If we are playing God, are we doing so rationally? Thinking specifically of frogs and condors, I wonder why we choose to save some species and not others. It's possible, I decide, to conjure up answers that suffice. The yellow-legged frog, for example, is a canary-in-the-mine kind of character that thrives when lake waters are healthy (and trout free) but dies off when acid rains bring too much pollution. Analyzing a frog's success tells us about a high-country lake's ecological well-being and also about the air we breathe. And as far as condors are concerned, they're, well, big. As I noted earlier, they're a signature bird in California, a psychological emblem of what is means to be wild and free. Even though saving them may be flying in the face of evolution, we like to think that such massive relics may still exist in the present and the future. Condors link us with the dinosaur past, an illusion that encourages us to seek preservation.

So we are saving certain animals because of a whole complex of reasons that ranges from the wholly scientific to the entirely personal. We save them because individual scientists choose to work with them — Roland and frogs, Curt and condors. If no one is interested in a particular scarce creature, it's likely to disappear. But in truth, the evolutionary process naturally dictates that certain species will go away and that others will thrive. While the current rapid pace may be out of step with evolutionary time, the process itself is inevitable.

Still, the critical question remains unanswered. Since humans appear to be responsible for much of the current retention and attrition, are we thinking about preservation versus extinction in any analytical way? Is our selection process random or planned? Happenstance or carefully conceived? Probably a little of both, a combination of accident and calculation, and I think that is what's happening in the American West today.

For example, the sufficiency or insufficiency of game birds is of great interest to sportsmen and hunters. Preservation is important, if only to provide more birds to shoot. Two birds with comparable breeding and bonding habits model two systems of population enhancement. The sage grouse, once plentiful in California and Nevada, is not listed as endangered but is much less common than biologists and hunters would like. The wild turkey, on the other hand, thinks rural California makes a dandy home. Finding mating turkeys, it turns out, is relatively easy; finding mating sage grouse takes some local knowledge.

Off to the east, a secondary highway bisects the sagebrush. An occasional truck hums past, lights dimly cutting through the night. Otherwise, silence. And darkness. And distances too far to measure, except along a rain-rutted two track with hood-high sagebrush on either side. At the first sign of daylight, just a dim whitening of the edge of the sky, meadowlarks begin to sing, a sure sign of spring in the desert. More daylight, enough to see across the cold empty landscape. It's time to hoist myself out the back of my truck. I join three friends, the four of us bundled in fleece like over-weight dolls. Dennis is already peering through his telescope. And pointing. I steady my own telescope carefully atop its tripod, then focus on a stretch of ground a couple of hundred yards from where we'd parked. Rose whispers, "There, over there, two, no three, they're moving around. Look below the notch."

Without the telescope, I can dimly see a little movement. I swivel the scope slightly to the left, refocus, and then I see two rocks that aren't rocks at all. They're sage grouse, huffing and puffing in full display, like two punk rockers with their coiffures standing on end, idling on a street corner, side by side but facing opposite directions, waiting for the girls to notice. Their tail feathers, brown like the desert dirt, flare in peacock spikes. What from a distance look like white Christmas ornaments—they're really just white feathers—hang in patterned echelons. Around their necks, Santa Claus muffs, growing larger when the cocks begin to boom. And boom they do, a kind of two-tone "hooop, huuuf" sound that comes when they expand their chests. "Hooop, huuuf," the sage grouse puff themselves out until they're almost twice their normal size. "Hooop, huuuf," their creamy sacs bulge with just a hint of yellow. "Hooop, huuuf." Their chests sag. No female in sight. All that preening energy for nothing.

When the sun finally lights up the scene, three more cocks wander into view. One turns, and chases a smaller bird away. Like fat billiard balls, they careen out of view. Looking back at the two show-offs, I can hardly spot them. They look like rocks again, two more brown objects in a miniature boulder field. Last night, when we arrived, we walked over to see first-hand the place where sage grouse have been returning for generations. Just a flat open space in the sagebrush, dotted with rocks the size of sage grouse. Called a lek, the area looks much like the rest of the desert that extends in every direction, but not exactly. It's grassier, with pink puffs of owl clover dotting the ground, and tufts of buckwheat poking through the groundcover. It's rockier, too, which helps camou-flage the birds.

A "lek," according to the *Oxford English Dictionary*, is a patch of ground used by certain birds during the breeding season, a setting for the males' display and their meeting with the females. Darwin coined the term in 1883. It comes from a Swedish word, *leka*, which means "to play." That's appropriate, I decide, as I watch the grouse caper in and out of the rocks. When they pause, they're practically invisible. On the move, or displaying their finery, or "hooop, huuufing" their sacs, they're eminently watchable. Other birds are keeping their eyes on them, too. A horned lark meanders past the strutting grouse. Intent on their promenade, the cocks hardly notice. Then two California quail tiptoe past our scopes, on their way to somewhere. The desert, so khaki and beige and ostensibly nondescript, is alive with birds this morning; some in pairs, others—like the meadowlarks—calling for mates. And there go the two biggest sage grouse, displaying their finery for all the world to see.

Unfortunately, the world on this April morning doesn't seem to contain any hens. No females to react to the scintillating display of fanned tails and deep-throat sighs. Most of the actual mating probably took place a month or so ago. The females are most certainly hunkered down on their nests in the sagebrush perhaps miles away, warming their eggs. The boys are strutting alone on the lek. But maybe, just maybe— they hope—one more female will stumble into the arena. Maybe, just maybe, the cocks will be attractive enough to mate one more time. I wonder if the peripheral sage grouse, the ones that keep wandering near the two center-fold six-pound hunks, are just beardless teen-agers, a little smaller, perhaps taking their cues from the more experienced adult males. The "master cocks," they're called, as I later learn from Fred Ryser's *Birds of the Great Basin*. Ryser explains, too, how often sage grouse are seen side by side, facing different directions, brushing each other with their vibrating wings and tails. What we're watching is typical "polarized territoriality," especially in late April after the hens have disappeared.

We try to count the visible birds, but it's hard because they rarely move all at once. Seven, no, nine or ten. "I think there are eleven," Rose decides. I never discern more than a handful at a time. Most of the time I stay focused on the two biggest show-offs, who seem to have the energy to go on and on and on. "Hooop, huuuf," they drum. "Hooop, huuuf." The others display briefly, but seem more interested in chasing each other around. Teenagers, I think again. Finally, one by one, they deflate, and squat amid the rocks. Or perch atop a rock, no longer round and fluffy but sleeker and more birdlike, with long pointed tails. The sun glistens off their feathers, as their tiny heads cock sideways. Listening. Checking out the arena, once again.

7:16 a.m. At some unknown provocation, they all fly off together. Twelve of them—we miscounted while they were on the ground—rise in formation like a fighter squadron ready for aerial combat. The sage grouse, jetting off to somewhere, disappear into the sky. They may end up five or ten miles away, but they'll be back tomorrow. Cocks return, I'm told, every day for almost two months, instinctively seeking the same lek where they and their ancestors have returned every year for centuries. To the identical spot, they return, to a tiny patch of rocks and grasses almost indiscernible from any other piece of desert. There, over and over, they will repeat the same display of finesse and feathers and finery.

By comparison, I would say that wild turkeys are more forthright and less romantic. Maybe because the "turkey" carries unfortunate connotations, maybe because I didn't need either binoculars or a telescope to watch their mating antics, I equate turkeys with their common barnyard kin. They're less flighty, more gregarious, perhaps dumber than most of their free-ranging avian counterparts. It's relatively easy to see them up close. Just below an escarpment named Turkey Ridge, I shared a California campsite with twenty-two of them. The flock meandered up the ravine toward my truck that was parked off to one side. The turkeys stopped to peck at the ground, to chase each other a bit, and to "gobble, gobble, gobble" at random intervals. They sounded almost like caricatures of themselves, the distinct gobbling sounds a sure sign that mating season was at hand. The males were on display, feathers fanned in arcs so wide that their wings dragged on the ground, making "S" curves in the dirt. Despite occasional altercations and digressions, the flock seemed to have a pattern in mind—up the dirt road until it dead-ended, a leisurely exploration of the hillside that culminates in Turkey Ridge, and perhaps a little turkey sex along the way.

I discovered I was in a bordello of sorts. Four turkeys were particularly interested in the ground behind my pick-up. Since it was early morning—the incessant gobbles had awakened me long before sunup—I was lying in my sleeping bag, peering out the open back of my truck, the perfect spot for a lounging voyeur. No need to climb out into the cold because, unlike the sage grouse, these turkeys strutted within a foot or two of the tailgate, apparently unconcerned about whoever might be watching. They, after all, were campground turkeys, so they must have been used to an audience. Three toms, one hen, the toms in full display. The largest, the one with the brightest red wattles and the thickest beard, gobbled and rattled and shook his tail feathers with glee. The display reminded me of an eighteenth-century promenade. Dandies, dressed in tight pants with perfumed lace at their throats, eying the ladies, choosing the damsel who would suffice for the next dance. Or is it the damsel who selects the flashiest beau?

The bright red wattled guy was victorious; he mounted the hen with great enthusiasm. I expected the two losers—or "jakes," as they are called—to wander away in disgust, but no, they arranged themselves on either side of the happy couple, as if they were yeoman of the guard protecting their king and queen from harm. While the hen peeped a kind of steady chirp, all three toms were strangely silent, though the two guardsmen dragged their wing feathers back and forth in the dirt almost in time to the rhythm of the pair. The scene was a kind of parody of the non-mating dance I watched the sage grouse do. I generally don't watch or write about pornographic activities, but this was just plain fascinating, as if a gavotte had been orchestrated to some beat I couldn't hear. The action didn't last long, though. When the deed was finished, the tom, the two jakes, and the hen all hustled away together, hurrying to catch the rest of their flock. The magic spell was broken; deflated, they looked just like turkeys.

California bird checklists call *Meleagris gallopavo* "a non-native species." Although wild turkeys may have lived in California during the late Pleistocene, all of the current dwellers have been introduced during the past forty years. I could find one instance from 1877, when wild turkeys were transported to Santa Cruz Island, but the bulk of the popular game birds were brought west in the 1960s and 1970s. Because the genetic line is unclear, experts disagree whether these new turkeys should be called "introduced non-natives," or "re-introduced natives." Whichever, like tamarisks and eucalyptus, they're thriving. California hunters are delighted; Nevada voyeurs are too. But the fact that wild turkeys are flourishing is more accidental than planned. They've adapted well, even to campgrounds. Meanwhile, the more skittish—and more particular about their mating territory—sage grouse seem to be struggling.

Why? A conservation biologist could probably recite the facts and figures behind these birds' relative successes. I serve occasionally on the Ph.D. committees of graduate students in conservation biology. That's where I've learned the most about radio transmitters and collars and the repetitive habits of birds. One student, who finished last fall, spent the past several years of her life studying the dispersal patterns of Australian Tree-Creepers, both White-Breasted and Brown. What she learned about their normal activities while searching for breeding partners will form the basis for a habitat conservation plan in the upland forests. Another student is in Brazil right now, tracking the nesting patterns of Buff-Breasted Plovers. She's trying to figure out how and why these birds adapt especially well to fields that are overgrazed. In both cases, the researchers' discoveries are directly applicable to future land use planning. Plotting the activities of contemporary California Condors and Greater Sage Grouse and Wild Turkeys and even Australian Tree-Creepers and Buff-Breasted Plovers isn't irrelevant. But all these activities seem to me randomly selective, accidental rather than analytically chosen.

I confess that I'm doing exactly the same thing as I write this chapter. I'm mimicking the sorts of selection patterns that seem to be taking place in the late twentieth- and early-twenty-first centuries. Frogs and condors? Why not? Steelhead and grizzlies would do just as well, or desert pupfish and desert tortoise, or tamarisk and purple sage. But I am under no illusion that my choices have been based on logic or any particular principle. Rather, I'm just trying to imitate on the page what we in fact are doing in the wild.

So far, my examples have focused on creatures protected somehow, even bred for success. Occasionally, however, nature randomly selects an animal for proliferation. A surprising example occurs where the front range of the Rocky Mountains meets the plains of eastern Colorado. Two early pioneers there were Joseph W. Bowles and James B. Grant. Bowles, with an engineer's vision of the future, dug a ditch from Morrison in the nearby foothills to farms and ranches east of Red Rocks. There he created waterways and reservoirs to irrigate the surrounding fields. Meanwhile, Grant and his family were busy amassing property, from 1,280 acres in 1878 to 2,227 acres in 1950. Now Denver voraciously is turning such old ranches, with their artificial ponds, into suburban pleasure palaces for humans and wildlife alike.

One such development is Grant Ranch, a planned community of 738 acres that includes Bowles Lake, an upper-middle-class oasis in the midst of typical suburban sprawl. When first built, more than a decade ago, the homes ranged in price from $150,000 to close to a million, but they're undoubtedly worth much more today. Walkways and bike paths wind in and out of the common areas that themselves curve around the picturesque "lakes" built by entrepreneur Bowles a century ago. Visiting friends who live in Grant Ranch, and strolling the various black-topped paths, I could see the attractiveness of retiring to such an insulated, designer-boutique locale. With so many amenities close at hand, a homeowner need never venture off the grounds.

One June day, with hot sun overhead and thunderheads just beginning to climb into the western sky, we rented paddle boats, fat sluggish pontoon things that barely steered. Our legs churning, we splashed around Bowles Lake, first sticking close to shore so we could gape at the more opulent houses that line the "beachfront," then heading toward an isthmus that separates Bowles from another reservoir to the north. Our backs to the clubhouse, tennis courts, pool, and dock, we turned our faces toward a place where nature and urban planning come together in a startling combination.

Bowles Lake is home to one of the largest great blue heron rookeries in the western United States. Buoys floating in the water told us to paddle no closer, so offshore we drifted, staring in amazement at the avian display. I counted forty-two chicks, though I suspect there were more. Including the parents, far more than a hundred herons altogether. The chicks, nearly full-grown and almost ready to fledge, were hanging off their nests and beating their wings in the still morning air, flapping incessantly but not flying yet. The herons were talking nonstop, too, a "cack cack cack cack" sound that resembled a low-level Morse code for birds. Sometimes two to a nest, but more often single dwellers, the chicks ornamented the uplifted branches of cottonwoods and Russian olives. With occasional territorial squawking, the place sounded and looked like some sort of inner-city tenement.

And indeed that's what, in effect, it is. Down the block, we found a companion aviary high-rise. In a single massive cottonwood, only a hundred yards or so away, was another rookery. There, dozens of baby cormorants were standing on their nests, too, not making as much noise as the great blue herons, but actively chirping in loud chirrups. Later I learned that herons and cormorants often nest side by side—never in the same tree, but often in the immediate vicinity. Meanwhile, we spotted more herons along the shoreline. It appeared as though they were giving and receiving fishing lessons, the adults teaching their chicks to dip here and duck there. Funny stilted creatures, herons look almost like awkward giraffes when they stand in the water. Even as they start to fly, they take off by lumbering upward like old overloaded cargo planes. Fully airborne, with their legs tucked invisibly away, they're more like stealth bombers, all sleek and speedy fast. Giraffes, cargo planes, stealth bombers—components out of place in a "planned community." Alongside Bowles Lake at Grant Ranch, however, birds and humans live together in happy proximity. And everyone is thriving.

A copy of *Life at Grant Ranch: An Owner's Manual* is handed to every purchaser of property in the suburban development. Not only do the pages explain all the rules and regulations of the enclave but they also boast about the intersections of wildlife and tame. Or at least the milder forms of wildlife. Although I'm sure a resident would not be amused by a coyote that snacked on the family cat, all the ranch dwellers seem enthusiastic about their rookery neighbors. Extolling the presence of the great blue herons, the manual also points out the botanic virtues of the place. It seems that the peachleaf willow is the *only* tree-sized native willow to be found on the property. At least one specimen of the original vegetation has been saved. Something to be proud of—one native plant, plus the excess of birds. So goes the neighborhood.

Sometimes, too, an area can be overrun by an astonishing population explosion. What happens when, without explanation, a wild, semi-scarce creature multiplies tenfold? A century ago, very few elephant seals remained alive. Like the condor, they were nearly extinct. Scientists estimate that only a small colony on Guadalupe Island, off the coast of Baja California, kept the gene pool alive. First Mexico and then the United States passed laws to protect the elephant seals, which had been widely hunted and killed for their rich oily blubber. The seals held their own, until the 1972 Marine Mammal Protection Act gave them further asylum. Then, slowly but surely, these mammals began to regenerate. The result is astonishing.

On November 25, 1990, a dozen or so elephant seals arrived unin-vited on the central California coast just south of the Piedras Blancas lighthouse. A month later, nearly a hundred more had joined them, and two months after that, nearly four hundred lounged on the narrow beach. In February of 1992, the first pup was born. In 2003, more than 2,600 pups came to life on the same narrow strand. Almost too many to count.

When I saw them in March that year, the pups were mostly asleep. The adults had departed for the open seas, leaving the "weaners," as they're called, on shore. The young, which weigh about seventy-five pounds at birth, suckle milk that is fifty-five percent fat, the richest of all mammalian lactation. While the pups are fattening themselves up, the mothers lose nearly a third of their weight. Then, when the pups are weaned, the mothers depart. The weaners have to teach themselves how to swim and, when they're finally hungry enough, how to fish. No maternal oversight for elephant seals. Meanwhile they sprawl on the beach, huffing and puffing, piling all together much like bratwurst on a tray at the local butcher's. The young males, especially, jostle each other and snort the miniature battle sounds that will be maximized when they're older.

I'm told that the mating season is much more exciting than watch-ing the weaners take their afternoon naps. The adult seals begin arriving in late fall, males first, then pregnant females. Their time on the beach together is spent jockeying for position, as alpha males weighing as much as five thousand pounds gather harems and fend off all comers. The Pismo Beach docent flyer calls the winter scene an elephant seal "Woodstock" of sorts. Once the young are born, the pushing and shoving grows even more intense. Because the females are impregnated the moment they finish lactation, the bulls are gathering the most attractive mothers. One male will glean a harem of perhaps fifty or a hundred females, while unsuccessful beta bulls "haunt" the harem perimeter. Once the mating process is complete, they all go off to sea again.

The life of an elephant seal is a paradox of sociability and isolation. On the beach, they're all together in an intensely intimate scene of parenting and sexuality. In the ocean, each seal swims alone. High frequency collars and time-depth recorders tell a great deal about elephant seal mobility. A *Comprehensive Guide* reports that seals rarely rest, diving to depths of 1000–2000 feet with only a minute or two of breathing time in between. They swim as much as ten thousand miles every year, making two round trips—they return to molt in the late spring, then depart again until late fall—from the beach at Piedras Blancas to the northern Pacific Ocean and back again. Because they dive so deeply, they face little competition for their oceanic food. That's why, without the pressures of seal hunting, they seem to be thriving today. Unlike truly endangered species, the elephant seals have adapted to the twenty-first century with great success, and without much help from humans other than the work of the docents who keep tourists from getting too close to the enormous mammals on the beach.

Paradoxically, the elephant seals now breed as prolifically as tamarisks, and more successfully than many managed populations. Their sudden appearance at Piedras Blancas indicates how little we actually know about the preservation of species under the conditions of modernity. That condors fly past the Pinnacles, that wild turkeys have mastered the invitation of Turkey Ridge, that great blue herons have found a subdivision to their liking, that yellow-legged frogs can thrive in the absence of trout, that elephant seals have taken over the beach at Piedras Blancas, that curlews continue to scream (or at least cry), and that at least a few herds of antelope graze freely—these facts are indicative not only of an ongoing adaptation and interaction between humans and the rest of the biological world but also of the random nature of the "science" of preservation. In the new West, we can expect contractions and expansions of territories to continue in predictable and unpredictable ways.

Humorist Andy Kerr sets the conundrum to music this way, in tune with "Home on the Range."

> Oh it will not be long 'til the livestock are gone,
> And the bighorn range without fear;
> When the native biotic will retake the exotic,
> And the streams again will run clear.

Perhaps in 2020, I'll see four dozen condors flying free. Or elephant seals covering every inch of beach from San Francisco to Los Angeles. Or no fan-tailed grouse and turkeys at all. Perhaps in 2020, I'll see vistas of cheat grass and tumbling tumbleweeds. Or waterways redolent with waving tamarisk fronds. Or no native grasses anywhere. A roll of the dice, though I like to think the dice are in our hands.

CHAPTER SIX

Stream Flows

Oh, give me a land where the bright diamond sand
Flows leisurely down the stream;
Where the graceful white swan goes gliding along
Like a maid in a heavenly dream.

I live in a desert. According to the National Weather Service, the Reno airport averages 7.5 inches of rainfall each year. Since I can see the airport from my house, I assume that's approximately the meager amount that falls on my deck in winter flurries or summer bursts. So why am I sitting at my desk on a sunny February morning, turning 514 pages of a Great Basin Research publication titled *Dictionary of Water Words*? Why, in fact, did Gary A. Horton, a "resource and financial economist," find so many water entries applicable to Nevada and to the rest of the West as well? More important, what might we learn about water in a water lingo dictionary?

I begin reading the entries for the letter A. "Abandonment" seems to be the operative term on the first page, as in "abandoned channel," "abandoned water right," "abandoned well." Right away, I recognize the book's anthropocentric thrust. Rather than focus on H_2O itself, Horton will itemize the ways that people operate in relationship to water. Or perhaps the ways that water indifferently operates in relationship to people? We'll see. Carefully, I copy down the first crucial definition. "Abandonment—To give up the right to make a beneficial use of water as authorized by a water appropriation." This double assumption not only suggests that some governmental entity can "authorize" the use of water but that someone is obligated to make beneficial use of the resource. Some particular entity of power authorizes the public to use water, provided that those in power deem the use as beneficial and wise. Given the vociferousness of the Wise Use Movement in the American West, a loose-knit group that equates "wise use" with mining and grazing—remember that a kitty litter mine on the outskirts of Reno may be called "beneficial" by a mining corporation—I cannot truthfully say that wise use is synonymous with beneficial. I wonder, in fact, what "beneficial" means in this context.

Turning to page 35, I discover the answer. In truth, there are several sorts of beneficial uses. The first is "the amount of water necessary when reasonable intelligence and diligence are used for a stated purpose." Personally, I think the words "intelligence" and "diligence" are slippery terms when applied to water usage in the West, but I'm willing to acknowledge the generic nature of these definitions. I can follow the human-centered logic of the second entry, too. "A use of water resulting in appreciable gain or benefit to the user." The third sort of beneficial use, however, startles me with its blatant disregard for subtlety. "Any use of water within or outside the state, that is reasonable and useful and beneficial to the *Appropriator* [Horton's capitalization and italics, not mine], and at the same time is consistent with the interests of the public of this state is the best utilization of water supplies."

Who, exactly, is this *Appropriator*? The *Dictionary*, with a circularity of logic so common to governmentalese, will tell me. The appropriator is the "one taking water from a watercourse under the authority of the state and applying it to *Beneficial Use*" (again, the capitalization and italics are Horton's, not mine, though I can't really castigate him any longer because I'm beginning to see that capitals and italics are being used to direct the reader to other entries in the book). So, back to beneficial.

What might this anonymous appropriator find beneficial? Horton answers with a list that orders the relative values as recognized by the state:

[1] domestic and municipal uses;
[2] industrial uses;
[3] irrigation;
[4] mining;
[5] hydroelectric power;
[6] navigation;
[7] recreation;
[8] stock raising;
[9] public parks;
[10] wildlife and game preserves.

The prioritizing replicates a nineteenth-century world view marched straight into the twenty-first century. When miners, ranchers, pioneers, and various stripes of entrepreneurs began settling the American West, the dearth of water proved to be a significant handicap. On most of the lands west of the hundredth meridian, water was and is a precious commodity. Immediately, "first come, first served" became not only the watchword but also the law. The California '49ers, for example, needed massive amounts of water to sluice for gold, while cattlemen and other agricultural interests required adequate access as well. In order to further their interests, the wealthiest westerners used their powers to influence the legal system. Even today, the law dictates water rights and water usage in ways that not only echo the priorities of the past but also signal the relative political strengths and weaknesses of the consumers.

While I trust that stock-raising would have ranked higher than eighth a hundred and fifty years ago, I don't doubt that wildlife would always have been tenth. Yet Horton himself realizes that times are changing. After defining "the cardinal principle" of the water appropriation doctrine as "a use of water that is, in general, productive of public benefit, and which promotes the peace, health, safety and welfare of the people of the State," he adds a qualifying statement. "Recent statutes in some states have expressly made the use of water for recreation, fish and wildlife purposes, or preservation of the environment a beneficial use."

Here, a 2002 publication acknowledges that "recent" laws—and presumably the people who enacted them—actually have recognized that water might be useful for something other than economic human consumption. Before I applaud the *Dictionary's* priorities, however, I would point out that "recreation" precedes "fish and wildlife purposes," which in turn precedes "preservation of the environment" in an apparent hierarchical ordering. Although adding this particular sentence to a "beneficial" entry is a step in the right direction, it turns out to be a very small anthropocentric step indeed. The sentence seems worth emphasizing, however, because, as written, it underscores changing water priorities in the twenty-first-century American West and intimates future reconsiderations of some sort or other. Water reallocations in Oregon's Klamath Basin, for example, court-ordered and so strongly advocated by the Klamath Tribes, exemplify current rethinking about the relative values of irrigation, hydroelectric power, salmon, water purity, ecosystem health, and the precedence of long-standing native rights. As the western population grows, might we choose to allocate water for beneficial uses other than commercial ones? Might we decide to differ from our western predecessors? Might we think in a more biocentric fashion?

With this notion in mind, I decide to look for biocentric terms in the *Dictionary of Water Words*. Perhaps a book published in 2002 will be forward-looking in more ways than one. So I open the book at random. Page 25 begins with "attenuation" and ends with "average annual flood damages." Nothing there. Page 69—"coal slurry pipeline," and "coastal state." Page 155—"floodproofing" to "floodway." Page 257—"mean annual runoff" to "meandering channels." Page 349—"recessional moraine," "recharge basin," and "recirculated water." Page 431—"tertiary wastewater treatment" to "thermal mass." And so it goes. Looking for flora and fauna, I find none described.

Thinking my sample might be flawed, I examine the even-numbered pages instead. On page 408—"stagnant basin" gives way to "Standard Industrial Classification Codes," a category that surely deserves its capitalization. Page 298—more capitals, as in "Office of Ocean and Coastal Resource Management." But there, at the bottom of page 298, I sight my first biological term. "Old growth," followed by a definition wholly absent of human beings. Page 190 yields another such example, not "groundwater vulnerability" but "guttation." At first glimpse, I don't think "guttation" meets the test, but it does. It's "the loss of water in liquid form from the uninjured leaf or stem of the plant," or "the exudation of water from leaves as a result of root pressure." A botanic function explained solely in biological terms. I'm so accustomed to the human-centered entries, though, that I can't resist wondering—what about human pressure? Might that result in ecological guttation, too? Pressuring myself and Gary Horton, I keep looking for more biocentric terms, but find none. Although it is possible that a few more are buried in the *Dictionary*'s pages, neither biology nor ecology is central to this vocabulary. Rather, the volume iterates its subtitle—*A Compilation of Technical Water, Water Quality, Environmental, Natural Resource, and Water-Related Terms.*

"Environmental" and "Natural Resource" pique my interest, but at this point I know that Horton is using these erstwhile biocentric words in wholly anthropocentric ways. The book simply focuses on the human side of water utilization. Meanwhile, I am finding water consumption concepts that surprise or even horrify me. "Makeup Water" sounds good, but turns out to be "water added to the flow of water used to cool condensers in electric power plants. This new water replaces condenser water lost during passage of the cooling water through cooling towers or discharged in blowdowns." Horton's definition raises two questions. Where does this new makeup water originate? Although the passage implies that such water is readily available, even in excess, I suspect it comes from the same source as the lost condenser water. A zero-sum game, obfuscated by the *Dictionary*. And, I wonder, what is a "blowdown"? Cross-referencing makes a blowdown sound innocuous. It's simply water used to prevent the buildup of solids, of the "portion of a recirculated water stream" that is "run to waste to avoid accumulation of impurities." Avoiding the accumulation of impurities sounds good to me, but the context remains unclear.

Less innocuous is another term I find—the "self-purification factor," which turns out to be "an indication of the ability of a stream to assimilate a waste discharge." There even is a mathematical formula to determine the ratio of the re-aeration and the rate of deoxygenation. Of course, I

don't know what this means, but I can definitely spell out the way the
text assumes that waste discharge is acceptable. The pages treat "waste"
as if it were a commonplace word. As an English professor who always
has been fascinated by vocabulary and by the authorial manipulation of
words and phrases, I am intrigued by the way Horton describes unnatural
functions in natural ways. "Phytoremediation," for example, which occurs
when "plants are used to remediate contaminated sites by removing
pollutants from soil and water." Or "Secondary standards," those "allowable
amounts of materials in air or water" unrelated to human health. Or
"Secondary wastewater treatment," which "is accomplished by bringing
together waste, bacteria, and oxygen in trickling filters or in the activated
sludge process." Somehow, I'm not especially relieved to know that some
unnamed plant might "remediate" an abstract source of pollution, or that
certain "allowable amounts of materials" are immaterial, or that secondary
wastewater treatment involves an "activated sludge process." What on
earth am I drinking?

Suddenly, I tire of the verbal gymnastics. Perhaps a walk along the
Truckee River, Reno's central water course, will cure my indoor blues.
The Truckee rises from the Sierra's Lake Tahoe and ends its hundred-
mile mountain-to-desert journey in treeless Pyramid Lake. En route, it flows
directly through Reno's metropolitan area. Just enough snow has fallen
in the mountains this winter so that the early February flow fills the
Truckee's banks from side to side, yet ricochets downstream in some sem-
blance of a controlled fall. I choose Idlewild Park for my stroll, applauding
again the city's founding fathers who preserved a haven alongside the
river. Over the years, in fact, Reno and her sister city, Sparks, have maintained river access, so that—by following a blacktopped pathway—anyone
can hike or bike or rollerblade from almost one end of the valley to the
other. Old cottonwoods shade much of the walk, which meanders west to
east from a residential setting, through Idlewild Park with its green soccer
and softball fields, along downtown casino-lined streets, past a lonely
stretch often filled with homeless denizens, out to the warehouse district
of Sparks, and then through open acreage (where the waste treatment
plant is visible across the river). In the works are plans to extend the pathway many more miles in both directions.

In the works, too, are plans for downtown redevelopment, a concept undoubtedly applicable to every city in America. In 2003, the Reno City Council authorized a kayak course. Previously, the downtown Truckee River had been captured between cement banks that straight-lined through the city. Now it twists and turns a bit, with routes on either side of slender Wingfield Island that provide whitewater for kayak beginners and racers alike. The north course is more challenging than the south; together they're called Whitewater Park. The construction also allows the river to expand here and there, so the flood danger is somewhat diminished. A rampaging river has been an issue since Reno first was settled at the end of the nineteenth century. At irregular intervals, whenever an exact combination of temperatures and rainfall occurs, the Truckee River blasts out of its channel and spreads across the valley like a shallow lake.

The last big flood occurred in early 1997, after a late December/ early January tropical storm pounded the Sierra Nevada. The "Hawaiian Express," or "Pineapple Connection," as weathermen like to say, dumped rain on the mountains and the city alike. In just six days, the Lake Tahoe Basin generated nearly one-third of its average annual run-off. Downstream, the water flowed at a rate of more than 18,000 cubic feet per second, cresting in downtown at nearly three feet higher than flood stage. Television and radio stations warned citizens to stay away, but of course we didn't. Standing on Sierra Street, I watched the river send waves of dirty water cascading down city boulevards and into city basements. Safely behind heaps of sandbags, I mused that someone could even kayak down First Street, if someone dared. Great sport for someone who lives on a hillside; far less entertaining for downtown business men and women. The legitimate kayak course is supposed to make flooding less likely. We'll see.

This year, though, the river looks healthy. Full enough; not too full. (Two weeks later, still in February, I am revising and extending this essay the day after 1.12 inches of rain fell in Reno, the most ever recorded on the 25th of the month. No flooding, because the cold temperatures brought snow to the mountains, but an episode nonetheless indicative of rapid weather changes that can pound this area at any time. Five more days, and a foot of snow fell in my front yard; five days after that, and outside it's nearly 70 degrees. Because 2004 climatology is unusual to date, I might continue this metronome of weather variations for pages.) Meanwhile, back on the banks of the Truckee.

Almost immediately, I put the *Dictionary of Water Words* out of my consciousness and concentrate instead on the biological constituents missing from the pages. Standing midriver on a rock, a dark cormorant surveys the scene. Stiffly, the bird turns its black head from side to side, watching and waiting. At the same time, a pair of mergansers floats past, taking advantage of the current to sweep them along. Closer to shore, seven—no, eight—mallards drift lazily in a backwash and dip their heads into the water in search of food. Those allowable waste products are nutritious, I guess. Even less exotic than the mallards are the Canada geese that inundate every available patch of park and golf course in Reno and Sparks. They're here, too, honking at each other and waiting for more humans to bring them more stale bread.

Across the river from where I'm walking, the Oxbow Nature Preserve parallels the north bank. A couple of years ago I visited it in the early morning with Alan Gubanich, an ornithologist from the university. He found more different birds in an hour than I might spot in an entire day. A single great blue heron even flapped itself into the air, while tiny rosy finches chattered in the wind. Alan waved his arms in the chilly a.m. breeze, pointing excitedly to first one feathered creature and then another. As our breaths streamed from our mouths, we didn't discuss abandonment or waste water treatment at all. If I had known about beneficial use, however, I might have thought the Oxbow Preserve fits the category.

Actually, I spend a lot of time walking beside the beneficial waters of Reno. And I have to admit that some of those waters developed from allocators allocating. Not far from my house, for example, man-made Virginia Lake offers a tiny bird sanctuary in the midst of the city. A 1930s New Deal Works Progress Administration Project, the local lake is just the right size for human and avian visitors. Dozens of walkers, young and old, usually crowd the mile-in-circumference path and fight the Canada geese for space. A list of the species I've spotted wouldn't take up as many pages as the *Dictionary*'s water words, but the number would be substantial. The 2002 Christmas Bird Count, conducted by the Audubon Society, totaled 93 separate species in the Truckee Meadows, this valley's pioneer and agricultural name, and 113 in 2003, 110 in 2004. The Truckee Meadows was and is a key stopover on the north-south fly-way. Showy snowy egrets, voracious pelicans, ruddy ducks and hooded mergansers, ugly old coots, and more western water birds common and exotic, flock to the river corridor and to other local riparian oases. Rarities come, too, a Eurasian Widgeon last December, for example. Such avian activity counters the notion that Nevada is nothing but empty desert.

But the main waterway, the Truckee River, the magnet that attracts wildlife and birds, today is as mechanically contrived and controlled as Virginia Lake. The *Dictionary of Water Words* defines a "river" as "a natural stream of fresh water that is larger than a brook or creek, has a perma-nent or seasonal flow, and moves in a definite channel toward a sea, lake, or another river." Once a natural stream, the Truckee River was then made unnatural, although it now flows in a quasi-natural state once again. Like so many other western rivers, this one is managed by humans. The amount of water, the speed of the water, the retention and dispersal of that water all are accompanied by a full complement of allocations, oversights, and arguments. The Truckee River, as a matter of fact, exem-plifies how so many waterways in the western United States came to be governmentally designed.

In the opening years of the twentieth century, elected officials were looking for ways to develop previously unarable parts of the West. A number of powerful senators and representatives settled upon water projects as the means by which to realign rivers located in "unsuitable" places, to harness and store water in order to solve the difficulties of unpredictable rainfall, to enable agriculture everywhere. Irrigation, on a massive scale, should effectively alleviate aridity. Thanks to Francis G. Newlands, a powerful United States legislator who held property in strategic, soon-to-be watered spots, the prototype took place in Nevada. In 1902, President Theodore Roosevelt signed the National Reclamation Act, which signaled the beginning of western water projects. The first, the Newlands Project, was authorized in 1903 and came into being in 1904–6. To bring water to the desert and to enable farmers to settle there successfully, the ambi-tious undertaking diverted Truckee River water away from Pyramid Lake and neighboring Winnemucca Lake and into the Carson River Basin. By building two dams, Lahontan along the Carson River and Derby along the Truckee, engineers could rechannel water to the potentially fertile fields of Fallon where farm crops such as alfalfa, hay, squash, cantaloupes, and tomatoes can successfully grow. Upstream storage was part of the design, too, so a series of small reservoirs was built between Lake Tahoe and Reno. In effect, the entire Truckee River basin was re-engineered.

Almost immediately, homesteaders settled on more than a hundred new ranches created out of irrigated desert landscape. Mining camps, like Tonopah and Goldfield to the south, provided ready markets for all the produce these farmers could grow. By 1910, however, the mining played out and so did the need for supplies. At the same time, certain estimates proved mistaken. Senator Newlands projected that the government would net nearly three million dollars in profit. Other analysts expected approximately 400,000 acres to be irrigable. But actual water was available only for about 87,500 acres annually. Spending more and more money in an attempt to make the Newlands Project viable, the government invested nearly eight million dollars in the first two decades. Then auditors discovered that more than half that amount had been spent improperly. After fruitless finger-pointing and investigations—and no profit whatsoever—the federal government decided to cut its losses and turn the operation over to local control. Legal wrangles continue to this day.

Meanwhile, as some of the desert and dollars turned green, the reduced water flow caused radical environmental disruption. By altering the course of the river, the engineers changed the face of the land, especially at the Truckee's Great Basin terminus. Winnemucca Lake dried up completely. Pyramid Lake lost more than forty-five feet of vertical shoreline, as its surface area diminished by nearly twenty-five percent. These lakes were important bird habitat, too. Once a key nesting ground, so crucial it was designated a bird refuge, dried-out Winnemucca Lake attracts no water fowl at all today. Its refuge designation has long since been decommissioned. And even though pelicans frequent the rookery on the pyramid-shaped island that caused John C. Frémont to choose Pyramid Lake's name, a land bridge now forms in dry seasons and gives predator coyotes clear access to the birds.

The Paiute Indians, who claim Pyramid Lake as their own, saw their fish supply shrivel when the native Lahontan cutthroat trout and the cui-ui suckers no longer could swim past Derby Dam to spawn. This tribal economic issue underscores the themes missing from the pages of the water *Dictionary*—the costs in both biological and human terms when beneficial use is dictated by allocators interested in economics instead of native rights. When technicians take over water distribution, politically powerless constituents necessarily suffer. By mid-century, Nevadans recognized the problems created by the Truckee River diversion, but for decades, no one could find a solution to satisfy anyone.

Fortunately, this particular story has a happier ending than many such western sagas. In 1990, another Nevada senator, Harry Reid, brokered a compromise that, while pleasing no one entirely, at least allows everyone a share of the available water. Public Law 101-618, also known as the Truckee-Carson-Pyramid Lake Water Settlement Act not only apportions water fairly among constituents in California, Nevada, and the Paiutes but it also protects and promotes relevant wetlands and fisheries. Upstream dams hold back the allocations until the watermaster can be sure that all parties receive a reasonable share of the resource. Four years after its passage, Eldon Hanneman caught a 21-pound 8-ounce Lahontan cutthroat trout in Pyramid Lake, a measure of the rapid recovery of this previously endangered fish. Another Gary A. Horton book, *Truckee River Chronology*, cites facts and figures for the century preceding the settlement and the years subsequent. Despite equipment maintenance problems and growth spirals along the river basin, the compact, at this point, seems to be working. Future negotiations are necessary, however, if the settlement is to remain viable as water priorities continue to change.

The issues concerning the Truckee River resemble hundreds of other water confrontations and negotiations throughout the West. It includes all the troubled components—tribal sovereignty that was ignored when the project began, endangered fish and wildlife, diminishing agricultural returns, twentieth-century population growth, industrial needs, desirable recreational habitat, environmental issues—that have been prevalent considerations wherever and whenever water projects have been constructed. Where the balladeer croons about a leisurely flowing stream, with bright diamond sand, a graceful white (I suppose trumpeter) swan, and a heavenly (I suppose perfectly imagined) maid, the reality is much less poetic. Dr. Higley, in fact, penned another water verse that has long since disappeared from the familiar version of "Home on the Range."

> Oh! give me a gale of the Solomon vale,
> Where the life streams with buoyancy flow;
> On the banks of the Beaver, where seldom if ever,
> Any poisonous herbage doth grow.

Little did Dr. Higley know what the future would hold!

From the appearance of the first pioneers until today and surely tomorrow, water has been a focal point for conflict and concern. As I think about the Truckee River case, I am reminded not only of the fact that this project preceded all the other government-sponsored waterworks in the West but that a parade of influential politicians staked their careers on intricate manipulations of western water. Francis Newlands, for example, was an organizer and a schemer who firmly believed that conservation meant the proper utilization of natural resources. As his biographer, William D. Rowley, writes, "Development was the key word in the Newlands vocabulary." Arguing vociferously for federal control of all irrigation projects, Newlands concurred with John Wesley Powell, saying that the entire western arid region should be considered as a single unit. State lines, in effect, were meaningless. Newlands disagreed with Powell, however, by romanticizing both the engineering and the outcomes. Repeatedly, Newlands promised that reclamation would allow a yeoman farmer to support his family on ten or fifteen acres of land, an idealistic notion that has never proved to be the case. As a matter of fact, most of Newlands's projections came to be embarrassingly inaccurate.

Even so, his words epitomize the vision shared by many politicians at the beginning of the twentieth century. When asked about the Reclamation Bureau's plans for the Colorado River, he answered succinctly, "Dam it, we must." When considering Hetch Hetchy and the question of whether or not water for San Francisco should take precedence over the sanctity of a national park, he readily sided with those who believed that anthropocentric usefulness should always come first. The importance

of recreational lands and aesthetics, in comparison to utility, was insignificant to men like Francis Newlands.

So how might he evaluate the Truckee River of the twenty-first
century? What might he say about its current beneficial use? In May of
2004, the first Reno River Festival was held on the Truckee's redesigned
banks. Expert kayakers from all over the world vied for prize money in
the Free Style competition and then in the Boaters Cross. On Saturday,
the free-stylers in snub-nosed watercraft showed off for the judges. In
sixty-second intervals, each contestant spun back and forth and upside
down in a single foam pile. The announcer compared the action to an
all-out sprint in place, with required moves such as cartwheels and back
and forward flips, and then free-wheeling, head-popping innovation. I never
quite understood the scoring—which seemed to give points for number
of moves and for difficulty and for acrobatics and for sustainability, and
which seemed to be as obtuse as the scoring for ice skating competitions—
but I've never seen a contest any more thrilling. The man who holds
the title of world champion turned out to be the winner, amassing more
than four hundred and fifty points during his last sixty seconds on the water.

The overall competition reminded me of the Olympics, with unnamed
skating or gymnastics judges marking mysterious cards. I could tell the
talented kayakers from the not-so-gifted, but among the top echelon the
feats all seemed the same. They performed the movements so quickly,
in fact, that I couldn't keep up with the announcers. Like skiers and
snowboarders, the kayakers needed fancy gear—snub-nosed kayaks, brightly
colored jackets and helmets, anything to spike the opposition. Despite
the one-upsmanship and the blatant playing to the crowd, the deadly
serious business of winning was clearly critical. The women were just as
focused as the men. They'd "hop and catch air," flip upside down, pivot
and pirouette, loop in midair. Listening to the announcers, I learned a
whole new vocabulary of water words. The self-explanatory "foam pile"
was one of my favorites, but I liked "Space Godzilla"—an aerial loop with
a ninety degree twist—and "Tricky-whu"—a combination splitwheel and
stern pirouette, too. All the action took place in the man-made "features,"
those rocks artificially put in place to replicate a free-flowing river and to
generate the best white water experience.

On Sunday, the competition grew more fierce. In a Boaters Cross, four or five paddlers start abreast of one another, then sweep down the river simultaneously. This involves elbows as well as paddles, as the kayakers zig and zag downstream. Again, I could see that the most talented tended to prevail, but occasionally one of the pros would find himself cross-current and entirely out of the race. The announcers egged them on, hyping the "carnage," the "combat," the "paddle battle." One of the women kayakers said, "It gets uppity out there." One of the men observed, "You have to deal with the other guy's boat climbing all over yours." The announcers applauded "the big nasty."

Meanwhile, rap music and equipment booths and food and beer turned the Reno River Festival into a water-side carnival. In all the years I've lived in Reno, I don't believe I've ever seen so many people lining the riverbanks and enjoying the surroundings. Thirsty, sun-burned, laughing, splashing, having a wonderful time. What would Francis Newlands have said? I suspect he would have applauded the money-making aspects of the enterprise. For him, the entrepreneurial spirit would have won the day—Fallon cantaloupes and alfalfa giving way to Reno Daggers and Water Waves and Prijons and Lotus. On this day at least, the most bene-ficial use meant kayaking and crowds.

I stopped by the booth of the Truckee River Yacht Club, an ironically-named group of volunteers dedicated to saving the Truckee from further degradation. I asked Susan Lynn, the yacht club's commodore, what she thought of the Festival. "I kind of like it," she smiled ruefully. "Look at all these people enjoying the river." Then she shrugged. "But it's our drinking water. And what about the fishing?" Susan Lynn and Francis Newlands, two quite different voices envisioning Truckee River water usage, are characteristic of their times. Newlands saw the river as the water dictionary might describe it, with all its possibilities for economic gain. Susan Lynn sees it as a green belt bisecting a concrete city, a place where modern urban dwellers can find refuge from all the cement. If I were to talk with a member of the Paiute tribe, even now, he or she would articulate a different concept, one where the cui-ui might prevail. The State Watermaster, still another vision. Indeed, almost no two Nevadans talk about the river in exactly the same way. Nor do they imagine its potential in exactly the same terms. The complex, multifaceted conundrum of water usage in the American West necessarily invites conflicting points of view.

Not long ago I read a new biography of Wayne Aspinall, the congressman from Colorado often labeled Mr. Western Waterworks by his constituents and by his enemies as well. First elected to Congress in 1949, Aspinall represented Grand Junction and the rest of Colorado's Western Slope for twenty-four years. Just as Francis Newlands can serve as a spokesman for early-twentieth-century utilitarians, so Wayne Aspinall can be characterized as someone who articulated the mid-twentieth-century attitudes of many westerners when they were evaluating their natural resources. Progress meant economic growth, and economic growth in the arid West depended on water's beneficial use. When confronted with arguments about the accompanying destruction of irreplaceable scenery, Aspinall's standard response was to say that there were thousands of places in his district every bit as beautiful as those being flooded.

Steven C. Schulte, author of *Wayne Aspinall and the Shaping of the American West*, definitively states that, "To Aspinall, conservation meant careful husbandry, not protection of resources." As chair of the House Irrigation and Reclamation subcommittee, and later as chair of the Interior and Insular Affairs committee, Aspinall played an instrumental role in negotiating most of the bills affecting the Colorado River. And as he grew more powerful, he grew craftier as well. A gifted politician who rarely made the same mistake twice, he almost single-handedly shepherded a long sequence of utilitarian water bills through Congress. Beneficial use, to Wayne Aspinall, was a term archetypically demonstrated in those public water works constructed by the Army Corps of Engineers. Abandonment, on the other hand, was antithetical to his nature.

One of Congressman Aspinall's chief adversaries was the Sierra Club's David Brower. The two went toe to toe over whether or not the Colorado River should be dammed at Echo Park. Brower won. But whenever Aspinall lost a fight, he made very sure that he won the next one. To read about his machinations is to trace the flip side of mid twentieth-century environmental politics, to hear the voices of the engineers and entrepreneurs and the politicians who enabled them. When David

Brower and Eliot Porter produced *The Place No One Knew*, the definitive book of photos and excerpted essays that propagandized the place that was to be inundated with Lake Powell's water, Aspinall replied that if he could take Porter on a western tour, "I could take him into numerous canyons in my district where he could get similar pictures with like narrations." Confronted with Brower's emotional outrage, Aspinall remained unmoved. In the eyes of Wayne Aspinall, places like Glen Canyon "were a dime a dozen in the West." Most environmentalists, myself included, disagree.

I've always been fascinated by the Colorado River controversies, especially the central debate over Glen Canyon and Echo Park. The contretemps occurred, I think, after an accidental series of "what ifs." What if President Franklin D. Roosevelt had not extended Utah and Colorado's Dinosaur National Monument to include uninhabited canyon country east of the archaeological quarry? Then the Bureau of Reclamation's plan to build a 529-foot-high dam within the newly sanctioned boundaries would not have caused such a philosophical uproar about the sanctity of national preserves. What if Bernard DeVoto had not written a forcefully argued article entitled "Shall We Let Them Ruin Our National Parks?" published first in the *Saturday Evening Post*, later condensed in *Reader's Digest*, and widely circulated? Without his argumentative words, perhaps the public would have been less aware of the issues.

What if the Vernal (Utah) Kiwanis Club and a regional booster group, the Aqualantes, had possessed more legislative savvy and more political clout? What if California lobbyists had not spent at least a million dollars, hoping to defeat the Upper Colorado Storage Project? What if the Bureau of Reclamation had presented scientifically accurate evaporation figures for the proposed 6.4 million acre-feet project instead of a series of flawed projections? What if David Brower had not testified before a House subcommittee and pointed out the Bureau's egregious miscalculations? What if Colorado Congressman Wayne Aspinall, Mr. Western Waterworks, had his way?

If all this were true, I could not camp at Echo Park. The setting of what many would call perhaps *the* major environmental battle of the twentieth century, Echo Park is a Pyrrhic victory icon—saved because of a principle, preserved at an incalculable cost. The story is a straightforward one. To protect the sanctity of a designated National Monument, men like Howard Zahniser of the Wilderness Society and David Brower of the Sierra Club argued forcefully and successfully to block construction of both an Echo Park dam and a nearby backup dam at Split Mountain. In order to win, however, they had to sacrifice another irreplaceable portion of the Colorado River, Glen Canyon, so that the burgeoning water needs of those states dependent upon the Colorado River could be met. In part to appease requirements of the popular Central Utah Project, in part to satisfy the Upper Colorado Compact, the conservationists' political and bureaucratic opponents insisted that a series of dams be built somewhere along the river. Unable to construct a reservoir at Echo Park, the Bureau of Reclamation would design Lake Powell and also claim Flaming Gorge.

I personally have always lamented the loss of Glen Canyon, "the place no one knew" that lies buried under Lake Powell's waters. Elsewhere, I've called Glen Canyon a personal touchstone for me, a special spot that symbolizes a West legislatively lost but still alive in my imagination. While I understand and accept the principle at stake when conservation spokesmen acquiesced, I have always wondered about the price our forefathers paid. Since I never knew, and current generations never can see classic Glen Canyon, we'll never determine exactly what vanished under water. I trust John Wesley Powell's initial views of the Colorado River; I partially believe the passionate descriptions written by Edward Abbey, Wallace Stegner, Bruce Berger, Katie Lee and countless others, although I suspect their memories may have been colored by the passage of time. What I can still ascertain first-hand, however, is the fading beauty of Echo Park. With a little effort, anyone can witness exactly what was saved in 1956.

My first view came when, leaning over a metal barrier at Harpers Corner, I peered down toward the confluence of the Yampa and the Green Rivers. The waters of the former cascade through withered rocks of time, yellow and darkest beige; the waters of the latter, through narrow walls of red. The point where the two rivers directly intersect, however, lies hidden behind the enormous prow of Steamboat Rock. John Wesley Powell originally described the "peninsular precipice with mural escarpment," and called it Echo Rock. Later visitors, more impressed by the shape than the sounds, amended the name of the formation to Steamboat. Powell's overall "echo" designation held fast, however, so Echo Park is the common appellation today. Even from my vertical distance, the huge monolith—carved into a stand-alone edifice by centuries of water power—looks impressive.

An immense promontory, Harpers Corner juts out between Echo Park and Whirlpool Canyon and offers a commanding view of Dinosaur country. On the horizon, a skyline of castles and moats marches east and west. I check my map, imagining more details than probably are visible. To the west, Split Mountain and the old dinosaur quarry, hidden from this perspective. To the east, the almost roadless—at least by modern definitions—country of the Yampa, where travel still is difficult. To the north, the Gates of Lodore and Browns Park and Swallow Canyon and Dutch John and Flaming Gorge. Now I wish I'd scrutinized the panorama more carefully. Less than a month after I stood on Harpers Corner and took notes for this chapter, a wildfire swallowed much of the terrain, blackening and charring exactly where I'd camped between Dutch John and Browns Park. On this morning the sky was somewhat murky, but the smoke was blowing in from a distance, from Denver and Durango and Glenwood Springs where wildfires were skyrocketing out of control. The immediate scenery was fire-free—relatively pristine, for the time being.

So were my immediate surroundings. How many cars in the Harpers Corner parking lot? Four. How many people walked out to the point, a distance of perhaps a mile? Five, while I was there. Comparing those numbers to Lake Powell's count of more than three million visitors each year with its annual financial intake of between four- and five-hundred million dollars, I understand the 1950s logic advanced by the Vernal Kiwanis Club and the Aqualantes. This isolated part of the West sought and continues to thirst after an influx of dollars. Even Mr. Harper had a hard time earning a living on the point, and the sheep I saw grazing a few miles back looked almost anemic. More numerous and horrifically healthy were the Mormon crickets that literally covered the pavement. As the Mormon settlers found out in 1845, these beastly creatures definitely have a deleterious effect on economic growth.

More than a hundred and fifty years later, the family ranch is still a tough way to earn a living. Much of the country in this part of southeastern Utah looks overgrazed and unproductive. The local boosters who supported an Echo Park Dam argued that the subsequent water accumulations would provide a phenomenal boost to their economy. Not only would the stockpiled water have supplied precious irrigation for the ranchers and farmers but the ensuing "lake" itself would have brought countless numbers of visitors and dollars. No matter how many people might float the river, my kind of low-cost ecological tourism will never match the industrial impact of houseboats and jet skis and all their necessary accoutrements. Ironically, Vernal's visitor count actually is increasing these days, largely because a blockbuster novel and hit movie, *Jurassic Park*, suddenly made dinosaur bones fascinating to children. The parking lot below the old quarry was almost totally filled with vehicles, compared to Harpers Corner's four, or Echo Park's dozen. Still, this corner of Utah waits for an economic boom that has yet to explode.

Echo Park itself, however, did turn out to be more crowded than I expected. Although the road there is appropriately rough, any high-clearance vehicle, preferably with four-wheel drive, can make its way down the ruts and washes. The popularity of the SUV has brought an increase in visitors to distant places like this. While not every flatlander would relish this particular route—the single-lane track coils off a cliff like a southwest sidewinder—only the first bend is eye-popping steep. After that, sinuous horseshoe curves replicate the twists of the river. I'll attest to the roughness— the tailgate of my pickup truck popped open on the rocky upslope and a lot of camping gear bounced into the dust—but I've driven many many more precipitous byways. Finally, this one straightens out along a bench that has been heavily grazed by cattle, then turns down Sand Canyon as a flooding river would do. All the incipient arches and varnished walls and voodoo shapes so familiar to canyon lovers appear as the cliffs steepen. Below the dry creek bed, Park Service signs point to the noteworthy places. Ancient pictographs, Whispering Cave, the old Chew ranch with its sturdy log cabins, its wayward corral, and a lovely old whitewashed house long since abandoned. The road improves to state route status. I wish I'd seen it all fifty years ago, before the signs, before the protective fence girding Harpers Corner, before the advent of SUVs. I envy my parents, who explored a jeepster Southwest I can never quite replicate.

Arriving at the inevitable modest campground, I find the usual amenities. Picnic tables and sculpted tent spots and fresh running water and the requisite outhouse, positioned somewhat away from the river and out of sight of passing rafters, sit amid the box elders and willows and tamarisks. A close inspection reveals the flaws of what should be a picturesque scene. Past decades of overgrazing have led to meager grasses, trampled now by too many visitors. I am astonished to see only a handful of native plants, and they're protected by wire cages. Trying to take hold in an unfortunately altered terrain, they cannot survive without human aid. How much has changed in this symbolic place, I decide, while arriving campers circle around and around, looking for the perfect site. I watch a tiny bird—a chipping sparrow—circling amid the grasses, hoping to find its supper. Dust blows before the ruffling wind, more dust than I would have found a half-century ago. Sequestered under the shade of an old juniper, I recall Jared Farmer's essay, "*Desert Solitaire* and the Literary Memory of an Imagined Place," where he suggests that Glen Canyon was in fact losing its pristine qualities even as the dam was being built. Too many river runners, seeking one last view of the glen, left too much trash behind. But memory has made the glen sound more and more idyllic as the years have passed. What has happened here in Echo Park would undoubtedly have happened in Glen Canyon, too. The main river corridor would have been loved to death.

I lean back in my lawn chair, and mouth a silent toast to David Brower. Not with gin, as he would have liked, but with Wild Turkey. Not perfect preservation, as he would have liked, but a special place nonetheless.

Wallace Stegner, as part of the campaign to save the confluence of the Yampa and the Green, edited *This Is Dinosaur: Echo Park Country and Its Magic Rivers*, another collection of essays arguing for preservation and disdained by Wayne Aspinall. Each article explores a different facet— the geology, the natural world, the prehistoric inhabitants, the water itself. Stegner's original foreword calls it a "fighting" book, and indeed the pages played a propagandistic role when distributed to members of Congress during the battle over the Bureau of Reclamation's plans. Stegner, the dean of Western American letters, wrote in 1955: "It is a better world with some buffalo left in it, a richer world with some gorgeous canyons unmarred by signboards, hot-dog stands, super highways, or high-tension lines, undrowned by power or irrigation reservoirs." Then he added prophetically, "If we preserved as parks only those places that have no economic possibilities, we would have no parks."

The citizens of Vernal, the nearest town to Dinosaur National Monument, and many park proponents of the twenty-first century would probably turn his pronouncement around. A park without an economic engine may well appeal to mountain climbers, backpackers, boaters, and bicyclists, but such visitors don't spend much money. In effect, a pristine park remains nominally worthless to the locals who need work. A reservoir is a much more desirable economic engine than a free-flowing river. Such is the ironic dilemma of the new rural West, where preservation and development are often at loggerheads, where "developed" natural resources become more inviting than acreage left alone.

Alongside the river, after the Yampa and Green have fused, a broad sandbar leaves space for boatmen to put in and take out their watercraft. With the water low, as in this rainless year, the bar is wide and trampled with footprints. Neither the current nor the wind has scoured it in months. In fact, the Yampa actually is closed to boaters because of insufficient flow, though river-runners are still allowed on the Green. Where I sit would be five or six hundred feet under water had the dam at Echo Park been constructed as planned. What I see before me illustrates the dilemma. Looking up and out, I regard a Steamboat Rock as stunning today as it was when Powell camped here in 1869. Off to one side towers a pipe organ wall, honeycombed apricot and black. Behind me, as the sun sinks in the west, deeper browns and ambers make checkerboard patterns. The back-lit facade looks as if an erratic giant knife had tried to slice different places in the cliff. Seen panoramically, my surroundings are as stunning as any canyon locale anywhere.

Viewed microscopically rather than macroscopically, however, the scene is somewhat less appealing. A motorcycle buzzes around the interior of the campground. A radio carries in the wind an undertone of hard rock music. A father and mother accompanied by their three children arrive noisily in a shiny new SUV. Piling out of the vehicle, they race to the water where they wade briefly—no rapids here—and giggle at their bravery. Then they speed away, having "seen" Echo Park in the space of less than an hour.

I am tempted to conclude that Echo Park wasn't worth Glen Canyon's sacrifice. It's lovely, to be sure, but the spot itself connotes none of the magic I expected. I know I'm not quite being fair, that I'm only looking at the ordinary campground-ness of the park itself, not at the twisting inner canyons where the river runs wild. But even the river doesn't flow as freely as it once did. The Green, dammed at Flaming Gorge; the Yampa, so low it can't be rafted. Would Glen Canyon have fared any better? I think not. So we have to be content with the symbolism, and a river's bend, a riffle, a sandstone steamboat prow, a sandbar, a tiny chipping sparrow, a gnarled juniper, a wall of varnished ocher.

Once more I lift my Sierra Club cup, toasting an Echo Park that's overused but somehow saved, celebrating a David Brower who stood up for a principle, and all the time musing about all the other western water battles yet to come. Given current drought conditions, given the complex prioritizing of water usage, given engineering innovations, given greed—I can only imagine the future disagreements, conflicts, deals cut, and political machinations.

What puzzles me most is the apparent repetition of past mistakes. In Nevada, for example, the same senator who played such a key role in restoring the Truckee River water to its own basin is now touting a Las Vegas scheme to import water from the eastern and central parts of the state. If the importation of Owens Valley water to Los Angeles taught nothing else, it showed the folly of moving water from one basin to another. Yet the pattern continues, in a kind of resource evaporation that always puzzles me. Perhaps a toast is overly optimistic.

But I'm an optimist by nature, and so I'd like to toast Francis Newlands and Wayne Aspinall with cheap red wine, acrid liquid the color of blood. For my communion with the entrepreneurs, the engineers, and the federal bureaucracy, I choose another sort of campground. Horseshoe Bend, a Wyoming marina—if that's not an oxymoron—that abuts the

Bighorn Canyon reservoir backed up behind Montana's Yellowtail Dam. Built in the 1960s, Yellowtail's construction coincided with Glen Canyon's. A highway sign at a local vantage point boasts that the dam "provides hydroelectric power to the region, water for irrigation and opportunities for recreation." While camped at Horseshoe Bend, I planned to take advantage of those promises.

Jack and Carla Rupert, from Michigan, were my campground hosts. Along with their two dogs, they oversee an enclave of sixty campsites, each large enough for a boat, a trailer, and a motor home or two. Horseshoe Bend once contained more than a hundred such sites, but when campers complained about the lack of space for their mechanical toys, C Loop was decommissioned. A well-signed Nature Trail still skirts its perimeter, but now tamarisk and even tiny cottonwoods sprout from the unused pavement. B Loop, still in operation, boasts an eighty-seat amphitheater, with large-screen video equipment, and stone-worked benches that show a careful workmanship. The excess picnic tables and benches from C Loop cluster beneath the lean-tos that shelter B Loop campers from the summer sun. A Loop, where the Ruperts park their Pace Arrow, has more lean-tos, more picnic tables and benches, and the same spectacular view of the Chugwater Formation, a red rock backdrop worthy of Utah or Arizona. Horsehoe Bend, in fact, is a model modern campground, with almost every facility—except showers—imaginable.

The next level downhill from A Loop is developed even further. It houses a full-service marina, plus boat docks and gasoline pumps, more restrooms, gazebos, more picnic tables, plastic-lined trash cans, a carefully-tended lawn, a fully equipped children's playground, and so much parking that there's even an overflow lot. Like the campground, the marina is a twenty-first-century model of its type. And beyond the marina, at the base of the Chugwater Formation, floats the dream destination. When the Bureau of Reclamation's engineers were designing Yellowtail Dam, they imagined a lake of purest blue. They imagined, in fact, what has turned out to be a mirage.

Horseshoe Bend is empty—devoid of water, devoid of boats. Between July 29, 2001, and the late summer of 2004, the launch days there have totaled six. That's *six* days when sufficient water supported boats on the reservoir, if there were any boats to support. I didn't see any. Invasive weeds cover the ostensible lake and the campground stands essentially empty. Only the Ruperts, my truck, and one other out-of-state vehicle took advantage of the facilities in mid-July. "Busiest weekend of the summer was the Fourth," said Jack. "Six groups here for a couple of nights." He shrugged, and went on to explain that he and Carla were leaving in a week. "Not much going on here. Not much to do." While I camped at the Horseshoe, the only thing stirring was the wind.

Like so many other waterways in the American West, the Wyoming/ Montana Bighorn Basin has always been a setting for Anglo-American water schemes. As early as 1900, Mormon settlers were planning a canal system, selling ditch stock and beginning excavation. First the Sidon Canal was built; then, in 1906, the Elk Canal brought service to Lovell— the Wyoming community closest now to Horseshoe Bend. Historian Charles Lindsay outlines the early development of water rights, canal construction, and water usage in the area. The pattern is typically western, although on a smaller scale and at least initially without the federal intervention found elsewhere. For a time, at least, the canal-works were sufficient. But the ranchers living in the basin dreamed of more. By 1932, engineers were proposing a dam for this area, too, although their designs were tabled for thirty years. Finally, in the 1960s, the early settlers' aspirations came to fruition, when the Yellowtail Dam brought large-scale water reclamation to this isolated section of the Rocky Mountain West. In 1967, construction was completed; in 1968, the dam dedication took place.

The dam itself is actually in Montana, although the reservoir backs seventy-one miles into Wyoming and ultimately forms Bighorn Lake— when there is sufficient water. The same overlook sign that boasts of the hydroelectric power, the irrigation, and the recreational opportunities also notes that at normal pool the lake covers 12,685 acres but that a thirty-foot drawdown can move the shoreline five miles away. For several months of the year, even when a drought isn't dominating the weather, the sign acknowledges that the water level may be too low to cover the ground. That's all right, though, because the sign goes on to explain that lack of water provides a breeding ground for amphibians and aquatic insects. I decide that's a euphemism for mosquitoes, and I wonder how a dry lake bed can foster hydroelectric power and provide irrigation and recreational opportunities. Before my eyes, I see only a channelized river, flowing tidily within its banks. Bighorn Lake, in the drought-stricken summer of 2004, seems to be only a figment of the sign's imagination. A figment of the reclamation engineers' imaginations, too, I'm afraid.

Tracing my way back along the reservoir toward the distant dam, I try to find the spot where the river turns into the lake. Not at Horseshoe Bend, where the ghost camp waits for campers who never arrive. Not at Crooked Creek, where another overlook suggests that an arm of the lake once covered a field where wild horses now graze. Not anywhere near town. "How has this all affected the Lovell economy?" I asked Jack Rupert. He shrugged again. Jim Staebler, the Park Service ranger staffing the Visitors Center desk, was more expansive. "Lots of folks expected the economy to pick up," he said. "Lots of disappointment around here." Then he sighed. "Lovell's shrinking. Businesses shutting down. Folks moving away." Brushing back his hair from his forehead, he repeated himself. "Lots of disappointment around here."

At Devils Overlook I finally could look down on a widened, pea-green river. Caught between canyon walls, that section was boatable but empty of boats. Only a meager flock of eight pelicans enjoyed the water. Meanwhile, a tiny ragamuffin herd of nine bighorn sheep grazed placidly nearby, their indifferent attitude as domesticated as the landscape. Farther north, Barrys Landing provides the last accessible boat launch until just above the dam, nearly fifty miles away. I counted five boat trailers. Pieces of dock, freshly stained, were piled along one edge of the parking lot, sitting high and dry. Two would-be floating outhouses sat on the pavement nearby. Jack Rupert told me that a bear had tried to claw its way into a truck just last week, but I saw no signs of life at all. The fish-cleaning station was locked.

Jim described the extreme measures enacted to keep the reservoir as usable as possible. During the winter of 2002–3, the boat ramps had been lowered, allowing launches to continue as long as the water didn't drop too low. Now, even that isn't enough. "7.91 feet to go," he said.

"When the patrol boats can't launch, we shut everything down. Another couple of weeks. Then the whole reservoir will be closed." He added, "The concessionaires pulled out years ago."

Three miles northwest of Barrys Landing, another fancy facility sits empty and unused. The Medicine Creek campground was built for boaters. Half a dozen fancy tent pads were leveled, each site with its own picnic table, lantern hook, and sturdy bear box. In fact, all the trash receptacles are bear-proof, and bear warnings are posted everywhere. I didn't see any sign of bear; I didn't see any sign of humans; I didn't see any sign of water at all. In fact, the tent sites now are accessible only overland. The dock and a gangplank and the necessary cabling lie beached in a meadow filled with more invasive weeds. Tamarisks, already shoulder-high, are taking hold. Other weeds, including an aggressive yellow thistle of some sort, are taking advantage of the soil, too. In fact, where the water once pooled, the ground was richly green, an invasive fuzz that was changing the nature of the landscape as surely as the waters did before.

At Lake Powell, too, an eclectic accumulation of lake detritus has been left behind by the recent drought. A friend spent a week there this summer, working on a clean-up crew, hauling trash from emerging canyons near Bullfrog and Hite. She and her companions took lots of pictures. Their drying lake bed looks just like this one—pale green against red rock, unnamed opportunistic plants surging into the dampness, canyon walls stained with watermarks, towering formations. A natural unnatural place.

As I wandered around the Medicine Creek campground, I wondered about the costs. Jim Staebler couldn't answer for sure, but I suspect the construction of these facilities was not inexpensive. Just as the campground at Horseshoe Bend was luxurious by modern campground standards, so this more primitive version was totally up-to-date. My tax dollars at work. I suppose the construction created local jobs, but I wasn't convinced that the outlay was worth it. The playground facilities at Horseshoe Bend, for example, were fancier than any I've seen in an inner city. And the restrooms obviously were cleaned daily, though no one seemed to be using them but me.

"If we build it, they will come," must have been the engineering mantra chanted subconsciously when the Yellowtails and the Glen Canyons, the Bighorn Lakes and the Lake Powells were built. But they won't come—it seems very clear to me—when the weather warms and the waters fail. Now all of the attached facilities sit idle, caught in a state of arrested decay. In the heat of summer, Bighorn Canyon temperatures climb well over 100 degrees. Without the lure of a lake, few campers seem willing to set foot nearby. I like my campsites relatively uncrowded, so in a perverse way I was pleased by these places. But I kept pondering the costs.

Back at Horseshoe Bend, lifting my glass of cheap red wine and staring out at the drydocked Chugwater Formation, I wondered if I was seeing a twenty-first-century vision of water in the West. Above the Chugwater stretches the Gypsum Springs formation, a source of those wallboards that provide Lovell's current industrial base. Then the Sundance, with its marine fossils. The Morrison, where dinosaurs once prowled. And finally, on top, the Pryor Conglomerate, covering the low range with gravel. All of this geology floats atop a dry lake-bed that doesn't belong there in the first place. The presence of absence, a sculptor might say.

Will every reservoir in the West some day evaporate into the arid air? Will our anthropocentric water words and our memories of Francis Newlands and Wayne Aspinall evaporate as well? David Brower would be surprised; Edward Abbey would approve; many of their followers would be delighted.

I'm left with my toast to the past and the future. It's hot July in a waterless world. Not a soul is in sight, though the no-see-ums assure me that I at least am present. The wind continues to gust through the empty campground, swirling dust and weeds. For an entire evening, I sit alone. In the morning, I hike up above the deserted loops to where I can look at Crooked Creek from another angle. Its oxbow meanders look as natural as can be, as if the lake were only a dream. And so it was. This pale landscape in a sea of sagebrush is the reality. The vanishing water evaporates along with the dreams, the two together lost in the wind.

CHAPTER SEVEN

Home on the Range

Then I would not exchange my home on the range,
Where the deer and the antelope play;
Where seldom is heard a discouraging word
And the skies are not cloudy all day.

"We name it Flaming Gorge." On May 26, 1867, John Wesley Powell and a small party of naturalists and cartographers steered their boats through a stretch of the Green River that flows from what is now southern Wyoming into what is now northern Utah. Flaming Gorge, with its sharp vermilion cliffs and its roiling white water, was spectacular. "On the right the rocks are broken and ragged," Powell wrote in his diary, "and the water fills the channel from cliff to cliff. Now the river turns abruptly around a point to the right, and the waters plunge swiftly down among great rocks." Ricocheting down the river, the men went on to "thread the narrow passage with exhilarating velocity, mounting the high waves, whose foaming crests dash over us, and plunging into the troughs, until we reach the quiet water below."

Sounds of seepage drip from the red canyon walls, an interior waterfall that deafens the river's rush. I tip my head back to survey the sturdy Flaming Gorge Dam rising 502 feet above me. Built by the U.S. Bureau of Reclamation and the Army Corps of Engineers at the same time they were fabricating the edifice at Glen Canyon, this dam looks secure enough. I'm still uneasy, however, about some things I learned yesterday on a visitors' tour. The concrete isn't fully cured, and won't be fully cured for a hundred years. After construction, when the engineers tried to stop the incessant seepage, they found they couldn't. When they added more cement, the ooze just moved farther out to the sides. Water seepage continues today at the incredible ooze rate of 430 gallons per minute! Shifting my eyes up and down the permeable walls, listening to the water draining porously down five-hundred-foot cliffs, I muse about the supposed invulnerability of modern engineering design.

Katie, our tour guide, tried to make our group feel secure. "A million cubic yards of concrete hold back the river" she said, "and the dam is surveyed regularly with lasers. We add more concrete whenever necessary." Her confident voice spewed facts and figures that attested to the efficacy of the arch-style dam, though my imagination kept alive the current seepage rate and the implied ineffectiveness of cement plugs. Katie also boasted about the internal "Selective Withdrawal Structure," an innovation that, by choosing water from various levels of the reservoir behind the dam, keeps the downstream temperature relatively constant. The science sounded complicated to me, but I could see the results—a river habitat perfectly suited to a sportsman's idea of Nirvana. Trout swarmed at the base of the dam like a frenzied mob of subway commuters. A nearby vending machine advertised fish food—twenty-five cents for a handful. Leaning over the railing, I cast a recognizable Pavlovian shadow. Even though I couldn't bring myself to pay a quarter to feed artificial fish food to non-native fish, the trout surmised otherwise. Mostly browns and rainbows, with an occasional cutthroat, too, the fish were as conditioned as goldfish in a pond. Eagerly, they somersaulted below us, expecting to be fed on schedule. Katie continued her spiel, letting us know that twenty thousand fish swim in each mile of the first seven miles below the dam. That's a hundred and forty thousand trout between the dam and Little Hole. No wonder fly fisherman swarm here, too.

On the lake behind the dam, speedboats and houseboats and sail-boats twist and turn in and out of the water-filled canyons, fjords, and bays. But just as Flaming Gorge's geological and political rhetoric is more subdued than Glen Canyon's purple prose, so too are the people who vacation there. It's a family kind of place. I saw more private boats than rentals, found more campgrounds than four-star accommodations, discovered more docks with a single gas pump or two than cumbersome marinas selling ski-jets and fast food.

At the upper reaches of the reservoir, brackish water and a drawn-down band of white detritus especially detracted from the scenery. And the Firehole campground, its distinctive red walls long since lost beneath the water, was shaded by tamarisks and Russian olives, two invasive trees that don't quite belong. I looked in vain for the sandstone amphitheater that Powell so meticulously described in "banded red and green" with "roseate flashes" and "iridescent gleams." Despite the visual alterations, I rather enjoyed the place. When a fierce morning thunderstorm gave way to gray clouds of cotton batting that blew into the shadows of a pale afternoon sun, I could almost envision Powell's easel.

More than a century after Powell's journey, Colin Fletcher published *River: One Man's Journey down the Colorado, Source to Sea*. To describe Flaming Gorge, he chose the phrase "disruption of harmonies." Further amplifying, he wrote, "passed . . . through the cadaver of the magnificent red canyon, whole and harmonious, that Powell had traversed. Its upper walls—all that remained—were still magnificent in their own way. If you looked at the scene without prejudice—that is, without imagination—and could somehow ignore the bleached bathtub ring, it was still a beautiful place. But it was deranged." I sympathize with his choice of words. "Disruption of harmonies" and "deranged" and "cadaver." His thoughts echo my own as I ponder the lake behind the Flaming Gorge dam.

I found an island that exemplifies today's characteristic scenery. Perhaps fifteen feet of white encircled its base, a bleached dead zone so typical of a drawn-down reservoir. Rising from the ring were perpendicular red cliffs, stained with natural weathering and tinctured with lichen. Above the cliffs and all across the top of the unnatural landform that now looks as if it's always been an island, junipers crowded thickly together.

Boaters might draw closer, might pull against the cliffs, might even dock on the far side and picnic there. Because my view is more distanced than Fletcher's, I can ignore the bathtub scour. So the island seems inviting, even attractive. I do enjoy the lake's scenery, I decide, peering at it from roadside pullouts and the ribbon of maintained trails along the rim. I just wish the landscape were more free-flowing and less constructed.

To get closer to the water, I left the man-made lake behind. Below the dam, I could either float the Green or hike the man-made trail that meanders 7.2 miles to Little Hole. Here, ironically, the water looks more like its name than it ever did in the past. Because almost all its silt collects in the reservoir behind the dam, today's Green runs green instead of its once distinctive Colorado red. It runs colder, too. The native fish, the squawfish and suckers and chub, have almost disappeared, supplanted by the trout that thrive in the lower temperature. Moreover, the river runs at a managed depth at a calculated speed. No more dangerous drops and unexpected holes, no "exhilarating velocity." Tourists find a mellow river here, its flow continuous and relatively unforbidding.

As I strolled along the trail, I paused often to sit by the riffling water. I people-watched. Metal concessionaire dories floated past, each with a blue or green life-jacketed guide rowing steadily and one or two orange-jacketed passengers sitting or standing fore and aft. The guide would turn the boat from bank to bank, seeking the best fishing spots that day, while the passengers cast their flies into the rippling stream. Catch and release. Catch and release. If a fish measures less than thirteen inches or more than twenty, it's a keeper. Otherwise, it must be set free. Most of these trout were midsized, ineligible for the frying pan. When I positioned myself correctly, though, I could see larger cutthroat and browns in the tree-shadowed holes along the bank. Catch and release. Catch and release. A great blue heron flexed its wings, caught successfully, and did not release.

As the day warmed up, inflated rafts and pontoon boats grew more numerous. Less fishing, more sightseeing and more laughter. Where the fishermen had been silent and serious, the rafters were more playful. A troop of Boy Scouts splashed happily by, while one-person pontoon hover-crafts spun down the river in their wake. About half-way between the dam and Little Hole, the banks flatten and the underbrush begins to thin. Approaching Little Hole, I almost thought the tide was out. Slime-covered stones mottle the river's eddies, and I even caught a whiff of lowtide odor in the inland ocean breeze. A flood would benefit the Green, I think. It needs cleansing, flushing, and scouring with wild water and fine red silt. It needs more freedom to flow at its own pace.

In 1839, Thomas Jefferson Farnham described how the Green ran through this spot, "sweeping in a beautiful curve from the north-west to the south-west part of it, where it breaks its way through the encircling mountains, between cliffs, one thousand feet in height, broken and hanging as if poised on the air. The area of the plain is thickly set with the rich mountain grasses, and dotted with little copses of cotton wood and willow trees." A plaque on a rock further explains that "Powell's camp site is believed to be located across the river" and cites an entry from George Bradley's 1869 diary. "The camp is green and grassy and our beds are made beneath two noble pines." Today I see a modern "primitive" campsite across the way, populated by campers who must have waded the shallow river. Sagebrush grows down to the stubbled site. A couple of picnic tables, maybe a dozen tents of yellow, green, gray, and beige, strewn gear, dogs, and June grasses bleached tan by the sun. On my side of the Green, an asphalt parking lot leads to a boat ramp and actually paves over most of the river access. A mile from Little Hole, I even found a high-tech woodchip outhouse, one more invention to make the modern wilderness more agreeable. The path itself had been thoroughly engineered, too. Whenever it veered dangerously near the water or crossed a potentially muddy bog, either riprap wire tubes filled with rocks or wooden boardwalks made the route easy. A hiker need never get her feet wet here.

With less underbrush, the river near Little Hole was directly acces-sible from the bank. Dozens of shoreside anglers took advantage of the proximity, fly casting and searching the shadows. I struck up a conversa-tion with two avid fishermen from Eugene, Oregon. "How's the fishing?" I ask. "Already caught two big cutthroat this morning," one brother answers. "Real cows," groans the other. "No fight at all. They just let themselves be reeled in." I joined the two men for a stream-side beer, and the brothers continued their tirade. "Not like Oregon trout that fight like hell! These are just lethargic." "Pretty scenery, though."

So there I was, hiking a carefully designed trail beside a peaceful, temperature-controlled, artificially colored river, watching people cast for farm-raised fish, cogitating an unnatural natural landscape best described as genetically engineered. But people seemed to be enjoying themselves. Even the Oregon anglers relished the mesmerizing catch-and-release routine predicated by lazy well-fed trout. Shading myself under the pink fronds of non-native saltcedar, looking up the blue-green river and down, enjoying this Technicolor day, I suddenly realized what I was seeing. Not the pristine wilderness first explored by William Ashley and the rendezvousing mountain men, not the wild-running river first mapped by Powell and his crew, but something quite different. A new designer West. I call it pay-per-view scenery.

Taxpayers paid for the dam that redefined the landscape of Flaming Gorge. We continue to pay for the upkeep of the dam and for government oversight of the nearby surroundings. We pay for the parking lots, for the well-constructed trail system, for someone to stock twenty thousand trout per mile, for the sweet-smelling outhouse. Many tourists pay even more for their wilderness experiences, levying taxes on themselves to buy fancy gear, rent boats, and hire guides with high-priced expertise. First we pay for reconstructed surroundings; then we pay for the means to enjoy such places. John Muir would be astonished.

But just as Muir paid little attention to the potential impact of visitors in Yosemite, and just as Edward Abbey ignored the marketing draw of *Desert Solitaire*, so do many tourists and writers refuse to look too closely at the implications of one's surroundings. It's easy to forget the artificiality and praise the aesthetics. Ann Zwinger remembers skimming "a clear, deep-green river shot with lines of crystalline sparks, absolutely enchanted canoeing. As we head into the early morning sun, swarms of midges catch the light like spinning gold dust. The river bottom is full of dark green moss; like the upper river, fresh from out of the glaciers, the water is so cold and so swift here that water mosses thrive, almost covering the bottom from bank to bank in some reaches." Her naturalist's eye observes the gravel patches "swept clear by brown trout that are now spawning, a useless gesture as all trout here must be stocked" because the water is so cold that it prevents natural reproduction, but she doesn't belabor the point. Even though she notices how "dried plants plaster the rocks, stranded by the river's present low level," she doesn't complain. Instead, she takes joy in the river's rapids and rolls and flourishes, focusing her writing on the happiness of the experience.

I think her reaction is fairly typical. For every David Brower lamenting the damming of the Colorado, there are dozens of writers who extol the virtues of a Lake Powell or a Flaming Gorge reengineered and there are hundreds of thousands of visitors each year who feel little guilt while enjoying the pay-per-view scenery. This is not to say that Ann Zwinger applauds the damming of the Colorado. Elsewhere, she is quite clear about her environmentalist leanings. Rather, it is to admit that at any given moment, any one of us is capable of enjoying an outdoor experience that has, in one way or another, been modified by an anthro-pocentric hand. I found myself doing so as I strolled above Little Hole, watching both the fishermen and the great blue heron successfully plying their trades. I found myself doing so a few months later, too. I confess my hypocrisy. I not only enjoy pay-per-view scenery but I some-times pay to do so.

At Lajitas, the Rio Grande flows muddily. Like the Colorado, the Rio Grande is a managed river. First, New Mexico drains off so much of its flow that little water remains. Then El Paso takes the rest. Sometimes along the Mexico/Texas border between El Paso and Presidio, almost no water runs at all. When Mexico adds a fresh share from the Rio Conchos, however, the river fills with enough water to float the Rio Grande through Big Bend country. Then Texas River Expeditions happily accom-modates tourists like me who will pay for the experience. Mike Black rowed us twenty miles. From Lajitas downstream through Santa Elena canyon, "Mikey" rowed constantly. Between Lajitas and the mouth of Santa Elena, the river drops only one hundred feet in twenty miles. Without Mikey's muscles to power the raft, we couldn't finish the trip in the limited daylight hours of winter. Paying for my scenic trip, I sat idly while Mikey worked hard.

The Rio Grande flowed mud-brown. The color of sewage, I thought, remembering what I'd been reading about sanitation along the river corridor. It must be tolerably free of poisons, though, because we could catalogue the wildlife. Mexican mallards swam in pairs. Black phoebes cavorted in the cold sunlight. A peregrine falcon, almost invisible, swiveled its head to watch us pass. Soft-shell turtles clattered off rocks, while Mikey's rhythmic splashing and dipping carried us softly down the river. Nine years of Texas drought have dried out the terrain, but fresh pockets of green graced niches near the water. Two kinds of reeds clustered along the edge—one natural, one tasseled and invasive, as lovely in its own way as the non-native saltcedar of the Colorado. I saw yellow trumpet flowers and rock thistle and wattles of mudrock daubed together. I witnessed geology exposed, blueprints of the land.

The route differs somewhat from its historic, and notorious, past. Justice William O. Douglas, in *Farewell to Texas: A Vanishing Wilderness*, quotes a 1905 beaver trapper named T. M. Meler who ran the Labyrinth in Santa Elena canyon. The punctuation and spelling are Meler's own. "SO WEE STARTED in but when wee gott a bot a mile down the river wee come to a rock drift that was 2 or 300 feet hy and the river fun under it. wee unloded our bots & started to packen over the drift. this taden us 2 days to gitt our bots over. wee had to take rops & pull our bots over the top of that rock pile which was 300 feet abuve the water."

Douglas also describes the Labyrinth by narrating the experience of Bud Duncan in 1963, who "was swept violently sideways into a crack between two large boulders, his boat, under the tremendous pressure of the river, bending into a U-shape." Two friends, following in a raft, were then sucked "sideways like a giant vacuum cleaner," as the water pulled them under Duncan's craft. The three men half-swam, half-crawled to a "precarious perch" until their companions successfully used ropes to drag them to safety. Although Douglas never recounts his own personal test of the Labyrinth, he confirms that "Santa Elena, is, indeed, a canyon to travel with the utmost respect." Floating from the slide to the mouth, he accedes, "is a picnic," but he does observe that "I have the feeling of being shut in, of being in a close-fitting box, of being stifled."

What a difference a drought makes. And what a difference to float
on a managed river. Rafting Santa Elena canyon today, especially after a
fresh influx of Rio Conchos water, is not much more challenging than
lolling on an air mattress in a backyard swimming pool. Mikey slid the
raft gently through the infamous rock slide. A whiffle, a turn to the left
and then to the right, a scrape, and we were through the tricky part. If I
hadn't read Douglas's book, I wouldn't have known the river here was
dangerous. Douglas's claustrophobic description of the canyon walls didn't
match my reaction, either. I tipped my head back, straining my neck as I
peered cliffside, imagining the river when summer cloudbursts send
waterfalls over and down the pour-offs. Mikey said that's when he likes
the canyon best. A bit of a coward, I enjoyed benign January. Once
embarked on this twenty-mile stretch of the river, there's no escape.
Between Lajitas and Santa Elena, the country is roadless and empty of
human habitation, the canyon walls steep enough to prevent anyone
from climbing much above the water, perpendicular enough to preclude
climbing out. Guides and park rangers tell of hair-raising mishaps, occasional
rescues and more frequent failures. I am content to let the expert row.

While Mikey maneuvers us downstream, however, I think about my
own hypocrisy. Just as the fishermen paid to float the Green, so I pay to
float the Rio Grande. And I am enjoying myself. Figuratively, I want to
cast stones at pay-per-view purveyors. Literally, it's not all that simple.
I'm actually grateful to Texas River Expeditions—just as I was appreciative
of Hells Canyon Adventures, Inc.—for taking me somewhere I can't see
on my own. I can even pretend this is a wilderness experience, though I
know better. I can pretend, too, that the Rio Grande is a free-flowing
river, though I know better. At least it's sort of the right color I tell myself,
until I remember that sewage. We don't see many people that day.

Twice during my stay at Lajitas, I boated across the river to eat
lunch in Mexico. No passport, no border patrol, no port of entry. Just a man
willing to ferry me across for a couple of dollars and a woman willing to
cook burritos and tacos for the touristos. Another form of pay-per-view
scenery? The local color—the rundown shacks, the crippled ostrich, the
scruffy dogs, the children with the runny noses, the dust hanging heavily
in the air. (My Mexican sojourns occurred in January 2001, when border

security was more lax than it apparently is today. A Texas friend tells me that those restaurants all are boarded up now and no one earns a penny from hungry sightseers. What a loss for everyone, I think.) That day, when I finished eating, I boated back across the river to Lajitas, the "Palm Springs of Texas" as defined by the resort brochure. That's where tourists, captives of security, spend their money in 2005. When I toasted our adventure in the bar, I kept the phrase "pay-per-view scenery" to myself.

As my sabbatical trip lengthened, my hypocrisy increased. After Lajitas, I drove to San Antonio. The incomparable River Walk that defines the city is another engineering feat, of course. Designed during the Great Depression and then implemented as funds became available—construction is ongoing, even today—the downtown canals are no less and no more an example of pay-per-view scenery than Lajitas or Flaming Gorge. This particular designer river flows in a cement-walled format. With restaurants and shops jammed colorfully together, the River Walk is a tremendous tourist attraction. I liked it more than I care to admit. In fact, I preferred it to the nearby Alamo with its movie-set aura and its blatant Anglocentrism. When I asked why the mission wasn't signed in Spanish as well as English, I was told that would be "too expensive." A Texas lady with big hair smirked at my concerns. So, by comparison, the pay per view promenade of the River Walk, like Reno's Whitewater Park, seemed less pretentious to me, more honestly commercial, more direct in its appeal. Nonetheless, I was enjoying a created landscape, a free-flowing stream façade.

And I wasn't home free. On the way back to Reno from San Antonio, I stopped in Las Vegas. I confess that I spent time on the Strip, drawn to the megafacilities and especially the Venetian, a quasi-Italian resort built since my last visit to Reno's sister city. There my notions of pay-per-view scenery came full circle. Inside the casino, a canal system replicating the arteries of Venice flows gently under bridges built to resemble Italian architecture and winds decadently among high-end shops and "open-air" restaurants. I write "open-air" facetiously because the entire panorama is enclosed under an artificial domed sky that changes from day to night, replete with faux clouds and pseudo-sunsets. "High end" is the appropriate adjective to use for the shopping venues, however, because I found imported

Venetian glass for sale, delicate footwear, glamorous fur stoles, quaint baubles, and diamonds and pearls worth thousands of dollars. Ripa de Monti, Mikimoto, Gandini, Simayof. Unlike the banks of the Rio Grande or even the walkways of San Antonio, the Venetian smells of money.

On the meandering water, gondoliers singing grand opera ferry visitors in floating gondolas from one end of the artificial canal to the other. More tourists, listening to the ardent sounds of *Aida* and *Rigoletto*, lean over railings and gawk at the paying customers. Pole and sing; pole and sing; catch and release in a different guise. Of course I wanted to be part of the action. Climbing onboard, I fastened my seatbelt (unlike the flotation vests worn on "real" watercraft, seatbelts were de rigueur here on the Venetian canal) and was ready to go. Umberto, clad in pseudo-Venetian garb—black and white striped T-shirt, black pants and shoes, straw boater with a red band, red sash and red handkerchief—was my guide. A basso profundo with a penchant for whispering sweet nothings between bursts of song, Umberto gently plied his trade. He told stories of his "native" Umbria, romantic tales quite probably scripted by the concessionaire. He sighed. When we paused underneath the Las Vegas copy of the arched Rialto Bridge, he bent down and gently kissed my hand. Then, switching to tales of early Las Vegas, his tone became more lively, his voice more urgent. The Venetian replaced the once fabulous Sands hotel, home to popular entertainers like Dean Martin, Jerry Lewis, Peter Lawford, and Sammy Davis, Jr. Investors built the rich new casino after the faded one was violently imploded with much entrepreneurial fanfare. Umberto chuckled at his reminiscences of the location's glamorous past. With a burst of basso energy, he belted out "Volare," one of the Rat Pack's signature songs. "Volare!"—flying high, fly, fly away. "Ah," I sighed. Pay-per-view scenery with a vengeance.

How many megabucks to land a Green River farm-raised trout in distant Utah? How many megabucks to support a musical gondola on an inland waterway? How many fortunes won and lost? I suppose I might extrapolate further. How far away from the conceptualization of the dam, the reservoir, and the trout playground of Flaming Gorge is the interior canal of the Las Vegas Venetian hotel? How far from a rowing river guide is a poling basso profundo who sings grand opera? And how many people in the new West of the twenty-first century don't know—or don't care about—the difference?

Not long ago I visited the High Desert Museum in Bend, Oregon. The Donald M. Kerr Birds of Prey Center invited me to "get an up-close look at some of nature's fiercest predators." Inside the facility, I found raptors filmed and raptors caged and raptors stuffed. A panel display allowed visitors to push a button and hear a raptor screech or stoop and squawk. Dutifully, I pushed the red-tail hawk button, then listened to the keening sound I hear nearly every day in our neighborhood (the plentiful quail make a delicious smorgasbord for hawks, I'm afraid). I pushed the great-horned owl button, then listened to the hoo-hooing I often hear on my roof in wintertime. The sounds were accurate enough, I guess, but vaguely tinny and out-of-key. And how many people in the new West of the twenty-first century don't know—or don't care about—the difference?

Fee Demo programs are the government's latest pay-per-view gimmick. Initiated in 1996, Fee Demo programs are administered by the Forest Service, the National Park Service, the Bureau of Land Management, and the Fish and Wildlife Service for purposes of bringing in additional revenue. "Congress directed the agencies to use the money to 'increase the quality of the visitor experience at public recreation areas and enhance the protection of resources,'" reports news correspondent April Reese. Although the experiment originally was supposed to last for two years, it hasn't gone away. Because the four land-management agencies increasingly must rely on fewer federal appropriations, they are instituting more and more consumer charges in order to cope with the shortfall.

Estimates of the fee demos' fiscal success vary. The Forest Service believes the programs take in approximately $35 million each year, while acknowledging that the cost of administering Fee Demos amounts to nearly $20 million annually. Most state and local government officials remain opposed to the program, arguing that it excludes low-income residents from enjoying what ought to be free access. Rural westerners, in particular, dislike any restrictions whatsoever on their use of public lands. Urban environmentalists denigrate the program, too, saying it prioritizes public amenities ahead of resource protection. And it's true that the list of benefits cited by April Reese in her 2003 article highlights such things as "repairing picnic tables, installing new fire pits," maintaining trails, installing new outhouses, and digging new water wells. Nowhere does she mention enhanced preservation or conservation.

I checked the federal recreation programs' website, and found a "blueprint" for the Forest Service's Fee Demo projects. The stated goal is clear—"Provide recreation sites, services, and settings that meet quality standards to enhance visitor experience and protect natural and cultural resources." The fine print, however, says little about resource management and a great deal about recreational services. Furthermore, the blueprint never admits that this method of funding was supposed to be an experiment followed by a conclusive assessment of the relative successes and failures. Rather, the blueprint assumes that "appropriations for recreation for the foreseeable future will not be enough to meet recreation infrastructure and service needs." Hence, a Fee Demo program in perpetuity.

Another United States Department of Agriculture link took me to "Accomplishments in Facility Enhancement." Of the five general categories and sample activities that followed, four were directly related to public amenities—maintenance, security and enforcement, interpretation and signing, visitor services and operations—and the fifth was specious. "Accomplishments in Resource Preservation and Enhancement" boasted of "the construction of a river take-out site on the Nantahala River" in North Carolina that not only made the fish "happier because their water is cleaner" but also "more than 150,000 river users are happier because their vehicles and gear are less muddy." While this example isn't a specifically "western" instance, I think the point is clear. When we pay per view in a fee demo situation, we are spending our money for anthropocentric rather than eco-centric purposes.

I could write pages and pages describing various examples of Fee Demo areas. Indeed, I've been taking notes throughout the West. Most often I've encountered parking fees. On a busy Fourth of July weekend, for example, I went hiking in Utah's Logan Canyon. It cost three dollars to park in the black-topped lot adjoining Tony Grove; the restrooms were free, although they clearly were state-of-the-art. My friends and I hiked through meadows and wildflowers up to a rolling ridgeline, then dropped down to White Pine Lake. Clouds overhead assembled and disassembled, as if the weather couldn't decide on sun or rain. Many strolling families appeared unable to decide, too, as they started up the trail with children and grandparents in tow, then chose not to tackle the elevation loss and gain necessary to complete the hike.

Still, the place was filled with Utahans out to enjoy the day. When we returned to the parking lot, we couldn't see a single empty spot. At the rate of three dollars per car, I tried to calculate the profit, but of course couldn't factor in the overhead costs. No matter, the Forest Service was making money. A few vehicles were parked just off-site, drivers and passengers hoping to avoid the charge. Even though a warning sign announced a $100 fine for noncompliance, I didn't see anyone enforcing the edict.

Was this jammed parking lot a successful Fee Demo demonstration? I don't know. As I say, I didn't see any ranger personnel to ask. It's hard to argue that three dollars is excessive, and it's hard to dispute the fact that a well-used area like Tony Grove needs facilities adequate to serve a burgeoning crop of visitors. On the other hand, we pay taxes, in part, to sustain public lands and public services. But what sufficed in the past may be insufficient in the years ahead. Surely this is the sort of conundrum that needs evaluation and assessment.

Hunting policies are changing, too. No longer can sportsmen enjoy the open range in the ways their unrestrained nineteenth- and early-twentieth-century counterparts did. Since I am not a hunter—although I'm an enthusiastic consumer of whatever anyone brings to my freezer—I'm not familiar with current fish and game regulations. But I recently had an opportunity to tour a western mecca for affluent hunters. Ted Turner owns thirteen ranches that model his commitment to the preservation of bison and to the expansion of the current bison population. Even so, those herds need to be culled, and even Turner needs a cash in-flow to support his wide-ranging western enterprises. So at certain times of year, he selectively invites well-to-do hunters onto his land.

Purchased in 1989 by Turner, the Flying D was the communications mogul's first big enterprise in the West. Comprised of more than 113,000 acres, it abuts the Spanish Peaks Wilderness south of Bozeman in central Montana. Two major streams provide plenty of water for the Flying D—Spanish Peaks Creek, which flows into the Gallatin River, and Cherry Creek, which flows into the Madison. From the high divide between the two drainages, I could see across nearly thirty miles of Ted Turner property. Below, in the "big valley," hundreds of bison placidly grazed.

With deep soil and good moisture and plenty of open space, the Flying D provides natural bison terrain. Mark Kossler, general manager, explains the current operation. Approximately every two months, modern-day "cowboys"—many of them women, all riding four-wheel ATVs—push the herd from one of eight 18,000-acre pastures to another. This movement mimics the natural bison pattern, where a herd would freely and widely wander in search of fresh forage, and allows for a period of high-density heavy grazing, followed by a longer period of rest. Mark shrugs his shoulders. "Yellowstone bison, worst overgrazing in the West. Into the dirt."

Rightly proud of his operation, Mark continues to explain Flying D Ranch ecology. "Bison are just like people," he says. "They'll eat the ice cream first, then the mashed potatoes, and leave the broccoli behind." I could tell he had recited this spiel dozens of times to dozens of tour groups—the ranch is off-limits to casual passers-by—but I nonetheless enjoyed his analogies. The hands try to move the herd with as little disruption as possible, though occasionally the bison balk. "We use burning and salting to move 'em along." The former pushes the herd in a certain direction; the latter pulls them. "But basically we stay out of their way," Mark stated firmly. Bison are smart creatures of habit. When disturbed, "they're a big fast mean horned ungulate!"

The bison hierarchy is matriarchal. A lead cow tends to step out in front, drawing the rest of the herd along. On public lands like Yellowstone, the gender ratio is about twenty cows to one bull. Here at the Flying D, the ratio is more like 1.5 to one because Turner wants to sell hunting opportunities—and trophy heads—every year. "Part of the carrying capacity here includes wildlife," Mark reports. In fact, there is a high economic payback for trophy hunting. Or, as Mark prefers, "a controlled harvest" rather than a hunt. The ranch remains economically viable because of this income.

Other wildlife on the ranch includes grizzlies, wolves, wolverines, mountain lions, bobcats, and whitetail and mule deer. Essentially, the Ted Turner goal is to "turn the clock back," to return the entire property to its pre-ranching condition and to encourage the proliferation of native species. After he bought the blocks of acreage that make up the current spread—some sixty or eighty inholdings—Turner tore down most of the interior buildings. He left the roads intact, although many of those roads gradually are disintegrating from disuse. He also left a few buildings around the perimeter—like the ranch house where Mark Kollmer and his family live—but generally the structures were destroyed when the properties were consolidated. I did spot one faded old schoolhouse, though, standing in isolation on a gentle slope, and asked why it was left untouched. In the flattening shadows of the autumn afternoon sun, it looked lonely and quaint. Apparently, Turner agreed with my description. As the buildings were being demolished, Mark was told to leave this one alone because it's "romantic."

Bison prefer a wide-ranging "view shed," a distance where they can see for miles. The Flying D suits them perfectly. So do Ted Turner's other properties. All together his ranches cover some two million acres and are home to some thirty-thousand cow bison. That is perhaps a tenth of the total number of bison in the American West today. Turner takes pride in the health of his herd. They're regularly vaccinated—Mark again casts an aspersion toward the Yellowstone herd, noting their propensity for brucellosis. Turner bison sold to restaurants are even grain-finished, although Mark says that he himself prefers eating grass-raised heifers. "We sold five hundred head last year, individually marketed, to a repeat clientele." A big grin lights up his face.

"It's a narrow line to walk," Mark points out, "to manage the land in ecologically sustainable and economically viable ways." He adds, however, that "we can only turn the clock back so far." Homesteaders planted timothy and smooth brome, which effectively took over the range. To eliminate these grasses would be impossible. Mark argues for "bio-righteousness" — as close as we can get to the ecology of the past.

I stepped away from our tour group and looked over the blonde rolling hills. Early snow already tinted the distant Spanish Peaks. Closer at hand, the yellowed grasses waved in a slight wind, and October clouds crossed over the sun. I remembered that the bison we passed a few miles back were already heavily coated for winter. The small herd glared at us, flexed their muscles, refused at first to get out of the way. I agree with Mark—those cow-calf pairs looked healthier than any bison I've ever seen anywhere. Thirty to forty acres per cow apparently provides a pretty satisfactory supper table.

This range looks healthy, too. A stringent conservation easement means it will never be subdivided, that the Ted Turner Foundation will manage the land in perpetuity. Many westerners disdain this arrogant consumption of acreage for private purposes, but I find myself less anta-gonistic. Mark's tour remarks have been persuasive. Pay per hunt doesn't seem so egregious after all. And haven't I just paid for this tour on the Flying D? Culpability once more.

In fact, I would say that this entire chapter reveals my own complicit participation in the economic forces endemic in treating the New West as a personal playground. Every time we city folk set foot on rural or public lands, we're driving an economic engine unimagined a hundred years ago. I'm not just talking about wilderness and wildlife, either. Paying customers are altering the farmlands, too. Around Walla Walla, Washington, where lima beans and corn and apple trees once thrived, fields of grapes abound today. Why? Because consumers like me enjoy fine wine, and the boutique wineries of the Walla Walla valley are ready to supply the demand.

I recall no wineries at all during my Whitman College days (and I'm sure we would have noticed if local wine had been available). In 1974, Gary Figgins remembered the tastes of his youth, when Italian emigrants Frank and Rose Leonetti fed their young grandson tiny sips of diluted homemade wine, and decided to plant a hillside with a little white reisling and cabernet sauvignon grapes. In 1978, Leonetti Cellars produced its first hand-crafted wine. The result was world class. My cousin's husband shared one precious bottle—as fine a full-bodied cabernet as I've ever tasted. Now more than fifty-five wineries can be found around Walla Walla, and more are being designed each year. I have visited only a handful, but I can attest to the uniform excellence of their products. Downtown, and within walking distance of Whitman College, I found Waterbrook and Forgeron Cellars. Driving a ways, I stopped at Pepper Bridge, where Tim, an energetic young man with contagious enthusiasm, extolled the soon-to-be benefits of a new adjacent tasting room. At Bergevin Lane, Annette, clad in a GAP T-shirt, showed me the vats and barrels lined up side by side. Out by the airport, I visited Dunham Cellars and Buty Winery, where a young couple are embarking on a new winemaking enterprise all their own. Everyone seemed to know everyone else, everyone took pride in his or her vintage. I happily tasted and paid, recognizing as I did so that this was a fortunate (rather than unfortunate) instance of pay-per-something in the West. Back home in Reno, I'm still enjoying my purchases.

Walla Walla, indeed, has changed. Located in the southeastern corner of Washington state, this is now a vacation destination not only for wine-lovers but for tourists who admire outdoor sculptures. On campus, as well as throughout the downtown area, a wide array of metal and ceramic artistry pose in front of buildings and along the streets. My favorite is called "Matilde on her way to the market." Designed by Nano Lopez in 2003, Matilde is a huge ox standing in front of the public library. She's carrying multiple fruits, vegetables, an iguana, a parrot, a frog, and a host of other exotic creatures. A chromatic rainbow of yellows and turquoises, Matilda epitomizes this community's change from general agriculture to boutique eclecticism. In many ways, the rest of the West is following the same pattern, at least where consumers and customers drive the economic engine. Matilda, ox turned art, is an emblem of that change. She may even be an abstraction of Ted Turner's bison and Flaming Gorge's trout. They're exactly the kind of Fee Demo twenty-first-century creatures that populate pay-per-view scenery.

If we accept the notion that we enjoy pay-per-view scenery in today's West, we must also admit that we visit such playgrounds with pay-per-play accessories. John Muir managed to scale California's tallest peaks with little more than a wooden walking stick for balance and a loaf of bread for sustenance. He took pride, in fact, in his minimalist mountain sojourns. The first Yosemite climbers scaled Half Dome using stiff, heavy ropes. Without benefit of springloaded cams or lightweight anchors, they relied on their climbing companions' bolts and belays for safety. Early skiers herringboned uphill, used skins to climb higher still, glided down ungroomed slopes cluttered with protuberant rocks and trees. When my parents tried to describe the thrill of riding the first rope tow, years and years before chairlifts arrived on the scene, I scoffed. In fact, I was embarrassed by their equipment—the clunky wooden skis, the cable-spring bindings, the hand-knit sweaters and caps. But for their generation of outdoor adventurers, fancy gear was unimaginable. Today's mountaineers, however, head for the hills laden with costly accoutrements.

Not long ago I surveyed a local purveyor of twenty-first-century high-tech equipment. Reno Mountain Sports is the kind of locally owned specialty store often found in communities catering to tourists and out-door aficionados. They sell their wares to anyone who wants the latest fashion or function, and to anyone who can afford such products. Twice a year—after ski season and late in the summer—much of the merchandise goes on sale, so I've been in the store looking for fleece bargains many times. But I've never actually perused the "hardware." What an eye-opener to someone who doesn't climb and doesn't kayak, and whose backpack is nearly thirty years old. What an eye-opener, too, to someone who remembers going to REI in Seattle when she was a little girl. My father had a membership card with only three digits; the shabby store, crammed with wooly paraphernalia, filled a single upstairs room. That was then, and this is now.

Given the age of my pack, I began my excursion through Reno Mountain Sports by looking at possible replacements. My favorites were the Ospreys, which not only come in S, M, and L with various carrying capacities but come in multiple series, too, from the "full feature pack for the serious backpacker" to the climbing and "cragging" and "snow play" packs for high-altitude mountaineers to the "everyday packs for active people." Each series boasts a name designed to attract an eager buyer. Crescent and Luna, Aether and Arial—those are the full-feature ones. Eclipse and Switch for the "active adventurer"; Vertigo and Ceres for "climbing alpinism"; Helios and Synchro for the casual consumer. As the website explains, the latter "stand apart in a world of boxy, cluttered book bags with no personality." The Vertigos, on the other hand, are packed with "all the features (but not the gimmicks) that every climber will appreciate." Relieved to learn these packs were gimmick-free, I did, however, wonder how "gimmick" might be defined. Compared to my tawdry old Alpenlite, these packs looked fairly gimmick-laden to me, with side pockets and zipper-expanders and extra attachments galore.

Actually, a single customer could buy three or four Ospreys, one for every weekday and weekend activity, and could choose a variety of spectacular colors, too. Bright oranges, lurid yellows, and electric blues, colors to be noticed, colors to stand out rather than fade into the scenery. Like a sixty-inch digital flat screen television set, these Ospreys are simultaneously functional and showy, practical and sexy, blending ostentation with utilitarianism in a way that characterizes much of the latest alpine gear. Like so many other items of gimmick-less equipment, these Ospreys are not particularly inexpensive, either.

My first pack was a hand-me-down Trapper Nelson with a wooden frame and a canvas packsack. Ill-fitting and heavy, it was absolutely serviceable. I hauled it up and down dozens of mountain trails, and never worried much about the fact that it wasn't shaped for a woman's body. By comparison, Ospreys' Luna Series is "specifically designed for the relatively shorter torsos, narrower shoulders and tighter curves of the feminine form." Its "flexible configurations" let a female backpacker choose frame, harness, and hipbelt sizes independently. Trapper Nelsons, as I recall, were sized big and bigger. And they were khaki drab, army leftovers guaranteed to camouflage anyone. My current backpack isn't that archaic, but the external frame dates it badly. So does the color, an earthtone amber that blends into any hillside anywhere. I suspect my pack isn't as comfortable as an Osprey, but I've never felt the need to replace something that's given satisfactory service. It figures. Just as my television screen is a retrograde nineteen inches, so my backpack reminds me of my parents' skis. Fortunately for Osprey, most consumers are not as frugal.

Enormous technical advances have been made in the sleeping-bag segment of outdoor gear, too. The most significant happened years ago, when Polarguard and Qualofil replaced kapok as the synthetic filler of choice. Down has always been the staple of heavy-duty winter bags. In fact I still have my mother's, a boxy affair with a heavy cotton cover that weighs far more than it should. Like most serious campers, I have two perfectly adequate sleeping bags of my own—a two-piece fiber-fill for summer temperatures and a sleek down one for the rest of the year. By looking at Reno Mountain Sports' new bags, though, I could see that my bags' shapes are out of date. An outfit called Big Agnes declares itself "the mother of comfort," designing bags for people "who believe that only long deceased pharaohs should sleep mummy style." Big Agnes also has created a complex layering system of bag, pad, and open hoods. Such a combination, the company reports, will allow the customer to create "a versatile year-round quiver that you can pluck from based on trip and temperature needs." Their down bags even have a bag-length pocket, where an insulated air core pad—today's euphemism for yesterday's air mattress—can be inserted easily. As with backpacks, it seems that today's sleeping bags and pads are only distant relatives of their ancestral origins.

I like the catalogue language that invites the consumer to pluck treasures from a well-stocked quiver. Big Agnes goes further, though, offering narrative explanations of all its products. "When a storm builds on the high plains of Wyoming and drops into northwestern Colorado it starts rolling just like an out of control semi. When it slams into Mt. Zirkel, you don't want to be there." But you do want to be tucked inside a Zirkel sleeping bag, the prose insists. "A sleeping bag with the name Zirkel has a lot to live up to. It demands superior quality and cutting edge performance." Or perhaps a camper would prefer something lighter, the catalogue suggests, a synthetic bag named Whiskey Park. "During the 1860s train crews rode the tracks of Northern Colorado in fear of Indians holding them up. During one particular run to deliver barrels of whiskey to the mountain town of Hahns Peak, the crew unloaded and buried their valuable cargo in what is now known as Whiskey Park. It is said that the whiskey has never been recovered." While it is unclear to me exactly what the story has to do with this particular sleeping bag, it surely intrigues the customer. Might I find whiskey hidden between the baffles?

I envision out-of-work English teachers hunched over word processors, backcountry equipment stacked by their sides, weaving stories and creating imagery that will compel buyers to buy, mixing their diction and syntax with inspiration and perspiration. How can anyone resist the Horse Theif (misspelled on page 9 of the 2004 Big Agnes catalogue—perhaps the copyeditors are not English majors, after all) or the Lost Ranger named for "one of the most inhospitable spots anywhere," or the Little Red "for young campers in training?" Big Agnes catches my attention in a big way.

More than the catalogue copy, however, I relish the various Series—capital S—with their flamboyant labels. Across the aisle from the packs and bags, I found the Camelbaks. Hydration packs are a recent invention to eliminate all the difficulties inherent in lifting a bottle of water to one's lips. Instead, a hiker or climber or snowboarder or bicycler can carry a pack filled with water, can sip through a siphon and leave his or her hands completely free. "Drink on the Move" is Camelbak's catch-phrase; "bite and sip," its mantra. The series names suggest a range of possible Camelbak conditions, from the mundane—Classic, Rocket, Siren, Rally—to the more exotic—SnowBound, Snow-Bowl, SnoDAWG, H.A.W.G., M.U.L.E., Peak Bagger, Rim Runner, BlowFish, TransAlp, StoAway—to the quite picturesque—Dry Trekker and FlashFlo and Un-Bottle. Hunters not only can choose Trophy, or Upland, or Woodland but may also select the appropriate shade of camouflage. So can the military, whose options include Sabre and Stealth and Ambush and Hot Shot. I am not making this up! Camelbak's website intimates that they welcome direct orders from all branches of the armed services.

Most Camelbaks, however, are more commonly red or glowing orange or blue. In fact, much of the hiking and backpacking equipment is tinted alike. The Nalgene water bottles, for example, show up in hot pink and chartreuse, as well as in rainbow shades of red, yellow, orange, blue, and green. There must be a shibboleth intoned by every equipment manufacturer: "If we color it, they will buy." I'll admit that these bottles are far more attractive than the metal canteens we used when we were kids. Perhaps more utilitarian, too, since a dropped Nalgene water bottle is generally quite visible. Still, I wonder why no one chooses gear that blends into the landscape? I bought a new backpacking tent about three years ago. It's show-stopper yellow. My old 1980s tent was beige and gray; I never could find it after dark.

Because I have a new one, I didn't spend much time with Reno Mountain Sports' tent display. I took time to admire the layout, however. Not only were tents set up on almost every piece of available floor space but they also hung upside down from the ceiling, like rip-stop bats clinging to the rafters. Technical advances have enabled manufacturers to design "superlight" tents and poles quite superior to the tarps that we strung between trees in the 1950s. Mountain Hardwear brags about its Easton aluminum alloy poles, "hardened to 96,000 psi for strength and rigidity and anodized for corrosion resistance and durability," a "nylon ripstop with silicone-coated outer and poly-urethane coated inner" fly, a canopy with "a special exterior titanium dioxide membrane that protects the fabric from UV radiation," zippers of "polyester coils, and durable nickel-plated sliders," shock cords of "natural grade rubber . . . wrapped in cotton, silicone-dipped, and sheathed in durable nylon." Thinking about my teenage camping days, I can recall long afternoons and evenings hunched under a sagging wet tarp. I remember digging trenches alongside my sleeping bag so water wouldn't pool, and swatting mosquitoes when I wasn't tightening the ragged lines holding the tarp semi-taut. Looking at today's tents, with their utilitarian accommodations, I wonder how and why we managed without aluminum alloy poles and UV protected membranes and polyester zippers. Considering the early settlers' amenities, which were even more sparse, I wonder how and why the West was ever settled by anyone.

The pioneers' food, for example, must have tasted awful. Diaries tell us of the monotonous diet—whatever could be shot, somehow mixed with flour or beans, washed down with muddy water. Nowadays, we treat our water for a host of unpleasant germs, and we use it to rehydrate a range of backpackers' food unimaginable even half a century ago. Chicken Polynesian, Tomato Chipotle Pasta, Teriyaki Beef, Shepherd's Pie with

Turkey, Leonard de Fettucini, Turkey Tetrazzini, Tequila Chicken, Kung Pao Chicken, Mountain Blackberry Cheesecake, Mixed Fruit Yogurt Mousse, Chocolate Hazelnut Bavarian Cream, Chocolate Peanut Butter Pie, Deep Dish Peach Crumble, Bananas Foster, French Vanilla Mousse, Taos Black Bean Relish. I'm back to catalogue rhetoric again, but I find the names quite tantalizing.

I came of age just as freeze-dried backpacking food came into being. Kiskees, a long-vanished Portland firm, was experimenting with dehydrated options. While I no longer can recall any of the erstwhile exotic names the company used to disguise the sameness of the dinners, I do remember that none of them was particularly palatable. However, I still think fondly of a lemon custard pudding mix that made dreadful puddings but wonderful snow cones. We carried it everywhere, dousing snowbanks with the yellow powder and gorging ourselves on the results. I suppose Chocolate Peanut Butter Pie or Chocolate Hazelnut Bavarian Cream might be just as satisfactory, but I'm not convinced.

Maybe it was the wood-smoke flavoring that distinguished so many of those youthful concoctions. Living in the Pacific Northwest and backpacking before the sport became a fad, I never imagined carrying a camp stove. There was always plenty of downed wood—sometimes dry, sometimes altogether too damp—to throw on an open fire. After a trip, our clothes reeked of smoke and our pots were blackened with soot. Even though we soaped the outsides of our cooking gear, a dark greasy residue still coated the pans. Stoves might have been a blessing, but we didn't know the difference. It's been years since I've cooked on an open fire in the mountains, years since I scrubbed a set of charcoaled pots. Even so, the most recent cook stove innovations are amazing to me. MSR—Mountain Safety Research—sets the standard. I actually own an MSR stove, an elderly version of the new Whisper Light that uses gas or kerosene. Mine can be highly temperamental; the new ones are supposed to be foolproof, or so the catalogue says. The newest MSR stove, the Pocket Rocket, uses a propane canister instead of liquid fuel and is even simpler to use. But what is most amazing about the Pocket Rocket is its weight. Three ounces. Three ounces! Of course the fuel canister adds to the load, but the idea of a three-ounce stove is astonishing.

When I think of the relative weights of today's backpacking gear, I understand why so many more people are drawn to the sport. Mike, the man who was demonstrating all the Reno Mountain Sports gear for me, told about a fellow who completed a California through-hike on the John Muir Trail last summer and carried less than ten pounds at a time. "Of course you give up something when you go that light," Mike pointed out. For sure, I thought to myself—warmth, decent food, real shelter, just about all the creature comforts. And yet, a ten-pound pack sounds mighty appealing.

Continuing to relish the comforts of home, I browsed next through the hangers of clothes. Shorts and shirts for every activity, rain and wind gear, a whole room full of ski pants and sweaters and parkas left over from last season. Most of the clothes looked as if they'd best fit an underweight eighteen-year-old, but that's another essay. Many of the outfits would be as stylish indoors as outdoors, and all of them were designed with comfort in mind—well, eighteen-year-old comfort, perhaps. Henry David Thoreau, more than a century and a half ago, warned readers about such excess. "We don garment after garment," he wrote in the "Economy" section of *Walden*, "as if we grew like exogenous plants by addition without. Our outside and often thin and fanciful clothes are our epidermis or false skin, which partakes not of our life, and may be stripped off here and there without fatal injury." Thoreau clearly would have appreciated neither Gramicci nor Royal Robbins. Writing "It is desirable that a man be clad so simply that he can lay his hands on himself in the dark," Thoreau underscores his strong opinions. He would surely have disdained today's Gore-Tex and Polar-tec options. Most of us, however, appreciate the moving comfort.

My favorite clothes are made by Patagonia, a firm with a local connection. Its huge mail-order warehouse and a conveniently cluttered outlet store sit alongside the Truckee River in west Reno. From the fleece vests to Capilene underwear, even at reduced rates, Patagonia clothes are more expensive than similar brands, but each item is made in an ecologically sound way.

The Patagonia on-line catalogue explains the company's rationale. "To us, quality means more than how a garment looks or functions: It also includes the way it affects the environment and quality of life. This means working to source materials and develop processes that minimize damage to the environment." Organic cotton is only the beginning. The company's goal is to create "a fully recyclable garment." For example:

> In 1993, we adopted fleece into our product line made from post consumer recycled plastic soda bottles. We were the first outdoor clothing manufacturer to do so. PCR clothing was a positive step toward a more sustainable system—one that uses fewer resources, discards less and better protects people's health. Today, we use PCR fleece in about 31 products, and we've saved some 86 million soda bottles from the trash heap. That's enough oil to fill the 40-gallon gas tank of the diminutive Chevy Suburban 20,000 times.

The website goes on to explain that PCR filament yarn is comprised entirely of waste products, of "post-consumer" and "post-industrial feed-stock," utilizing not only soda bottles but also polyester uniforms and polymer factory waste products. The website also brags about Patagonia's commitment to environmental activism. The company donates ten percent of its pre-tax profits to grassroots groups "who take radical and strategic steps to protect habitat, wilderness and biodiversity." Money spent on Patagonia clothing, the company line infers, is money well spent.

The website, in fact, buys into another Henry David Thoreau admonition. "The childish and savage taste of men and women for new patterns keeps how many shaking and squinting through kaleidoscopes that they may discover the particular figure which this generation requires to-day. The manufacturers have learned that this taste is merely whimsical." Ah, words of wisdom from an 1854 prognosticator. Counting the number of Gramicci shorts and pants in my closet, I recognize that my personal kaleidoscope of color and fabric and design fully mimics Thoreau's warning. As in so many other ways—though he could not have foreseen the thousands of clothing options available today—Thoreau saw into a future that has come true. How might he have reacted to the Patagonia productions?

Like many of its peers, Patagonia also puts a personal face on its products. The catalogues and the website are filled with personal anecdotes about the men and women who work for the company and about their personal adventures in the out-of-doors. "Patagoniacs," they call themselves, "an eclectic bunch." Morlee Griswold, the director of direct mail, is a University of Nevada graduate who grew up in the Silver State, where her great-grandfather was one of the earliest governors. Since she once was a student of mine, I searched out her profile—"a mail-order maven turned itinerant kayaker," the website reports. The Spring 2004 Patagonia catalogue includes an essay by Morlee that describes the nine-day World Kayak Surf Championship competition in which she competed as a member of Team US West. "The water is more bubble than liquid," she writes. "I drop into 'The Zone.' The crowds on the cliff become inconsequential and the other competitors vaporize. It's just me, my boat and my paddle." Because I've known Morlee for more than twenty-five years, I readily visualize her version of "The Zone." I still remember a wild drive through the desert in her tiny VW bug, bouncing along a washed-out road as if it were zoned for highway speeds. I also can picture her words floating through the imaginations of nameless Patagonia catalogue readers, psychologically drawing them into a bubble that not only buoys up their spirits but also compels them to buy the products available. A *Mademoiselle* or *Esquire* narrative for grown-ups, I believe, promising glamour and success.

The Petzl catalogue that advertises climbing equipment goes even further, using the magic of poetry to lure its readers into a make-believe world of physical prowess. After I graduated from college, I attempted to succeed in that kingdom of alpine enthusiasts. I signed up for the Seattle Mountaineers' basic climbing course, dutifully attended every session, practiced diligently, passed the written exam, flailed my way through the physical tests, and then vowed to never climb again. I actually was quite proficient on the beginner routes—the ones a foot or two off the ground. But incipient acrophobia got the better of me whenever I was clinging to a cliff. Forcing myself to practice falling on belay was absolute torture; rappelling into an icy crevasse was even worse. My career as a climber was very short-lived.

Opening the Petzl catalogue of acrophobic attachments confirmed my decision. In its pages, however, someone might suffer psychic seduction from the poetry that accompanies the hardware.

If no barriers . . .
Behind the sum of doubts, dream:
Use solar sails.
Ride the strings that curve space.
Follow the magnetic tides
on the trajectory of a particle of energy.
Each barrier that today seems to pin us to the floor of the universe
Will be lifted, maybe, tomorrow.

If I use Petzl products, no barriers will prevent me from achieving my goals. Mixing my metaphors—solar sails, tides, trajectories, floors, and universes—I will succeed. Uneasy about a "trajectory" that might "pin us [me] to the floor," I find my decision to forego mountain climbing reaffirmed. The images continue to bombard me, knocking the "barriers" out of the way.

As so many barriers have been lifted.
And as still continue to be lifted
The sum of doubts and non-responses,
That are replayed between the climber and the terrain.
To use solar sails?
To follow magnetic tides?
On the tangible scale of a simple rock wall,
We are capable of exploring our whole universe.
And of endlessly transfiguring it.

I'm having trouble parsing this one. "And as still continue to be lifted /The sum of doubts and non-responses?" My non-response is to be puzzled. Dumbfounded by the oxymoronic notion of more solar sails and more tides beating themselves "on the tangible scale of a simple rock wall," I'm glad I don't have to teach this particular poem to a group of college sophomores. Photographs of spiderwebs, of leaf veins, and of a climber ascending a vertical wall accompany the verse, while the preceding page sells prusik pulleys and the following one advertises Petzl's carabiner range. As in the Patagonia catalogue, Petzl's sales enticement alternates the sublime and the mundane, juxtaposes the dream defined and the devices for getting there. Aspiration is the watchword; accomplishment, the goal; rhetoric, the cloud-cover of the real. The prosaic lines cannot be parsed. Rather, they iterate a seductive dreambeat that promises endless transfiguration, whatever that might be.

Between the carabiners and the harnesses, another poem marks the way. This time, the visual design is end set, each line braced against the right-hand margin, as if the goal were predetermined while the achievement pathway remains open to everyone. A bold-faced "**Other suns**" invites the catalogue reader into the text.

> **Other suns**
> To set out.
> To go toward.
> To leave for.
> Not just to watch others setting out.
> To take ones [sic] own turn to set out. To leave for. Not to stay.
> To set out to sketch the outline of new worlds.
> To give a name to the changing and the unknown.
> And also to gather the Lost and the Distant
> Into the fold of the tangible and the present.
> To set out.
> To go forward.
> Toward other plural suns.
> To set out.
> To go away.
> To go forward to worlds whose name the mind does not know.

Although I may question the melodiousness of this verse—and the lost apostrophe suggests again that diligent English teachers may not have been involved in the creative effort—I hear the intentional rhythm, the drumbeat of "to set out" repeated over and over again. On this page, the photographs are more directly human—hikers trekking somewhere, a truck hauling their gear, a letter box in a foreign country. However, a luscious blood-orange horizon fills the opposite page, balancing the poetic delineation. Again, every image propels the customer forward, urging him or her to seek "the plural suns" while at the same time subliminally suggesting that Petzl equipment will pave the way. The poem's one-liners eliminate complexity, too—although my Microsoft grammar checker doesn't like the ways they parse—their meanings as simple and direct as a climbing route to the top, or so Petzl would have the consumer believe. "To set out" is to achieve, especially with the proper Petzl gear. A cynic might interpret "To set out" as synonymous with "to get out" one's credit card, but this is poetry, after all.

Clearly, this catalogue was not cheap to produce. With color panels on almost every page and with almost as many pages devoted to ambient pictures and poetry as to products, here is a "medium is the message" kind of sales pitch. And even though the verses are neither sophisticated nor complex, they get the point across. With Petzl hardware, the consumer can go absolutely anywhere. Dreams, reality, it's all the same with Petzl.

When Mike showed me the latest climbing gear at Reno Mountain Sports, he explained that the creation of the cam was the single most important climbing innovation in recent years. Spring-hinged, a cam anchors itself in ways that even I might find secure. Mike showed me how a cam works, and we both laughed at my attempts to describe one. An artificial claw for a bird of prey; a bouncer's brass knuckle (singular); a tinker toy on steroids. Finally, Mike sent me home with some catalogues so I could learn more about these innovations. But when I opened the Petzl catalogue, I found no cams at all. Fernand Petzl, a metal worker who also was a canyoneer, began developing climbing and rappelling tools in the 1930s. The catalogue lists his "incredible series of technical 'firsts': the first device for protecting rappel descents, the first climbing harnesses, the first headlamps with the battery case carried on the head." It doesn't mention cams. Are they too enabling for Petzl heroics? I need to find out.

The Metolius catalogue contains cams by the dozens, in various shapes and sizes. It pictures other climbing treasures, too. Super chalk, for example, and waste cases containing trademarked Pooh Powder and refillable WAG bag kits. An editor once told me that Ten Speed Press's best-selling book was the one titled *How to Shit in the Woods*. I guess Pooh Powder and refillable WAG bag kits would render that how-to text totally obsolete. Still, it's intriguing to find such a fixation in an otherwise romanticized venue. Metolius's catalogue is fascinating for another reason, too. It devotes more than twenty pages to artificial holds—screw-on corners and plates and rails and modulars and grips that can be mounted on indoor climbing walls, so the climber need never venture outside at all. They're for practice and conditioning, of course, the climber's version of a treadmill, but I must confess that I am as dismayed by indoor ascents as I am by the adjudication of bodily functions. I guess I ought to adjust my image of out-of-work English teachers generating catalogue copy. Instead, I imagine a much larger seven dwarfs' workshop, where engineers happily design slinky toys for grown-ups. Alongside those artful contrivers, incipient poets are hammering gimmicks, and everyone is singing harmoniously, or recycling rounds.

Given both the designers' and purchasers' propensities, almost every mountaineering necessity eventually gets refurbished or reengineered, leaving the old equipment obsolete. The continuous upgrading of hiking and climbing and bicycling and skiing gear feeds into today's consumer-driven marketplace as effectively as Palm Pilots and cell phones with photographic capabilities. We willingly pay per play, eager to sport the latest gimmick as we enjoy the out-of-doors. "No gimmicks," Osprey boasted, but who can argue with the weight of a three-ounce stove, or the efficient comfort of a fleece vest made from plastic soda bottles? Who can disdain cams and carabiners, or a mosquito-proof tent and gourmet food? I might make fun of the impulse to buy, but I eagerly peruse the REI and the Sierra Trading Post catalogues when they arrive. I know there's room in my closet for another pair of boots.

With pay-per-view scenery and pay-per-play gear, we are changing the nature of our wilderness experiences. When we rearrange the landscape so that the red Colorado turns green and trout flourish where warm-water fish used to thrive; when we rely on guides to take us into grizzly corners of the West and outfitters to safely negotiate the rapids; when we spend hundreds of dollars on fanciful boutique clothing and perhaps thousands of dollars on colorful, lightweight, high-tech gear; when money and merchandizing finally dictate the relative success of each outdoor adventure— then we have turned the experience of wilderness into a commodity. When we pay per view and pay per play, we pay—I think—a higher price than we might imagine.

Refrain: The Owyhee

Home, home on the range,
Where the deer and the antelope play;
Where seldom is heard a discouraging word
And the skies are not cloudy all day.

L ike any small child, I loved throwing objects into water. At Kalaloch alongside the Pacific Ocean, I would heave driftwood into the waves and watch the tide carry the gnarled wood out to sea. At Summerland in Canada, I'd skip flat stones across the surface of Lake Okanagan; five, six, seven times, they'd bounce. At Hood Canal, I'd roll rocks upside down into the salty foam, just to see tiny crabs disperse in every direction. At Green Lake in Seattle, I'd toss pebbles into the stagnant water, and watch concentric circles grow into larger rings. If *Oh, Give Me a Home* has a design other than the touchstone verses of the old traditional song, that pattern might be called concentric circles, as though words had been tossed onto the land and repetitive rings had been the result.

The thematic repetitions themselves say something about the American West—that it is a distinct philosophical place where certain motifs splash and circle, disperse and reform anew. Pioneer notions of making homes in the wilderness have become contemporary thoughts about how we might make the remaining "wilderness" hospitable to its flora, to its fauna, and to ourselves. Skies glitter; precious metals gleam; forest fires glow. Pesky tamarisk and tumbleweed can roll into any scene. Condors, bison, turkeys, elephant seals appear and disappear and reappear again. Water tumbling freely down a mountainside can flatten into managed reservoir waters, can change the shape of drops into new sorts of aquatic playgrounds. From San Francisco to Seattle to San Antonio, distinctly western communities welcome new generations of urban dwellers, while Lake Tahoe and Big Sky invite new tides of "rural" residents, too. Although none of us will embrace all the variations on a theme, there's continuity in the repetitions, comfort in the concentric circles. The balladeer repeated his chorus after every verse of "Home on the Range." I want to repeat my refrain only once, in Owyhee country, where so many patterns of the West can ripple into word splashes and teleological rings.

The Owyhee is that isolated spot where Nevada and Oregon and Idaho all come together on the map, where perhaps ten thousand people live permanently, and where city dwellers like me love to explore and want to protect. After three Hawaiian fur trappers got lost there in 1818, other white explorers began referring to the region as the Hawaii canyon country. But, as so often happened in the empty West, someone couldn't spell. So Owyhee the place became, and the Owyhee it remains. It's the largest unprotected roadless area in the lower forty-eight states, more than four million acres of solitude and sagebrush and splendor.

The early years of the Owyhee contained all the stuff of legends. Volcanic eruptions and massive lava flows set the stage. Pioneers arrived; the Indians rebelled; a bloody massacre resulted. Then a gold and silver strike generated Silver City, a boomtown that became a ghost town that now attracts thousands of vacationers and gawking tourists. There was a military presence in the old days, and a haul road built in the middle of nowhere. The family ranches in the Owyhee have been handed down for generations. One of the West's largest herds of California bighorn sheep lives there, too, as do nesting eagles. Salmon even used to swim in this desert, until dams barred their spawning routes. Away from the water, miles of sagebrush, tumbleweeds, and sand comprise spectacular scenery that

includes one of the deepest canyons in North America (and one of the
most desolate). So spectacular is the Owyhee, in fact, that it has now
become the focal point for what is known as the Owyhee Initiative, a
comprehensive land-use policy put together by a coalition of conservationists, ranchers, scientists, and politicians. If the Owyhee Initiative becomes
law, the compromise may be a model for future planning, with its ripples—
its agreements and its disagreements—felt throughout the American West.
If it fails, the misfire will signal how far apart remain the distances among
western political, economic, and environmental points of view.

More than 14 million years ago, molten lava lay underneath the region.
A series of eruptions and land shifts carved gorges where the Owyhee,
the Bruneau, and the Jarbidge rivers flow in deep rhyolite-walled canyons.
"It's the largest exposed basalt area in the world," says Spencer Woods, a
local geology buff. He describes the nearby Swisher Mountain flows as
"world class stuff." Gesturing broadly at our surroundings, he explains
the current theory about a glowing Neocene "hot spot" that moved east
from Fort McDermitt to Yellowstone at a pace of about an inch a year.
The Owyhee, with its upturned geological landscape, was right in the
middle of the hot spot's path. Looking around me at the remains of
molten rock and ash, I find the cataclysm hard to imagine. A thousand
times greater than the 1980 eruption of Mt. St. Helens, one bio-pic
brochure proclaims.

   After the fireworks subsided, plants and animals took advantage of
the rich volcanic soil left behind. Fossils indicate such species as the
saber-toothed salmon, scimitar-toothed cats, giant beaver, grison, coyotes,
wolverine, and horses. Although the exotic creatures have long since
disappeared, many significant fauna remain. The current animal population includes not only what might be expected but also most of the
rare species indigenous to the sagebrush West. Biologists call the Owyhee
good "anchor" country, where California bighorn, sage grouse, Columbia
spotted frogs, loggerheaded shrikes, and ferruginous hawks all successfully cling to life.

   But not every endangered species has survived. Cynthia Yates, an
aquatic scientist, described for me one facet of human interference. The

Owyhee dam, located south of the confluence where the Owyhee River runs into the Snake River, was finished in 1912. At the time, it was the tallest dam in the country. Before its completion, Chinook salmon spawned upstream all the way to Tuscarora, an ersatz ghost town in northern Nevada where several well-known artists now live. After the dam was built without a fishladder, no salmon could return to their spawning grounds. Rainbow trout were planted to replace them. Today, the species composition in the river is totally different than it was in the nineteenth century. "Now it's mostly bass and carp," she said, grimacing. "And bull-frogs. An invasive species," she added. "Near where the river flows into the reservoir, there are more bullfrogs than you can count." Cynthia talked about grazing, too, and described the strategies used to satisfy the ranchers and the increasing numbers of rafters and vacationing visitors who don't want to encounter cumbersome herds. They move the cattle by March, "one year on, one year off."

Despite such public lands management, further ecological disaster is pending. Non-native plant seeds from cattle and excessive ORV use are degrading the Owyhee bluebunch wheatgrass biome. As might be expected, cheat grass, Russian thistle, and tumble mustard are "the main culprits," although whitetop, knapweed, and yellow star thistle are increasingly present, too. These invasive weeds not only "out-compete" the native plants for water and habitat but also "inhibit" wildlife feeding and reproduction. Moreover, their presence is affecting the natural burn frequencies in the Owyhee, reducing the recurrence of fire "from a historical rate of every 60–110 years, to a devastating 3–5 year cycle."

Inside the Owyhee Country Historical Museum, I saw pictorial evidence of the most recent large-scale conflagration. The Rough Diamond fire blazed out of control in August of 2001. Six planes, including two giant C-130s, dropped a steady stream of water and retardant on the flames. One museum wall is covered with sequential pictures of the burn and the aerial firefighting support. Labeled "even in disaster there is beauty," the photographs show an "empty" landscape devoid of human communities, yet so despoiled by overgrazing that it is vulnerable to rampaging fires and then dependent on a human presence to put those fires out. The naked beauty of the pictures seems to me a tacit commentary on the land itself.

Actually, humans have been present in the Owyhee for perhaps fifteen thousand years, although Europeans discovered the place only a couple of centuries ago. While fur trappers and avid miners entered the canyon depths to seek their fortunes, others stayed on higher ground. The Snake River plateau became a major route for pioneers heading from Fort Hall to the Oregon Territory. I find it hard to believe that one of the grimmest nineteenth-century pioneer calamities took place near the banks of the Owyhee River. In grade school we learned about the Whitman massacre at Washington state's Waiilatpu mission site, but we were never taught about what's called "the Utter disaster." In 1860, a small group of families and dragoons set out from Fort Hall, even as they fretted about the Indians who had tormented local travelers for the past two years. Sure enough, a band of Snake Indians soon surrounded the small wagon train and began stealing cattle and food. Before long, the Snakes attacked the embattled party directly. A gunfight erupted. Twenty of the travelers were killed, another six died later, and four were kidnapped by the Indians and never found. The remaining twelve stumbled away without food or water. When tracked down by rescuers several weeks later, the survivors were consuming the human remains of their relatives in a scene reminiscent of the Donner party debacle fourteen years before.

Everyone, I think, has heard of the infamous Donners; few, I daresay, have heard of the Utters and their companions. This says something about the way we westerners perpetuate sensationalism. When an event takes place in an out-of-the-way location, far from newspapers' prying reporters, the details well may vanish into history. The Donner survivors ended up in Sacramento, where news could be dispersed rapidly. In the distant Owyhee, communication was sparse. Lieutenant Marcus A. Reno, of later Little Bighorn fame, discovered one group of bodies "unburied, showing marks of torture, too develish for any human beings to inflict except Indians." Captain Frederick T. Dent found the dozen who endured, plus five partially consumed corpses, a "scene of horror." These cavalrymen wrote little about their findings; the survivors either chose not to tell their macabre tale or recalled the debacle imprecisely in later years.

I tell the story of "the Utter disaster"—labeled that, I think, because of the hyperbolic ring of the words—not only to point out the desolation of the Owyhee country then and now, but also to underscore the paucity of knowledge about the indigenous tribes of the region. In my research, I could find a whole book about the sensational debacle, *The Utter Disaster on the Oregon Trail*, but only subchapters and vague allusions to the native presence. The lack of Owyhee Indian stories, other than lurid ones, clearly reflects a nineteenth- and early-twentieth-century purview when "the red men were pressed from this part of the West." Mike Hanley, in *Owyhee Trails: The West's Forgotten Corner*, mentions the Bannocks and Shoshones and Paiutes and Snakes more than once, but always in a violent context. His chapter titled "The Tribes Strike Back" ends in telling fashion—"gradually, by the end of 1868 the Indians were subdued, temporarily at least, and their lands opened for grazing. As the word spread, it brought in the cattlemen . . . ." Hanley does describe one more uprising a decade later, but after the two chiefs were killed "the hostiles scattered in small bands." The narrative of his book then quickly returns to the "more significant actions" of the area's mineral and ranching enterprises.

Once, when camped at a place called Three Forks, where the main branches of the Owyhee River converge, I heard Mike Hanley talk about the old fort that used to be there. Indians hidden in the buttes would fire hot lead down on the soldiers holed up inside. Mike told us that we could find bullets in the rocks, or at least bullet holes and chips and chinks, if we climbed up the basalt spires. Thirty-six Indians killed, maybe. Rather like Massacre Cave in Canyon de Chelly, I thought to myself as I listened. He pushed his white felt hat back on his forehead, brushed his stringy blond mustache with a forefinger, then solemnly nodded his head. "Dangerous country hereabouts," he said. "Three years ago one of my buddies drowned, right over there, moving cows off the river." Pushing at his hat again, Mike continued with more stories of settlers, of sheep-herders and cattlemen, of strike-it-rich dreamers attracted by the lure of Silver City in the nearby mountains of Idaho, of the wives and children who made the Owyhee their home.

Ledges of both gold and silver were discovered on the sides of War Eagle Mountain in 1863. Almost immediately, miners and shopkeepers laid out a Silver City townsite. At its outer edge they placed the powder storage, safely distant from where the church, the school, the hotel, the cemetery, the meat market, the brewery, the mansions, the Masonic Lodge would be located. All these places remain visible today because Silver City has never really vanished. Even after the mineral productivity diminished, a few people stayed on. Vacationers were drawn to the area, and many families have spent summers there for generations. My friend Ken Langton, for example, accompanied his grandparents to Silver City when he was a boy, still owns their summer residence, and still vacations there himself. When I visited Silver City, the old Stoddard house — a mansion really, ornately decorated with gingerbread trim — was being auctioned off. I never learned the sales price, but later heard it would take millions more to make it habitable. Something about the sewage. But the action drew dozens of bidders who filled the local old hotel that weekend.

Interesting Buildings in Silver City, Idaho, a guidebook published by Helen Nettleton in 1971, takes tourists past aging and refurbished houses. Reading history while I walked among them, I noticed two very different sites. One was Our Lady of Tears Catholic Church, which originally had seventeen cathedral windows of leaded glass until vandals broke them out. Today, the church remains in service, opening on certain summer days that are announced well in advance, although not when I was there. Ironically, the Brewery Vat, though long unused, is equally well-preserved. Painted white with bright red, yellow, and green trim, it sits not far from the abandoned Hawes Bazaar and a meat market closed behind intricately carved doors. Apparently, the beer was quite tasty. Mike Hanley writes that the "Queen City," Silver City's moniker, boasted ten brothels in its heyday, but I could find no evidence on site.

I camped in a campground at the edge of downtown, where Chinatown used to be located and where I was surrounded by ORV and ATV enthusiasts. These people — mostly kids, their parents, and a lot of retirees — take their recreation seriously. The militaristic machines were gun-metal gray, camouflage, and khaki brown. Flying American flags fore and aft, they growled up and down the dirt roads left behind by the mineral exploration. The noise at times was deafening. It's tempting to generalize about the participants riding on the mountain. Their mechanical toys looked brand-new, while their camping equipment and their trailers looked old and well-used, jerry-rigged almost. Futuristic machinery; ancient personal gear. Not even any helmets. The lanky men and round women, who might be unfairly characterized as outdoors workers and indoors homemakers, seemed to have spent their recreational dollars differently than my friends and I do. These vacationers were more utilitarian than I, actually using the landscape whereas I was just tiptoeing through it. Two consumptive Wests, perhaps the nineteenth century juxtaposed against the twenty-first.

I walked along the dusty streets, and thought about what I was seeing. By Central City, Colorado, or Virginia City, Nevada, standards, this "city" isn't overcrowded. If Silver City were closer to a large population center, like Denver or San Francisco, it surely would be a boutique resort. However, only Boise and its environs are close at hand. And in the winter, deep snows deluge the place. With the advent of snowmobiles, the winter analogue of summer's sporting vehicles, Silver City is more accessible now, but blizzards still dictate who goes where and when. So, too, does land ownership circumscribe Silver City's development possibilities. Some of the area is still under patent by mining corporations, while much of the remainder belongs to the federal government. Only by purchasing something like the Stoddard mansion can a newcomer buy into the scene.

Meanwhile, mining continues to play a major role in this part of Idaho's Owyhee County. On the road to Silver City, I drove past the biggest earthen dam in Idaho, a set of tailings 255 feet high that holds minerals, rather than water, in suspension. I understand the DeLamar Mine, owned by NERCO, eventually will be 330 feet high, with a capacity for twenty million more tons of earth. So even though the diggings on War Eagle Mountain are long since defunct, and the accompanying mine at Ruby City long since washed out by floods, mining is still critical to the rural Idaho economy. As it remains throughout the twenty-first-century West.

East of Silver City, the road winds between earthtone rocks twisted like cinnamon crullers or French braids before dropping steeply down to the distant dry plateau. My memory of that drive, however, summons up the invaders more than the natural terrain. Mormon crickets almost completely covered any exposed dirt. So called because they inundated early Mormon settlements, these insects have voracious appetites. They even eat each other. Driving over them, I could hear their bodies tinkling against the side of the truck as the tires squashed them into a gummy paste. So many smashed Mormon cricket corpses actually make a road slippery. Elsewhere I've had fun slithering from side to side, seeing how many of the ugly creatures I might destroy at a time, but here the drop-off was too steep for such nonsense. Instead, I kept the truck at a slow and steady speed, and thought about animal incursions.

The West, in part, was born of ranching. Most observers would say that sheep and cattle are a natural part of the landscape, now, though many would argue that the numbers are no longer cost-effective. Owyhee country is rich in this vein of history. For the old-timers' stories I turned back to Mike Hanley, a fourth-generation man who has heard many a tale about the cattlemen and the Basque sheepherders who fought for subsistence. Their successes and failures differ little from the highs and lows encountered everywhere throughout the intermountain West. Floods and drought, governmental encouragement and federal interference, outsiders and insiders, feast or famine. Early on, when native grasses still prevailed, the ranching was quite profitable. Longhorn cattle, trailed in from Texas, proved to be a sturdy stock that adapted well to the high desert. Then the snows of 1888–89—later called the "Great Equalizer"—obliterated whole herds and forced many ranchers out of business. Throughout the West, in fact, that monumental winter wrought economic devastation. Sheep followed next, especially in Jordan Valley where the Basque language almost seemed "the town's predominant tongue." According to Mike, widespread moonshining provided a steady income, too. Many Owyhee sheep and cattle operations stayed marginally profitable, until Prohibition ended and the 1930s brought both the depression and new federal guidelines for the ranching business.

Mike writes at length about the Taylor Grazing Act of 1934, which forced changes in the ways cattlemen and sheepherders could access the public lands. Indiscriminate use was no longer permitted, and grazing was severely reduced. Where ranchers had considered the open range their own, governmental rules and regulations now decreed otherwise. Mike's father, for example, was restricted from 613 animal units per month (AUMs) to 386. The Bureau of Land Management "put the clamps on

the ranchers," Mike summarizes. After that, he opines, "livestock must give
way to wildlife and lovers of the out of doors." Nonetheless, ranching
remains an important way of life for many men and women who call the
Owyhee home.

> Out where the skies are a little bluer,
> Out where a friendship's a little truer,
> That's where Owyhee and the West begin.

writes Mildretta Adams about this special place, as she idealizes the landscape around her. Like her fellow versifiers on the opposite end of the
state, she views Idaho as the best of all possible worlds.

I wish I could quote an Owyhee poem that includes the word "home";
I'm sure there must be one somewhere. The closest correlation I could
discover locally, however, invokes a different sort of sanctuary. Titled "In
the Owyhee Sage Hills" and penned by Esther Brubacher, it nonetheless echoes the words and values of the other rural verses I've found.

> Out in Owyhee's sage clad hills,
> A little graveyard stands,
> Builded by the Pioneers
> With work-worn loving hands.
>
> Its flowers are the sage's bloom
> Its music the winds that play
> Along the crosses gleaming white
> In the night watch—and the day.
>
> I've stood at night in the moonlight
> By these graves out in the west,
> It seems there is given unto these
> A place of tranquil rest.
>
> The winds they blow more gently here,
> And sometimes here, at night,
> A little bird sings plaintively
> From the wooden crosses white.

What matter where we sleep at last,
Love is the same and true,
Whether in marble vaults or here,
Where sage is wet with dew.

"Builded by the pioneers," and flowered with purple sage, the cemetery becomes a place of safety, solitude, and "tranquil rest." If this is a dirge for those pioneers who have passed before her, Brubacher also acclaims the Owyhee as a loving sanctuary, an eternal home-place for those who connect with the land. Present-day explorers would agree.

Stepping carefully, I shoulder my way through Great Basin wild rye that occasionally closes over my head. Although cattle have grazed this Owyhee canyon for years, they no longer stay put, so the trailing herds haven't done much recent damage. I spot only desiccated cow pies, find no fresh ones underfoot. When I'm not ducking my head through the grasses, or looking for traces of cattle, or making very sure I'm not putting my foot down on a sleeping rattlesnake, I catalog the flowers. One perfect desert primrose, for example, and hundreds of whites and yellows and pale lavenders. Orange mallow, and creamy buckwheat. Frosted green sage, a different variety than I've seen before, with soft nubbins like flaccid walnuts. It's late spring, and tiny bits of color stipple the greenery of this so-called dry desert scene.

A dozen paces away, the east fork of the Owyhee River parallels my meanderings. In this year of drought, the water runs remarkably shallow. After wading across, I sprawl on a bank of grass and look back on the blackened basalt cliffs to the west. Against the greenery of spring-time that tints the arcing curves of most of the landscape, the rough-ened cliffs stand ominously dark. I imagine basalt zippers on a green velvet dress, zippers placed by an errant seamstress who cannot straighten out her work and so tries again and again until the material is puckered piecemeal, caught by her ancient Singer. Big country, as far as I can see. A red tail hawk sweeps overhead, and yellow-headed blackbirds cater-waul nearby.

Does this particular spot qualify as wilderness? Not according to the strictest definition, the 1964 Wilderness Act that separates wild landscape from human intercession. Between the river and the closest cliffs, a dilapidated old road winds sporadically up the grade. Where it hasn't fallen in on itself, carefully constructed rockwork holds the track in place. Back across the river, a little farther upstream, another section of road still navigable by four-wheel drive twists down to the water. An old toll road, the route was built in 1866 so mail could be moved, supplies hauled more cheaply from Sacramento, and, most important of all, so bullion could be carried west from the thriving Idaho mines. All these tracks indicate man's presence.

My truck is parked where the old fort once stood. After driving twenty or thirty miles on a dirt road—maps and odometers disagree—I camped alongside more than a hundred other Owyhee enthusiasts who had come to Three Forks for the same reason. We are attending a Sierra Club rendezvous sponsored by club chapters in Idaho, Nevada, and Oregon and co-hosted by the Sierra Club High Desert Committee. A website and e-mails invited us to "join desert enthusiasts and newcomers to experience the natural wonders of the Owyhee Canyonlands. Come connect with the land and the people working to protect this very special treasure in Oregon's high desert." In small groups, we trekked up and down and in the river by day, then all the activists joined together in the evenings to hear more about this suddenly crowded wilderness study area.

Roger Singer, a Sierra Club staffer then based in Idaho, handed out brochures and gave us some facts and figures. Overall, the Owyhee is a nine-million-acre ecosystem. He repeated what I already knew, that the section extending from Oregon into Idaho and Nevada is the largest unprotected roadless area in the lower forty-eight states. Despite the apparent human history near Three Forks and along the dirt roads we drove to get here, most of the remaining Owyhee does qualify as modern wilderness. A lot of inaccessible terrain still remains. Much of the land, an area nearly twice the size of Yellowstone National Park, is undeveloped. The Idaho portion contains over 700,000 acres of Wilderness Study areas, with 288 miles of recommended Wild and Scenic River Canyons. The BLM, which manages fifteen WSAs within Oregon's share of the Owyhee, too, recommended just over 300,000 total acres for wilderness designation. Conservationists contradict those bureaucratic findings, arguing that at least 1.3 million acres should be set aside. Nevada also boasts inaccessible Owyhee country worth preserving, surprisingly deep coulees and canyons, infrequently explored. Here is an opportunity to steward an enormous—and reasonably intact—ecosystem.

I tried to pay close attention to all the numbers, and to the attendant conservation strategies, but I must admit my mind was wandering. Scattered clouds, sunlit from both below and above, drifted together and apart; directly overhead, a crescent moon occasionally glimmered. It was a photographer's dream sky, one I could picture in an Ansel Adams frame. When I tried to imagine the reality of Indians hidden in the nearby black-brown cliffs, firing down on our crowd, I couldn't project the fast-moving reel. Then I thought about this place in silence, without the crowd of people who so ironically were assembled here to make the Owyhee safe from further development. Contrarily, I then envisioned even more crowds, like the Grand Canyon grandparents and moms and dads and children and pets who might come to see a place that vies with red rock for depth and distance and just plain awesomeness. Here, too, a landscape could be loved to death.

What, exactly, do we mean by wilderness? I asked myself again, thinking back to the zippered basalt cliffs with the unzippered roads cutting up to the plateau. In narrow bureaucratic terms, this section of the Owyhee, with its rich historic and prehistoric centuries of habitation, isn't wilderness at all. Human hands have touched the landscape for thousands of years. Even so, I feel a sense of wildness here: the wildness that comes from camping a couple of dozen miles from pavement; the wildness that comes from the designer notes of a spring meadowlark and the piercing alarm of an angry plover; the wildness that comes with the brown and white curl of a swift-flowing river; the wildness that comes from a stiff uphill hike, followed by a long soak in a hot springs pool; the wildness that comes from wandering alone up a narrow tributary, stepping in and out of the shallows, and breathing deeply of the unpolluted air.

Where I hiked earlier today, hot waterfalls cascade down both sides of the canyon. Too many waterslides to count slip over the rocks and into the river below. In between, natural hot tubs—some tepid, some as warm as 90 degrees—pool above and below each other. As the hours passed, dozens of would-be preservationists gathered there, turning the hillside of waterfalls into a condominium of baths. An old German shorthair named Birdie, her shaggy black and white coat mottled with gray, limped after her master and then lay snoozing in the sun. So crippled she could hardly walk, though she still could swim at a steady pace, she reminded me of the land itself—ungroomed and very ancient. And worth preserving.

William Cronon argues that "wilderness is not quite what it seems." Rather, it is a human construct, a product more of the human imagination than of a reality untouched by human hand. "[T]here is nothing natural about the concept of wilderness," he writes in a chapter of *Uncommon Ground: Rethinking the Human Place in Nature* titled "The Trouble with Wilderness." "It is entirely a creation of the culture that holds it dear, a product of the very history it seeks to deny." I suppose his observation holds true in the Owyhee, where we imagine we're camped in a wilderness setting and where in fact there technically is no wilderness at all, although the country just south of us is very wild indeed and we seek to protect and extend its wilderness status. Perhaps we need to rethink our definitions.

The 1964 Wilderness Act specifically says that wilderness is "an area where the earth and its community of life are untrammeled by man." Historically, Three Forks has been extensively "trammeled"—first by Indian settlement, then as an outpost for the cavalry and by mineral exploration, road-building, cattle and cowboys. So if wilderness is a place essentially untouched by man, this particular place doesn't fit into a governmental wilderness schema. But what if we turned that sentence around? What if we said that wilderness is wild landscape that profoundly touches man? Such a conclusion, while still anthropocentric and subjective, reverses the subject and object. Instead of man acting, or not acting, upon such land, wilderness becomes an expression of how the land acts upon man. With such a definition in mind, we can remain philosophical, yet think and act in practical terms.

The Owyhee touches me profoundly. After the three forks come together, the water tumbles through a canyon almost as deep as the Grand Canyon. Kayakers and rafters alike enjoy its tumultuous course. The more distant view from above—comparable to what onlookers see when they peer over the Grand Canyon rim—looks down on the complexities of an enormous jigsaw puzzle. Black and greens, layers of basalt pillared together, different colors and shapes than in the American Southwest, but the viewer has the same sense of gazing on infinite time and space. The difference? Here, thousands of feet above the flowing river, I could actually hear the rushing water echo upward from the canyon floor. No one else was crowding the overlook, no voices could be heard, so even from such a distance the river dominated the semi-silence. Its whitewater sounds prevailed. Imagine standing on Yavapai Point, looking down at the Colorado River, and actually hearing the water cascading downstream.

Later that day, an inverted view from the bottom of the gorge looking up reminded me of the Grand Canyon, too. The black cliffs guarding the river are just as Hellish, just as nether-worldly as those of the more famous inner gorge. But no Phantom or Kirkwood ranches await those who brave the Owyhee. It's a primitive place, where Winnebagos would get into trouble and where amenities are absent. Much of the Owyhee does fit part of the 1964 wilderness definition, with its "outstanding opportunities for solitude or a primitive and unconfined type of recreation." Other sections, like Three Forks, don't meet a second requirement, that "the imprint of man's work" is "substantially unnoticeable." Taken together, however, the entire ecosystem is a relatively intact laboratory, a precious place where the integrity of what is wild may be preserved.

Many conservationists agree with me, and they're fighting ferociously to protect this corner of the West. In 1997, a group of environmentalists sued the BLM, "arguing that 68 grazing permits stretching across 1 million acres had been issued without adequate environmental access." They won, and in 2002 the BLM cut back allotments well beyond Mike Hanley's father's critical AUM drop in 1934. After this most recent court decision, ranchers and conservationists and the Shoshone Paiute Tribal government began working together, drafting what is known as the Owyhee Initiative, a compromise plan that values both the ecosystem and a way of life.

Six key areas form the collaborative cornerstone. First, a Board of Directors will oversee implementation of the Initiative. Second, an additional Advisory Council will be composed of interests not represented on the Board. Theoretically, tribal, cultural, historic, agricultural, recreational, vehicular, environmental, conservation, local-state-federal government, and multiple-use voices will be heard. Third, a Peer Science Review Process will be implemented. Fourth, a Conservation and Research Center will coordinate on-the-ground activities. Fifth, legislation will resolve specific turf battles, naming particular rivers as "wild and scenic," particular acreage as "designated wilderness," and releasing others to multiple-use management. Sixth, the BLM will monitor all on- and off-road travel, so that indiscriminate cross-country encroachment will be stopped. While pragmatists insist that the Initiative is a genuine solution to most of the land-use conflicts in the Owyhee, other partisan voices dislike its parameters intensely. Hardliners don't like what's happening—staunch environmentalists and old-time ranchers are equally dismayed at the necessary compromises. Their disagreements and debates echo the land-use disputes of generations, as the Old West continues to bump headlong into the new.

Like so many western locales, the Owyhee invites a vastness of responses. Hubert Howe Bancroft, in his "History of the Pacific States," articulates the contrast. "To the weary traveler crossing the dreary, monotonous and arid plains of Owyhee, the emerald and picturesque ranches, sequestered in the deep canyons of the creek, are a source of joy and beauty." He must not have visited the overgrazed pastures high above the coulees. One day I drove out on a hiccup of a road to the confluence of the West Little Owyhee with the main fork. I felt as if I were stairmastering to the end of the earth, though I passed salt licks and barbed-wire fences left and right. Two sleek jet fighters boomed overhead when I got out of the truck where the road dead-ended, but silence soon prevailed. There, I stood and looked across an ineffable rim of buttresses and buttes and basalt emptiness. Only on Utah's Kaiparowitz Plateau have I feasted my eyes on so many miles absolutely devoid of human habitation.

Parking our trucks—it's always a good idea to convoy two vehicles together in the Owyhee—my friends and I then hiked down to the river, where we walked on shifting oxbow sandbars and waded knee-deep in chill green water that twisted and turned through towering basalt formations worthy of a national park. Easter Island run amok, I thought, laughing to myself. Downstream, the canyon walls finally foreclose any further hiking, although whitewater sportsmen often enjoy the river when it runs high with springtime snowmelt. My friends in the other truck, in fact, went back the following May and kayaked through the gorge. That's still on my agenda.

The verticals and horizontals pull the land in two directions here, just as the conservation-oriented environmentalists and conservative ranchers do when they fight about biomes and ecosystems versus animal unit months. Some say the Owyhee Initiative holds out a promise of better days ahead, with a compromise that brings the angles all together. A *High Country News* article by Robyn Morrison quotes a long-time voting member of the Idaho Conservation League, John McCarthy. "'There's no brow-beating, no stand-offishness,' McCarthy says. 'I'm more familiar (with timber-issue meetings) out in the forest, where you meet with people and there's a lot of positioning, pissing on stumps, sniffing around and people being huffy and angry. (In the Owyhee) it's not that way at all. These people realize that some kind of change needs to happen.'" Conversation and compromise, as in the Klamath Basin to the west, hopefully can lead to fuller utilization and understanding. The Wilderness Society and the Nature Conservancy have signed off on the proposed legislation here; the Sierra Club has not.

Twice I've been to the Sierra Club's conservationist rendezvous at Three Forks. That's where I met Mike Hanley who, despite the biases of his heritage, is as eager as anyone to reach a satisfactory statement of stewardship. Other local men and women came to talk with the city folk from Reno, Portland, and Boise, too. We shared our beer and wine; they shared homemade Basque sausage; everyone shared conversation. William Cronon would have been pleased by the exchange, which focused solely on finding common ground and forging mutual understanding. Wilderness, home, a combination of the two—what is worth sustaining is worthy of discussion. Yet deep divisions remain. Solving land-use dilemmas in the American West will never be an easy task because the currents of conflicting points of view so often run contrary to each other. In every chapter of *Oh, Give Me a Home*, concentric circles emerge and diverge,

touch and dissipate. When a colleague pointed out the physical impos-
sibility of my imagery in the preceding sentence, I laughed and said,
"That's the point."

Leaving Three Forks, I drove the regally named Owyhee Uplands Back
Country Byway, a scenic route touted by an Idaho Chamber of Commerce.
Trucking east, I followed the signs that direct ambitious drivers along a
hundred more miles of dirt road—some graded, some washboard, some mud,
some powdered with alkali. The way winds up toward Juniper Mountain
and trails through well-kept ranches and patterned fields, meanders
across the stark high country, then drops into dryness until it reaches the
well-irrigated Snake River basin. The land along the road is varied—
some luscious and green, some overgrazed and shriveled, some badly
burned by a recent fire, and some fallow in the warm June sun. While
the panorama was unreeling in clips of Technicolor film, I came to another
"click" moment, a mirrored antithesis of that Wyoming cattle drive along
parched pavement where dudes dutifully trailed the herd. This one was
more organic, though. Here, pink phlox covered the bladed sides of the
road; yellow mules-ears brought more color to the fenced areas that had
been chained and grazed. Down from the junipered hills, a gully curved
under the dirt road where a splash of water tumbled freely in the sunlight.
High up on the flank of the mountain, miniscule patches of snow still
hung in the shade. Meanwhile, a lone antelope, spotting the truck, turned
and raced a hundred yards or so, then stopped to peer back at the possible danger. At the same time two cowboys on horseback, wearing leather
chaps, Levis, Stetsons, red bandanas at their throats, rode in from the west.
Three nondescript dogs loped alongside. As I stopped to watch the scene
unfurl, a single meadowlark trilled up-and-down notes to spring.
    For nearly an hour, I enjoyed this New West version of a "home on
the range." Not wilderness exactly, but a kind of romantic wildness that
touched my imagination. The cowboys and dogs trotted off toward the
horizon, while the birds of spring kept up their musical calls. Alongside
my truck, the nameless creek bubbled and glittered in the rays of the
sun. A still pool eddied behind a log, where water-scooters flitted back
and forth across the surface. The shadow of a trout contorted sideways.

Sounds of spring and silence alternated in the air. A West of my imagination—yes; but a very real rural West of the twenty-first century, too.

One well worth our dreams, I think. I'll not give up my "home on
the range" or my home in the West quite yet, I hum silently. Tossing a
piece of sage into the water, I watch the ripples grow.

Sources and Suggestions for Further Reading

Chorus: Introduction

Like all the old-time ditties sung by generations of balladeers, the verses of "Home on the Range" are various, some with incremental differences, others with significant changes. For this book, I chose the well-known version printed in *Cowboy Songs and Other Frontier Ballads: Revised and Enlarged*, collected by John A. Lomax and Alan Lomax (New York: Macmillan, 1938). A black saloon keeper in San Antonio gave the editors the music as it is reprinted in their book. The words are identical with those in the 1910 edition of *Cowboy Songs*, which were gleaned from many different sources. It differs somewhat from the 1870s Brewster M. Higley version and from the later William and Mary Goodwin version. Both of these can be found at *www.50states.com/songs/kansas.htm*. The official story of the original composition and early playing history is outlined at *www.ku.edu/heritage/kssights/home/official.htm*.

"For a time," the Lomaxes say, "'Home on the Range' was the most popular song on the air," and was pirated with great regularity. In fact, a lawsuit for a half-million dollars was brought "on copyright" in 1934, an enormous sum for the early part of the twentieth century. William and Mary Goodwin claimed they wrote the song in Colorado in 1904. Their version includes Rocky Mountain lines like "Oh, give me the park where the prairie dogs bark / And the mountain all covered with snow" and "Oh, give me the mine where the prospectors find /The gold in its own native land." The Goodwin suit failed when the Kansas origins of the song were thoroughly documented. Now in the public domain, "Home on the Range" remains a symbolic remnant of settlers and cowboys yearning for their special place. The official state song of Kansas since 1947, the verses nonetheless speak to all of us who feel at home in the American West.

Edward Abbey thought so, too. Apparently, his last journal entry, written just before he died in 1989, was a ditty titled "The Kowboy and His Kow." Later printed in *Earth Apples: The Poetry of Edward Abbey*, edited by David Petersen (New York: St. Martin's Press, 1994), this satirical version yearns for a cow-less home on the range. "Where seldom is heard a bawling beef herd / And the flies are not swarming all day." The second stanza pictures a home "where the grizzer bears roam /Where the bighorn and wapiti play," then more graphically denounces the reality of cows. It's amusing, but perhaps not as deadly ironic as a cartoon I found more recently. Penned by Steve Benson for United Features Syndicate, it appeared in the *Seattle Post-Intelligencer* on Monday, November 25, 2002.

> Oh, give me a home where all the cows roam
> And George Bush does what cattlemen say
> Where seldom is heard the ~~environment~~ word
> And the streams are polluted all day
> Graze, graze out the range
> Where the plants and the water have changed
> Where what has occurred is because there's a herd
> Of elephants having their way.

I appreciate the levity used to describe what in truth is a very serious matter. Hopefully, a book like this one brings further attention to the many ways we are denigrating the lands and viewscapes our offspring will inherit. May its ripples circle far and wide.

More seriously, an important part of my thinking about the "Chorus" came from my reading of Yi-Fu Tuan's *Space and Place: The Perspective of Experience* (Minneapolis: University of Minnesota Press, 1977). I highly recommend all of his books, but this one is especially relevant to a "home on the range." The phrase "geography of hope" comes from Wallace Stegner's 1969 "Coda: Wilderness Letter," found in *The Sound of Mountain Water: The Changing American West* (New York: Penguin, 1997). The two quotations from snake poems can be found in *The Complete Poems of Emily Dickinson*, edited by Thomas H. Johnson (Boston: Little, Brown and Company, 1960) and *The Complete Poems of D. H. Lawrence*, edited by Vivian de Sola Pinto and Warren Roberts (New York: Viking Books, 1964).

Chapter One: Oh, Give Me a Home

The stories of my parents and grandparents come mostly from my memory. I meant to have my Aunt Nancy read the draft of this chapter, but unfortunately she passed away before I sent her the pages. Now there is no one left from my parents' generation to take me to task if my recollections are inaccurate. Although I have a distant relative, Teri Cassias, who generously has shared her research about my grandfather Keller's genealogy, I no longer have any contact with my maternal grandmother's side of the family. Unlike the prolific Ronalds, the more recent Kellers and Smiths remained childless. I remember my mother's stories, however, and her effusive praise for Wallace Stegner's 1971 novel, *Angle of Repose* (New York: Penguin, 1992).

In Summerland, British Columbia, I spent time at the municipal museum, where I found a replica of an early-twentieth-century tent home and where I found the Okanagan History Index most intriguing in its descriptions of the people who first came to southeastern British Columbia. Sherril Foster's *According to the Giant* (Summerland, B.C.: Okanagan Annie Productions, 1998) recounts many details of early Summerland settlement. My Aunt Maggie's granddaughter and my father's cousin, Louise Atkinson, provided not only helpful conversations about her family but also delightful hospitality at the Lake Okanagan beach home I remember so well from my childhood vacations there. Thanks, too, to long-time Western Literature Association friend Laurie Ricou, whose book *The Arbutus/Madrone Files: Reading the Pacific Northwest* (Corvallis:

Oregon State University Press, 2002) reminded me of so many familial Washington/British Columbia connections and contrasts. Ferenc Morton Szasz's informative *Scots in the North American West, 1790–1917* (Norman: University of Oklahoma Press, 2000) explains the very successful settlement patterns of other families like mine.

I first read Grace Jordan's *Home Below Hell's Canyon* (Lincoln: University of Nebraska Press, 1962) more than twenty-five years ago, when the publication of women's narratives about western settlement was just becoming popular. Because I found her book so provocative in its sense of place and of home, I began investigating the countryside around Hells Canyon and reading the surprising number of books written about this isolated corner of the United States. Washington Irving's *Astoria: or Anecdotes of an Enterprise Beyond the Rocky Mountains* (1836, edited by Edgeley W. Todd, rpt. Norman: University of Oklahoma Press, 1964) offers the first description I could find, but Robert G. Bailey's *Hell's Canyon: Seeing Idaho through a Scrap Book* (Lewiston, Idaho: R. G. Bailey Printing Co., 1942) was perhaps the first local piece published. It was followed by Johnny Carrey, Cort Conley, and Ace Barton's *Snake River of Hells Canyon* (Cambridge, Idaho: Backeddy Books, 1979), which continues the anecdotal and informational pattern of narrating stories and describing sites along the Snake.

More recently, two women's books have added to Grace Jordan's perceptions of home below the inner gorge. Bonnie Sterling's *The Sterling Years* (Halfway, Ore.: Hells Canyon Publishing, 1995) focuses on a twentieth-century family's wanderings throughout the West, while Doris Wilson's *Life in Hells Canyon: A Private View* (Middleton, Idaho: CHJ Publishing, 2002) gives a more explicit description of canyon life. The latter includes copies of many newspaper articles articulating the landowners' difficulties with the government after the National Recreation Area was established.

A number of websites give up-to-date travel and tourist information. I found *www.gorp.com/gorp/resource/us_river/or_snake.htm* particularly useful for its detailed description of every item of interest along the river corridor. At the same time, *www.tcfn.org/tctour/parks/HellsCanyonNRA/heritage.html* outlines much of the legislative history. Tim Palmer's book,

The Snake River: Window to the West (Washington, D.C.: Island Press, 1991), not only provides a great deal of statistical information about the entire river course but also includes many narrative passages about the author's own experiences along the Snake, including eleven days in Hells Canyon. T. Louise Freeman-Toole's *Standing Up to the Rock* (Lincoln: University of Nebraska Press, 2001) offers a more extended and more personalized examination of today's Hells Canyon country.

Two collections of essays that consider notions of house and home in more abstract and theoretical terms are *Home: A Place in the World*, edited by Arien Mack (New York: New York University Press, 1993) and *At Home: An Anthropology of Domestic Space*, edited by Irene Cieraad (Syracuse: Syracuse University Press, 1999). In the Mack book, the individual contributions by Simon Schama, John Hollander, Joseph Rykwert, and Tamara K. Hareven were especially useful to my thinking. So, too, Edward Abbey's essays in *The Journey Home* (New York: E. P. Dutton, 1977) that express his initial conceptualizations of what home in the West might mean. *The Poetry of Robert Frost: The Collected Poems, Complete and Unabridged*, edited by Edward Connery Lathem (New York: Henry Holt and Company) is the definitive edition of Robert Frost's poems, but in fact "The Death of the Hired Man" is available in almost any anthology of modern American poetry.

Finally, I'd like to thank Stanlynn Daugherty, founder of Hurricane Creek Llamas, for her hospitality, for her beasts of burden, and for her enthusiasm about this part of the country. I find it hard to believe that I attended college less than a hundred miles from Hells Canyon, and never saw the place until many years later. What a loss.

Chapter Two: Cities and Air

Once again I thank my cousin, Nancy Kieburtz, for our shared childhood adventures. Sometimes our memories differ, but we both recall that I was the one who always got the two of us in trouble. Anyone interested in further descriptions of Seattle sites both past and present will enjoy *Reading Seattle: The City in Prose*, edited by Peter Donahue and John Trombold (Seattle: University of Washington Press, 2004), which contains brief narratives by more than forty different writers. Nannie C.

Alderson and Helena Huntington Smith, in a 1942 narrative A *Bride Goes West* (Lincoln: University of Nebraska Press, 1969) helped my Miles City recollections. So did the Miles City website, *www.mcchamber.com*.

In Page, Arizona, I relied on many tourist brochures, like "Birthplace of Lake Powell," and, surprisingly, on a set of informative displays on the Rim Trail that circles the city. I also spent time at the Glen Canyon Dam Visitors Center, and at the John Wesley Powell Museum where the then-director, Julia Betz, once again gave me valuable insights about her city and her region. Quotes from early Page residents accompany the museum displays. Anyone who wants to understand the full history of the area should read Russell Martin's *A Story That Stands Like a Dam: Glen Canyon and the Struggle for the Soul of the West* (New York: Henry Holt and Company, 1989). Jared Farmer's *Glen Canyon Dammed: Inventing Lake Powell and the Canyon Country* (Tucson: University of Arizona Press, 1999) provides an analysis of how various authors have written differently about the place. More recently, Charles Wilkinson's *Fire on the Plateau* (Tucson: University of Arizona Press, 2001) confronts the long-range implications of development there.

I thank Margaret Eissler, whose parents took care of Parsons Lodge for many years and who feels that she was raised there. Her invitation to participate in the 2004 Parsons Memorial Lodge Summer Series led me to camp at Tuolumne Meadows campground for a week, which in turn led to the thoughts incorporated in this chapter. Elizabeth Stone O'Neill's *Meadow in the Sky: A History of Yosemite's Tuolumne Meadows Region* (Groveland, Calif.: Albicaulis Press, 1993) particularizes the past (including quotations from early Yosemite aficionados like William Brewer and Joseph LeConte), as does Keith A. Trexler's *The Tioga Road: A History 1883–1961* ([s.l.]:Yosemite Natural History Association, 1980). Many, many books have been written about the historic dilemmas faced by the National Park Service. I found Dyan Zaslowsky and T. H. Watkins' *These American Lands: Parks, Wilderness, and the Public Lands* (Washington, D.C.: Wilderness Society, 1994) and Bob R. O'Brien's *Our National Parks and the Search for Sustainability* (Austin: University of Texas Press,

1999) the most useful. For historic reasons, Alfred Runte's *National Parks: The American Experience* (Lincoln: University of Nebraska Press, 1979) is worth consulting, too.

Dozens of recently published books tell stories of various horrific wildfires. Norman Maclean, with his *Young Men and Fire: A True Story of the Mann Gulch Fire* (Chicago: University of Chicago Press, 1992) was perhaps the first "creative" writer to begin analyzing the processes by which a blowup occurs. He consulted computer modeling that would have been unavailable at the time of the fire itself. His other well-known book, *A River Runs Through It and Other Stories* (Chicago: University of Chicago Press, 1976) includes a narration of Maclean's own experiences as a young firefighter. Maclean's son, John N. Maclean, tells of another major blowup in *Fire on the Mountain: The True Story of the South Canyon Fire* (New York: Washington Square Press, 1999). Historian Stephen J. Pyne has written several important books about fire. I found *Fire on the Rim: A Firefighter's Season at the Grand Canyon* (New York: Ballantine Books, 1989) and *Year of the Fires: The Story of the Great Fires of 1910* (New York: Viking, 2001) especially helpful for this chapter, but I can recommend any of his others as well. Ivan Doig's *English Creek* (New York: Athenaeum Press, 1984) contains a lively account of pre–World War II fire-fighting in the West. And I'm grateful to Richard Slotkin for his useful terminology and thought-provoking commentary in his 1973 *Regeneration through Violence: The Mythology of the American Frontier, 1600–1860* (rpt. Norman: University of Oklahoma Press, 2000).

David Carle's *Burning Questions: America's Fight with Nature's Fire* (Westport, Conn.: Praeger, 2002) is an up-to-date analysis of where we are today as government officials speculate and make policies about how best to handle wildfires. Mary Ann Franke, in *Yellowstone in the Afterglow: Lessons from the Fires* (Mammoth Hot Springs, Wyo.: Yellowstone Center for Resources, 2000), explains why and how the Yellowstone conflagration of 1988 helped establish the rules and regulations currently followed. Despite Franke's revelations about the media, newspapers nonetheless are valuable sources for on-the-spot reporting. I used the May 31, 2003 *Reno Gazette-Journal*, the June 25, 2002 *Glenwood Springs Post Independent* and the June 28, 2002 *Rocky Mountain News* for details of individual fires. A powerful overview of wildfire conundrums in the contemporary West can be found in the May 26, 2003 edition of *High Country News*. I can also recommend *Forest Magazine* for further information. Corey Lewis's article, "Bearing Witness," in the September/ October 2000 issue addresses the particular problems with illegal timber harvests. Government quotations were taken from *Fire and the Changing Land* (Washington, D.C.: United States Department of Agriculture, 1989). Conversations with Bill Bishop and Corey Lewis helped give immediacy to what I had been thinking about fires in the West.

In San Francisco, I mostly relied on my own experiences and memories, although I carefully read Rand Richards's *Historic San Francisco: A Concise History and Guide* (San Francisco: Heritage House Publishers, 2001) before my last trip there. Many other excellent guidebooks are available, but generally I follow my instincts while walking the city streets. However, I do carry Olmsted's "Street-Walker's Guide to San Francisco" (Berkeley: Olmsted & Bros. Map Co, no date). For more general scholarly considerations of the contemporary urban scene, I recommend *The American West: Interactions, Intersections, and Injunctions*, edited by Gordon Morris Bakken and Brenda Farrington (New York: Garland Publishing, 2001). Recent theorizing by spatial geographers like Edward W. Soja, in *Postmodern Geographies: The Reassertion of Space in Critical Social Theory* (New York: Verso, 1989), John Brinckerhoff Jackson, in *A Sense of Place, a Sense of Time* (New Haven: Yale University Press, 1994), and David Harvey in both *The Condition of Postmodernity* (Oxford: Basil Blackwell, 1989) and *Spaces of Hope* (Berkeley: University of California Press, 2000), added to my understanding of urban spaces and places. However, I ended up utilizing none of their language or definitions in *Oh, Give Me a Home*.

Chapter Three: Pressed from the West

More than two hundred Medicine Wheels can be found in the western United States and western Canada and, although a great many guesses have been made about the origins, no one has yet been proven correct.

David Hurst Thomas gives two coherent—if repetitive—overviews in *Exploring Ancient Native America: An Archaeological Guide* (New York: Macmillan, 1994) and in *Exploring Native North America* (New York: Oxford University Press, 2000). Most of my direct information came from the Bighorn Mountains site of the Medicine Wheel itself, and from talking with an on-site northern Arapahoe ranger, Cassie Spider Wolf.

Although my visits to Canyon de Chelly provide the basis for the first part of this chapter, I refreshed my memories by looking at Charles D. Winters's photographs in *Crossing between Worlds: The Navajos of Canyon de Chelly* (Santa Fe: School of American Research Press, 1997) and reading the text by Jeanne M. Simonelli. The history, the archaeology, and the anthropological information came from Campbell Grant's *Canyon de Chelly: Its People and Rock Art* (Tucson: University of Arizona Press, 1978). Grant's thorough discussion of Lieutenant Narbona's raid on Massacre Cave was especially helpful. The William Clark quotation was taken from Volume 3 of *The Journals of the Lewis and Clark Expedition*, edited by Gary E. Moulton (Lincoln: University of Nebraska Press, 1987). Finally, I learned the stories of Spider Woman from Kelli Carmean's *Spider Woman Walks This Land: Traditional Cultural Properties and the Navajo Nation* (Walnut Creek, Calif.: Altamira Press, 2002), though I heard them first while hiking through Canyon de Chelly in 1977.

A book titled *Tourism and Gaming on American Indian Lands*, edited by Alan A. Lew and George A. Van Otten (New York: Cognizant Communication Corporation, 1998), not only provided me with an overall background about Indian gaming but suggested further ways in which tourism is impacting the native populations. The Institute of Governmental Studies at the University of California also contains useful information on "Indian Gaming in California" at their website, *www.igs.berkeley.edu/library/htIndianGaming.htm*. To learn about Thunder Valley more specifically, I began with the website of the United Auburn Indian Community, *www.auburnrancheria.com*. There I found a copy of the lengthy May 2004 article by Steve Wiegand that provided so many historic anecdotes about the tribe. My thanks to Bill Eadington, an economics professor at the University of Nevada, Reno, and a long-time friend and colleague, whose world-renowned expertise in gaming helped me negotiate the tables and the terminology. He paved the way for my conversations with Doug Elmets and Greg Baker, who offered many insights into the impact of gaming successes on the United Auburn Indian Community. James May posted "Comprehensive Indian gaming report released," in the June 28, 2005, issue of *Indian Country Today*, and the *Reno Gazette-Journal* follow-up appeared on July 15, 2005. Mark Pilarshki's weekly column in the *Reno Gazette-Journal* provided a number of more folksy insights. I was particularly fascinated by the one printed in the February 17–23, 2005, version of "Best Bets," which assessed the complicated uses of RFID chips in the gaming industry.

I genuinely appreciate the generous amount of time Klamath Basin tribal members spent with me. Elwood Miller, Jr., and Taylor David were especially helpful. For written materials on the Klamath Tribes, I used two approved 2001 handouts—"History of the Klamath Tribes," researched and written by Barbara Alatorre, and "The Klamath Tribes— A Cultural Description," compiled by the Klamath Tribes Culture and Heritage Department. Tribal chairman Allen Foreman's e'waam cere- mony words are printed in volume 21, issue 3 of *Klamath News*, the tribe's official publication. Edward C. Wolf's *Klamath Heartlands: A Guide to the Klamath Reservation Forest Plan* (Portland, Ore.: Ecotrust, 2004) spells out more details of tribal hopes for their homeland.

On the more literary side, I can recommend William Kittredge's pictorial essays in *Balancing Water: Restoring the Klamath Basin*, with photographs by Tupper Ansel Blake and Madeleine Graham Blake (Berke- ley: University of California Press, 2000). Readers might enjoy Sherman Alexie's *Indian Killer* (New York: Warner Books, 1996), with its keen casino asides, too. I also read Rick Steber's *Buy the Chief a Cadillac* (Prineville, Ore.: Bonanza Publishing, 2005), which portrays a gruesome picture of Termination days. Filled with stereotypes, it nonetheless offers an apparently widespread attitude toward pre-casino, pre-economic-develop- ment Indian life in Chiloquin. Tribal members dislike it intensely.

Finally, I want to acknowledge two theoretical books that led me to ask hard questions about Euro-American tourism in aboriginal lands and cultures: Mary Louise Pratt's *Imperial Eyes: Travel Writing and Trans- culture* (London: Routledge, 1992) and Renato Rosaldo's *Culture and*

Truth: The Remaking of Social Analysis (Boston: Beacon Press, 1989). Although neither writes specifically of Chapter Three's topics, both suggest new ways of looking at old ways of seeing.

Chapter Four: Glittering Stars

My general information about the three Southwest power plants came from two books already cited in Chapter Two of this section: Russell Martin's *A Story That Stands Like a Dam* and Charles Wilkinson's *Fire on the Plateau*. Specific facts about the Mohave Power Plant can be found at many different websites. I used two of them, *www.epa.gov/region09/air/mohave/visfact.html* and *www.iwla.org/reports/parktext.html*. My favorite paperback collection of Gerard Manley Hopkins's poems and prose is the Penguin edition edited by W. H. Garner in 1953.

When I visited the Big Sky resort and toured the area, I picked up countless flyers, brochures, and newspapers that no doubt were dated as soon as I brought them home. The Boyne USA Resort website gives up-to-the-minute prices and potentials, *www.bigskyresort.com*, as does the website of Big Sky Properties, *www.bigskyprop.com*. Essential to my understanding of the history of the place was Rick and Susie Graetz's *Big Sky: From Indian Trails to the Tram* (privately published, no date).

My thanks to Tom Budlong, who thoroughly indoctrinated me as he explained the ongoing effects of current heap leach cyanide mining practices. He can be reached at *TomBudlong@adelphia.net*, and would welcome anyone who wants to be part of his e-mail list serve, Friends of the Panamints. On the other side of the equation, Canyon Resources materials can be found at *www.canyonresources.com*. Information about gold prices, at *www.goldprices.com*, is relevant to the debate. The Mineral Policy Center's *Golden Dreams, Poisoned Streams: How Reckless Mining Pollutes America's Waters, and How We Can Stop It*, written by Carlos D. Da Rosa, J.D., and James S. Lyon and edited by Philip M. Hocker (Washington, D.C.: 1997) is, too.

Three popular science books helped me understand the complexities of cloud formations—John A. Day's *The Science of Weather* (Reading, Mass.: Addison-Wesley Publishing Company, 1966), Robert Greenler's *Rainbows, Halos, and Glories* (Cambridge: Cambridge University Press,

1980), and Abraham Resnick's *Due to the Weather: Ways the Elements Affect Our Lives* (Westport, Conn.: Greenwood Press, 2000).

A recent overview by William R. Cotton and Roger A. Pielke, *Human Impacts on Weather and Climate* (Cambridge: Cambridge University Press, 1995) discusses not only cloud seeding but global warming as well. I chose not to dig into the complexities of the latter, but can highly recommend the tenth anniversary edition of Bill McKibbens's *The End of Nature* (New York: Anchor Books, 1997) to anyone who wishes to read a nontechnical consideration of the attendant problems of global climate change. I found Arnett S. Dennis's *Weather Modification by Cloud Seeding* (New York: Academic Press, Inc., 1980) worth skim-reading but somewhat dated. More up-to-date is *Weather Modification: Some Facts about Seeding Clouds* (Fresno, Calif.: Weather Modification Association, 1992), the October 2000 issue of *North Dakota Water*, and the 2004 Desert Research Institute's "Report on the Nevada State Cloud Seeding Program." Two relevant websites are the DRI's *www.cloudseeding.dri.edu* and North American Weather Consultants, Inc.'s *www.nawcinc.com*. Even more helpful were my conversations with Arlen Huggins (the uncredited author of the 2004 DRI report), who is the cornerstone of the current DRI cloud-seeding program, my quick airport airplane tour with Brandon and Jason, and my memories of talking with John Hallett many years ago. It's always a delight for this humanist to consult with colleagues in a scientific field.

It's delightful, too, to read the words of an old literary friend, Mark Twain, whose 1872 *Roughing It* (New York: New American Library, 1962) remains a Nevada literary classic. The now ironic quote that "nobody does anything about" the weather generally is attributed to Twain, too. Originally cited in a Charles D. Warner editorial in the August 27, 1897, *Hartford Courant*, many versions of it appear (Warner's quote, *Bartlett's Quotations*, and the blurb on the cover of "Atmospheric Water," that special issue of *North Dakota Water*, all print different words — I chose Bartlett's for these pages).

Chapter Five: Flowers and Flocks

One morning, after a heavy winter snow, I discovered a backyard highway of animal tracks beaten brown into the white. Several somethings had been trudging from under my deck to the fenceline and back again. Their paw prints stood out sharply. I turned on my computer, looked up animal tracks on the web, and found a dozen possibilities. Then, as we all are prone to do when sitting in front of the computer, I kept on googling, checking out all the plants and animals I was considering for this chapter.

Several key sites explain the spread of invasive weeds. Good places to begin are *www.blm.gov/resources* and *www.blm.gov/weeds* and *www. usgs.gov/invasive_species*, while *www.ext.colostate.edu* offers more particular details. All display extensive menus that can be followed with ease. Several books were helpful, too, especially *Invasive Plants of California's Wildlands*, edited by Carla C. Bossard, John M. Randall, and Marc C. Hoshovsky (Berkeley: University of California Press, 2000), which thoroughly describes every plant that is causing trouble in the Golden State. *Plant Invaders: The Threat to Natural Ecosystems*, by Quentin C. B. Cronk and Janice L. Fuller (London: Chapman & Hall, 1995) gave me even more specialized plant information. A Fact Book published by the Federal Interagency Committee for the Management of Noxious and Exotic Weeds, titled *Invasive Plants: Changing the Landscape of America* (Washington, D.C., 1998), outlined the overall scope of the problem. The University of Nevada, Reno Cooperative Extension posters collected in *Wanted—Dead, Not Alive!* (n.d.) made the problem more amusing.

Peter Brussard, from the university's conservation biology program read a draft of this chapter and made several helpful suggestions. He also shared his copy of Ecological Studies Volume 58, *Ecology of Biological Invasions of North America and Hawaii*, edited by H. A. Mooney and J. A. Drake (New York: Springer-Verlag, 1986), a most helpful addition to my reading. Many editions of Willa Cather's 1927 novel *Death Comes for the Archbishop* exist, but the definitive scholarly one was published by the University of Nebraska Press in 1999. Martha Summerhayes's early western adventures can be found in *Vanished Arizona: Recollections of My Army Life* (Philadelphia: Lippincott, 1908). Bob and Maria Snedden graciously took me along part of Mrs. Summerhayes's river route in their pontoon boat, and offered some very warm hospitality at their lovely

Martinez Lake home. Anyone interested in the problems involved with the chemical control of invasive weeds should begin with Rachel Carson's 1962 *Silent Spring* (Boston: Houghton Mifflin Company, 1987).

My understanding of endangered species was expanded by what I found on various web pages, too. Again, the BLM, USGS, and Colorado State University sites were most useful for an overview. I learned about mountain yellow-legged frogs, however, from *www.mylfrog.com* (which now seems to be off-line), and about condors from *www.ventanaws. org/condors*. I heard anecdotal vignettes from Roland Knapp, of the Sierra Nevada Aquatic Research Laboratory and Curt Mykut, who works for the Ventana Wilderness Society. I thank Rose Strickland and Dennis Ghigliari, too, long-time Reno friends who have hiked me to many wonderful Great Basin places, including the sage grouse lek. I am also grateful to my long-time Colorado friends, Shirley Hamilton and Brooks Clouser, for their Grant Ranch hospitality. They not only squired me around the property but also loaned me their copy of *Life at Grant Ranch: An Owner's Manual* (no publishing information available). Carole and Phil Adams's booklet, *Elephant Seals* (San Luis Obispo: Central Coast Press, 1999) explained everything I ever wanted to know about these creatures, and more. For sage grouse and wild turkeys, I googled the internet and got generalizations. More helpful was Fred A. Ryser, Jr.'s *Birds of the Great Basin* (Reno: University of Nevada Press, 1985). For another description of sage grouse preening and other colorful bird observations, I recommend Chris Cokino's *Hope Is a Thing with Feathers: A Personal Chronicle of Vanished Birds* (New York: Warner Books, 2001).

Less specific about the invasive plants and endangered species, but more crucial to my thinking about the issues at large were two important books. Dan Flores's *The Natural West: Environmental History in the Great Plains and Rocky Mountains* (Norman: University of Oklahoma Press, 2001) should be on everybody's reading list, for it wisely considers all sides of what turns out to be an untenable assumption. Was there ever any such place as a West untouched by human hands? *Protecting the Endangered Species in the United States: Biological Needs, Political Realities, Economic Choices*, edited by Jason F. Shogren and John Tschirhart (New York: Cambridge University Press, 2001), raised equally provocative questions about how we hierarchically decide what species to protect. Although I didn't use Mark Gerard Hengesbaugh's *Creatures of Habitat: The Changing Nature of Wildlife and Wild Places in Utah and the Intermountain West* (Logan: Utah State University Press, 2001) for this chapter, I can recommend his book to anyone interested in further assessment of habitat changes in the West. I also would suggest John Muir's *The Mountains of California* (New York: Century Company, 1894) for an early picture of the High Sierras and the Range of Light.

I found the Andy Kerr ditty at *www.andykerr.net/ChieftainCols/Col20.html*. And, by the way, the tracks in my urban backyard belonged to raccoons.

Chapter Six: Stream Flows

When I asked Kate Berry, a colleague from the University of Nevada, Reno, geography department, to read a draft of this chapter, she told me about another essay which more moderately riffs the excesses of water words. I want to acknowledge it here — Ed Quillan's "What Size Shoe Does an Acre-Foot Wear?" in *Western Water Made Simple* (Washington, D.C.: Island Press, 1987), even though I didn't see Quillan's piece until after my chapter had been written. My own essay owes its origins to *Dictionary of Water Words: A Compilation of Technical Water, Water Quality, Environmental, Natural Resource, and Water-Related Terms*. It was researched, written, compiled, and edited by Gary A. Horton, resource and financial economist (Reno: Great Basin Research, 2002). While he worked for the state of Nevada, Horton compiled two other useful Nevada Water Basin Information and Chronology Studies, *The Flood of 1997* and a *Truckee River Chronology*. For a more descriptive portrayal of Truckee River issues, including many photographs and an extended personal essay about people and place, I highly recommend Robert Dawson, Peter Goin, and Mary Webb's *A Doubtful River* (Reno: University of Nevada Press, 2000). The Audubon Christmas bird count statistics can be accessed at *www.audubon.org/bird/cbc/*.

I think that any examination of western water issues ought to begin with Donald Worster's *Rivers of Empire: Water, Aridity, and the Growth of the American West* (New York: Pantheon Books, 1985). Philip L. Fradkin's

A *River No More* (Berkeley: University of California Press, 1996) helps explain the course of the Colorado River, while Steven C. Schulte's *Wayne Aspinall and the Shaping of the American West* (Boulder: University Press of Colorado, 2002) outlines the political maneuvering. Closer to home, I learned the story of the Newlands Project from John M. Townley's *Turn This Water Into Gold* (Reno: Nevada Historical Society, 1998) and the gist of the recent Truckee River accords from Richard L. Acton's unpublished Ph.D. dissertation, "Peace or Truce: The Truckee-Carson-Pyramid Lake Water Rights Settlement Act" (University of Nevada, Reno, 2002). For an historic view of the politician behind the original project, William D. Rowley's *Reclaiming the Arid West: The Career of Francis G. Newlands* (Bloomington: Indiana University Press, 1996) is indispensable. For helping me put all the Nevada pieces together, I appreciated Kate Berry's "Of Blood and Water" (*Journal of the Southwest* 39, Spring 1997, 79-111). Thanks to Susan Lynn, too, of the Truckee River Yacht Club.

One of my pre-publication readers said he'd heard enough about the Colorado River; another advised me to "get out of the American Southwest." I can't stop thinking about the place, however, partly because it's so important to how we talk about water in the West and partly because it's that philosophical and emotional "touchstone" I keep coming back to in my own writing. In *GhostWest*, I mused about Lake Powell itself, and looked at the words of all the writers who have dwelled on Glen Canyon, too. Here, I backed up a bit to consider the underpinnings of western water policy, then turned my sights in the other direction to imagine what those original policies might mean for the future.

Two excellent studies of the Echo Park controversy complement each other, and should be consulted by anyone interested in the historic dispute. Mark W. T. Harvey's *A Symbol of Wilderness: Echo Park and the American Conservation Movement* (Albuquerque: University of New Mexico Press, 1994; rpt. Seattle: University of Washington Press, 2000, with a foreword by William Cronon) sets a high scholarly standard, while Jon M. Cosco's *Echo Park: Struggle for Preservation* (Boulder, Colo.: Johnson Books, 1995, with a foreword by David Brower) offers additional anecdotal evidence. To understand the place itself, I studied the *Dinosaur River Guide* (Boulder City, Nev.: Westwater Books, 1973) and, of course,

Wallace Stegner's *This Is Dinosaur: Echo Park Country and Its Magic Rivers* (Alfred Knopf, 1955; Boulder, Colo.: Roberts Rinehart, Inc., no date). To help me picture it a century before, I turned to my old favorite, John Wesley Powell's 1875 *The Exploration of the Colorado River and Its Canyons* (New York: Penguin Books, 1987). Jared Farmer's "*Desert Solitaire* and the Literary Memory of an Imagined Place," published in the Summer 2003 issue of *Western American Literature*, is the best speculative piece about an un-dammed Glen Canyon that I have read. Its provocative assessment certainly influenced my own conjectures.

Charles Lindsay's *The Big Horn Basin* (Lincoln: University of Nebraska diss. offprint, 1930) tells of a colorful Bighorn Basin history, as do the many National Park Service brochures I picked up in my travels. I'm also grateful to Jack Rupert and to Jim Staebler for their lengthy Bighorn conversations. Their two perspectives—one a seasonal employee's and the other a careerist interpretive ranger's—were most helpful in understanding the complexities facing the Park Service today.

Chapter Seven: Home on the Range

When I visited Flaming Gorge, I was struck by the extraordinary comparison between the current scenery and the places described by John Wesley Powell in *The Exploration of the Colorado River and Its Canyons* (see Chapter Two in this section for publication information). Almost anywhere along the Colorado, in fact, it is instructive to remember Powell's words. Two contemporary river writers of note are Colin Fletcher, in *River: One Man's Journey down the Colorado, Source to Sea* (New York: Vintage Departures, 1998) and Ann Zwinger, in *Run, River, Run* (Tucson: University of Arizona Press, 1984), which includes the Thomas Jefferson Farnham quote. Fletcher and Zwinger have both written books about the Grand Canyon, too, books that are well worth perusing—Fletcher's *The Man Who Walked through Time: The Story of the First Trip Afoot through the Grand Canyon* (New York: Vintage, 1989) and Zwinger's *Downcanyon: A Naturalist Explores the Colorado River through Grand Canyon* (Tucson: University of Arizona Press, 1995). For descriptions of ephemeral scenery of a different sort, I highly recommend William O. Douglass's *Farewell to Texas: A Vanishing Wilderness* (New York: McGraw-Hill, 1967). The "Visitors' Guide to the High Desert Museum" is an on-site handout given to everyone who enters the Bend, Oregon, facility, and I thank Mark Kossler, general manager of Ted Turner's Flying D Ranch, for his helpful tour narration. I also thank Mark Busby, editor of *Southwestern American Literature*, where an early version of the first half of this chapter appeared in Fall 2002.

April Reese's September 11, 2003, land letter, published in Volume 10 of *Recreation* (Environmental and Energy Publishing) gives an excellent overview of different points of view about the efficacy of Fee Demo programs. For an advocacy stance, *www.fs.fed.us/recreation/programs/feedemo/projects* leads to an array of governmental papers and policies.

I hope I can spend more time in Walla Walla, for I only touched the surface when I was there. To learn more about the Walla Walla wine industry, I suggest beginning with *www.leonetticellar.com*, and then continuing with a tasting vacation in the vicinity. My cousin and her husband, Caroljean and Don Parker, generously pointed me in the right directions. I thank them for their vintage expertise, their warm hospitality, and their superb wine cellar.

Henry David Thoreau's *Walden*—the definitive scholarly text can be found in the Norton Critical Edition edited by William Rossi (New York: W. W. Norton and Company, 1966)—sets the tone for pay-per-play equipment. Although I picked up many 2004 outdoor equipment catalogues at Reno Mountain Sports, they're just like the Big Sky Resort brochures—out of date within a few months. I suggest checking the relevant websites to find the latest information about the latest gear: *www.thenorthface.com*, *www.ospreypacks.com*, *www.camelbak.com*, *www.bigagnes.com*, *www.msrgear.com*, *www.patagonia.com*, *www.metoliusclimbing.com*. The Petzl catalogue, which contains no publishing information at all, is worth perusing separately. Two outdoor equipment giants worth visiting are Sierra Trading Post (yes, I bought a new pair of boots there just last month) and REI, which has been in business since 1938 and has grown enormously over the years.

Refrain: The Owyhee

I've been thinking about wilderness most of my life, perhaps ever since I read Henry David Thoreau's nineteenth-century words, "We need the tonic of wildness," and considered the connections and differences between the two locutions—wilderness and wildness. William Cronon's recent theoretical discussion in *Uncommon Ground: Rethinking the Human Place in Nature* (New York: W. W. Norton, 1996) is a provocative starting place for twenty-first-century contemplation. So is Linda Graber's *Wilderness as Sacred Space* (Washington, D. C.: Association of American Geographers, 1976). A number of subsequent historian environmentalists have taken Cronon to task or split hairs with his observations. I recommend the journal *Environmental History* for samples of the ongoing debate.

Owyhee Trails: The West's Forgotten Corner, by Mike Hanley with Ellis Lucia (Caldwell, Idaho: Caxton Printers, 1999) offers the best generalized overview of the Owyhee and its historic residents. For two very recent personal memoirs about the Nevada side of the region, I highly recommend both Dennis Parks's *Living in the Country Growing Weird: A Deep Rural Adventure* (Reno: University of Nevada Press, 2001) and Gregory Martin's *Mountain City* (New York: North Point Press, 2000).

For more history, I read Donald H. Shannon's *The Utter Disaster on the Oregon Trail* (Caldwell, Idaho: Caxton Printers, 1993). When I was exploring Silver City, I found Helen Nettleton's *Interesting Buildings in Silver City, Idaho* (Homedale, Idaho: Owyhee Publishing Company, 1971; rpt. 1998) invaluable. At the library, I discovered a small collection of books by women writers about their family's Owyhee days—Mabel Foreman Phillips's *The Ranch on Castle Creek* (124 pp; no publishing information available), Marian Lowe Quackenbush's *Air, Sunlight and a Bit of Land* (Fairfield, Wash.: Ye Galleon Press, 1982), and Mildretta Adams's *Historic Silver City: The Story of the Owyhees* (Homedale, Idaho: The Owyhee Chronicle, 1960). Each was fascinating in its own way. I also consulted *A Historical, Descriptive and Commercial Directory of Owyhee County, Idaho* (Silver City, Idaho: Press of the Owyhee Avalanche, 1898; facsimile reproduction, Seattle: Shorey Book Store, 1966). Its publication apparently was made possible by Mildretta Adams (see above), and its pages contain the Hubert Howe Bancroft quotation. Another book of local color is Earl J. Larrison's *Owyhee: The Life of a Northern Desert* (Caldwell, Idaho: Caxton, 1957).

Many of my facts and figures about the Owyhee came from conservationist brochures, most of which contain no publication information. One is called "The Owyhee-Bruneau Canyonlands;" another, "Owyhee Canyonlands." I also used data from a variety of activist e-mails, particularly ones touting the yearly rendezvous. At those outdoor gatherings, I was able to listen to a number of different voices—Mike Hanley, Spencer Woods, Cynthia Yates, Roger Singer. All together, they put the land-use issues into context. A *High Country News* article by Robyn Morrison, "Riding the Middle Path" (*HCN* 35: December 8, 2003, 6–11) gives some telling insights about the Owyhee Initiative process from an objective journalist's point of view.

Most of all, I want to thank the concerned men and women who have donated so much time and energy to preserving the Owyhee. Mike McCurry deserves special accolades, not only for his hard work but also for steering me over some *very* bumpy backcountry roads. He grew up in the Owyhee, and loves it dearly. Without his guidance, I would never have ventured so far off the beaten track.

As with all the references, statistics, and commentary throughout *Oh, Give Me a Home*, my Owyhee information is changing by the minute. Though the landscape itself remains the same, the voices—their arguments and their solutions—modify and mutate and modulate. Likewise, the conditions of the land. A drought one year can give way to record snowfall the next. Perhaps that's part of being western, too, adapting to inevitable change.

Finally, I'd like to thank the University of Nevada, Reno, for its extended generosity in giving me sufficient time and ample resources. With the university's support, my writing has been an easier task. I've already acknowledged the help of various colleagues who checked the accuracy of individual chapters, but I also want to thank two other thoughtful long-distance readers of specific sections—Leonard Finegold and Muriel Davis. The University of Oklahoma Press found referees who offered solid suggestions that improved *Oh, Give Me a Home*. I would thank them here, but except for David Robertson I don't know their names. I'm most grateful to Scott Casper, Mary Webb, and Eryn Branch who read drafts of the entire manuscript and who asked the questions that need to be asked, the ones that transform lots of pages into a coherent book. Eve and Bill Quesnel were proofreaders superb. Lois Snedden, as always, deserves the most thanks of all.